Classroom collaboration

Phillida Salmon
and
Hilary Claire

Routledge & Kegan Paul
London, Boston, Melbourne and Henley

First published in 1984
by Routledge & Kegan Paul plc

39 Store Street, London WC1E 7DD, England

9 Park Street, Boston, Mass. 02108, USA

464 St Kilda Road, Melbourne,
Victoria 3004, Australia, and

Broadway House, Newtown Road,
Henley-on-Thames, Oxon RG9 1EN, England

Printed in Great Britain by
Redwood Burn Limited,
Trowbridge, Wiltshire

Library of Congress Cataloguing in Publication Data

Salmon, Phillida.
Classroom collaboration.
(Routledge education books)
Bibliography: p.
Includes index.
1. Education, Secondary—Curricula—Case studies.
2. Interaction analysis in education—Case studies.
I. Claire, Hilary, 1941–   .   II. Title.   III. Series.
LB1628.S34   1984   373.19   83–17759

ISBN 0–7100–9957–6

Classroom collaboration

Routledge Education Books

Advisory editor: John Eggleston
Professor of Education
University of Keele

Contents

Acknowledgments

This book arises out of a three-year research project
funded by the Social Science Research Council, without
whose financial backing the study could not have been conducted.

We have many other debts.   The idea for the research
developed out of work done by the Institute's English
Department, and in particular from the inspiration and
support of Harold Rosen.   Tony Burgess, Neil Ryder, Anne
Diack, and other members of the English Department's Collaborative Learning Group, provided a helpful and responsive forum for discussion in the early stages of our work
work.   Other Institute colleagues, particularly Bob
Hartley, Lesley Smith and Harvey Goldstein, gave time and
thought to our concerns and methods.   Colin Hindley, as
Professor of Child Development, generously allowed Phil
Salmon three years' half-time secondment to the study.

The research was greatly enriched by the contributions
of two people outside the project team.   Campbell
Matthews, of Shoreditch College of Education, gave us the
full text of a transcript made with members of Mac's
class, together with his own funny and illuminating observations.   We were also able to draw fully on material
gathered from Mac's class by Sally Davies, a Brunel University student who did her work placement with us.

Dilys Davies was helpful in carrying out one of our
assessments in Rachel's class.   Other people acted as
consultants for specific aspects of the work, among whom
Mohammed Tikly made a particularly large contribution to
our understanding of multi-cultural aspects of the curriculum.

    Brenda Nathan, part-time secretary to the project, con-
tributed much more than secretarial skills.   The final
writing-up of the work could not have been achieved without the editorial judgment and personal support of Eve
Wade.

    Unfortunately, we may not name the teachers and pupils
whose contribution to the study was the greatest of all.
We can only acknowledge anonymously the two head teachers
who allowed us into their schools and the many other
teachers who advised and helped us.   Above all, we are
indebted to the four teachers who worked collaboratively
with us, and who, despite the enormous pressures on them,
continued to give us full personal access to themselves
and their classrooms, and who, both during and after the
project, offered us their insights and reflections on the
material we gathered.   Finally, the study rests also on
the interest and generosity with which the pupils met our
research enquiry.

Chapter 1

The concerns of the study

Traditionally, school learning has been seen as the transmission of a body of knowledge - as teachers passing on
their expertise to pupils. This view makes certain
assumptions about children and teachers, and about how
people come to know. One of these assumptions is that,
in the situation of school learning, the teacher has knowledge, while the child is ignorant. This fits with the
convention that communication should be largely one-way,
from teacher to pupils, since pupils are seen as receiving
rather than constructing their understanding of the curriculum. Implicit in a knowledge-transmission view of
education is also the idea that what is learned in school
is an impersonal body of knowledge, existing independently
of the particular human beings there. This idea makes
legitimate the separation of school knowledge from out-of-
school experience, and the exclusion from classroom concerns of personal feelings and personal relationships.

Many secondary teachers would themselves strongly dis-
pute this definition of their work. Yet, in some ways,
it is deeply entrenched in secondary school practice.
The gearing of the curriculum to external examinations
means that teachers must provide inputs for testable out-
puts. The separation into compartments of school knowledge confirms its impersonal character, and, additionally,
creates a timetable in which there is little continuity of
human relationships, and social encounters are transient
and short-term. The organization of learning carries
heavy pressures on teachers to control and manage pupils -
pressures which are most easily met by making learning
individualized and demanding that children play a largely
passive and silent part in the classroom.

It must surely be time to question the assumptions on

which these practices rest.   There is by now a substantial body of writing and research which challenges the
view of education as knowledge-transmission, and shows the
fertility of alternative definitions.   Sociologists of
education such as Keddie (1973) and Young (1971) have
shown the political basis which underlies the reproduction
of knowledge in school, and the function which education-
as-transmission can serve in social control and mainten-
ance of the status quo.   Other writers have questioned
the anonymity of knowledge, by examining the meaning of
the school curriculum for particular groups of young
people.   The work of Willis (1977) makes clear the irrelevance of school learning for many working class boys,
while writers such as Searle (1978) have illuminated the
ethnocentric character of the curriculum and the kinds of
radical reconstruction that are needed if minority ethnic
pupils are to be engaged in classroom learning.   Other
research, considering the differential significance of the
curriculum for boys and for girls, has revealed the extent
to which Maths and Science, for instance, are inter-pene-
trated by differential gender expectations (for instance,
Deem, 1980).

On another level, many writers have considered traditional teaching modes, and examined the ways in which they
can act to alienate pupils.   The work of Barnes (1976 and
1977) has been seminal in showing how these modes are in-
imical to real personal learning, which depends on much
freer and more open kinds of communication.   James (1977)
argues that learning methodologies are particularly crucial in multi-racial classrooms where content and method
are essentially inseparable.   The educational fertility
of non-traditional modes, within such classrooms, is shown
in a recent study by Richmond (1982).   In examining the
hidden agenda of classroom teaching, Spender (1982) demon-
strates the extent to which, by the ways they engage with
their pupils, teachers convey different messages to boys
and girls.   The processes of classroom learning are also
mediated by pupils themselves, and particularly by pupils
acting together.   This perspective informs a study by
Furlong (1976), who shows how unofficial, often covert
pupil-pupil interchanges are used to construct moment-to-
moment definitions of the classroom situation - definitions which carry very different kinds of response to the
teacher.

Teachers who acknowledge these kinds of considerations,
and who reject a transmission model of education, are inevitably entailed in developing alternative learning

methods.   These methods perhaps necessarily involve some
form of collaborative learning.   As yet, there has been
little published work on collaborative classroom modes.
The two short books by Barnes (1976) and Barnes and Todd
(1977) have, however, been very influential.   In them,
Barnes gives an account of his own work in setting up
small groups, in a variety of curriculum areas, in which
pupils worked together without the direction of a teacher.
Barnes's own focus has been concerned with the kinds of
talk generated by collaborative, as against traditional,
learning situations.   His argument, essentially, is that
small group talk has the exploratory character necessary
for personally meaningful learning.   Only by thinking
aloud, acknowledging uncertainty, formulating tentative
ideas, comparing interpretations and negotiating differences - only by these means can learners shape meanings for
themselves and others, and thereby arrive at real understanding.   This kind of free, active, exploration of
knowledge, though it can happen in talk among equals, is
constrained by expository teaching, with its implicit
demand for the correct answer.   For this reason, restrict-
ing pupil participation inhibits just those kinds of learning which teachers generally see as most important.

There are also other reasons why collaborative modes
may be critical if real learning is to occur.   As Schutz
(1932) has remarked, 'We achieve reflective awareness when
we try to act on someone whose implicit beliefs are different from our own.'   From this point of view, traditional teacher exposition, with its emphasis on consensus
and discouragement of idiosyncratic interpretations, may
be very un-developing intellectually.   Conversely, a
free-for-all among pupils, in which differences of viewpoint are bound to arise, is potentially much more stimulating.

Relatively free talk amongst pupils also has the potential for extending the narrow boundaries of classroom
knowledge.   Since children often inhabit similar everyday
worlds - worlds typically unlike that of the teacher -
their out-of-school experience is likely to form part of
their common currency.   Without being anchored within
real-life situations and concerns, educational knowledge
is bound to remain encapsulated and academic - if, indeed,
it is assimilated at all.

Collaborative classroom modes are rooted in a view of
learning which rejects the passive role assigned to pupils
by the traditional model.   Similarly, where the tradi-

tional view denies the significance of social relationships in the classroom, collaborative methods, on the contrary, make these the very basis of learning. Far from
seeing children's relationships as irrelevant to classroom
practice, or as a source of potential disruption in learning, a collaborative ethos presupposes the need to build
learning experiences out of the positive feeling between
children.   Potentially, this means more than an acknowledgment of existing pupil friendships. To the extent
that teachers, in devising classroom collaborative ven-
tures, are prepared to set up pupil groupings that go
beyond established friendship patterns, collaborative
learning is likely to develop positive bonds more widely
among pupils.   This possibility seems particularly significant in the context of inner-city schools, where there
is often mutual mistrust and hostility, across lines of
race, class, gender, or academic ability.

Finally, collaborative modes carry very different political messages from traditional ones - and thereby must
give rise to different political outcomes.   Where
straight teacher exposition essentially vests power in
teachers, small group working disperses authority within
the classroom, giving children responsibility and power to
organize their own learning.   This has particular implications for the situation of working class and minority
group pupils, as well as girls.   The appropriation of the
classroom for themselves by particular pupil groups is unlikely to happen in learning contexts which mobilize the
power of all the children in them.

For all these reasons, it seems important to study the
potential of collaborative learning modes within secondary
school classrooms.   To put such study to good use, it is
necessary to cast the investigation within a conceptual
framework which has some generality.   Many psychological
theories have been used to underpin the traditional model
of learning, and the methods which derive from it.   For
example, the information processing model in psychology
supports the idea that knowledge is received rather than
constructed, and that what is learned is something essentially independent of the individual learner.   The learning theory approach, also influential in education, portrays learning as a mechanical process, in which learners
need to be prodded or bribed by extrinsic incentives, and
knowledge consists of associations to be 'stamped in'.

A collaborative approach to learning makes sense only
within a theoretical position in which people are seen as

essentially social, and essentially active.   Such a view
is basic to Kelly's personal construct theory (see
Bannister and Fransella, 1980), in which the starting-
point is that human beings constantly strive to make sense
of their lives, in ways which involve continual reference
to others.   What this implies, for a definition of learning in its widest sense, is illustrated in another book
(Salmon, 1980).   For an examination of collaborative
classroom modes, however, the most critical aspect of the
theory is probably its emphasis on the frames of reference
in terms of which people act, and in particular, on the
commonality and sociality across different frames of reference.   These terms refer to the relationships between
the ways in which different people see things.   Commonality means the degree of similarity between the perceptions
of different individuals.   As emerges from work like that
of Furlong (1976), pupils do not always interpret classroom events in the way that their teacher does.   Nor do
different pupils always have a similar view of classroom
learning, as Hargreaves (1967) has shown, from his study
of pupil subcultures.   Sociality refers to a different
aspect: the degree to which people understand each
others' views.   Classroom communication, if it is to be
effective, must depend on mutual understanding; otherwise, as Torode (1977) describes, teachers' messages are
not received as intended, nor, as Driver (1982) shows, are
pupils' messages understood by teachers.

From this theoretical perspective, classroom learning
involves the meeting of a number of different frames of
reference - those of the teacher and the pupils.   Traditional modes of teaching pay insufficient attention to
pupils' frames of reference, and pre-empt the teacher's
but define this in standard, very limited ways.   Collaborative learning modes, on the contrary, remove the abso-
lute priority of the teacher's frame of reference and
allow for possibilities of idiosyncratic meanings, and
openness to change.   They also make pupils' frames of
reference central, as constituting the material for exploration, and joint negotiation of change.   Unlike traditional methods, collaborative modes presuppose different
frames of meaning among different pupils.

In terms of this theoretical approach, the goals of
collaborative learning are the achieving of commonality
and sociality, both between teachers and pupils, and
between pupils.   Commonality, or common ground, represents, from this point of view, not just a consensus about
specific aspects of the curriculum, but a shared under-

standing of its wider meaning and value.   Potentially,
collaborative modes achieve a widening of commonality
among pupils who, through working together, find themselves sharing and exchanging personal experience.   Less
directly, such modes, by freeing the teacher from an
authoritarian role, may enable her to communicate more
fully and openly with pupils, thereby enlarging the sphere
of shared meaning.

Collaborative methods can also serve social goals,
which, in this theoretical framework, are defined as the
development of sociality - mutual understanding.   Sociality is perhaps very ill-served in traditional classrooms,
which not only act to turn the teacher from a unique
person into a stereotyped role, but can perpetuate
or even create polarities between pupils.   Collaborative
learning offers the possibility of overcoming barriers to
mutual personal recognition.   By endorsing the existence
of social relationships in the classroom, and seeking to
extend positive feeling beyond existing cliques, teachers
may be able to overcome antipathy and incomprehension
among pupils, and develop real mutual understanding.
Similarly, the less formal, more spontaneous response to
pupils which collaborative settings demand from teachers,
offers the chance that teachers and pupils will encounter
each other more personally, and achieve greater sociality.

These concerns predicated an investigation which, as
far as possible, illuminated the frames of reference which
teachers and pupils brought to the classrooms they worked
in.   Inevitably, this entailed a close-focus, small-scale
study, in which some justice could be done to individual
viewpoints.   Within the context of the four classrooms we
studied, we explored the meanings which pupils, and the
teacher, brought to the situation.   For all four teachers,
committed to collaborative learning modes, we tried to
assess how far these modes were effectively creating
common ground and mutual understanding.

Chapter 2

The conduct of the study

THE SCOPE OF THE STUDY

The investigation we planned was necessarily a small scale
one.   There were practical reasons for this, in terms of
the time scale and personnel covered by SSRC funding.
The research period was three years.   The research team
consisted of three people.   Phil, the study's director,
was seconded on a half time basis.   Hilary, the research
officer, was the only full-time member of the team.
Brenda, the project secretary, worked two days a week.
Such practical constraints made it unrealistic to attempt
any large scale research, encompassing a wide range of
contexts, or large numbers of pupils and teachers.

More fundamentally, our own purposes themselves predicated an investigation which was essentially intensive
rather than extensive.   Our concern with exploring, as
fully as possible, the meanings which the teacher and her
pupils brought to their classroom context, meant that we
needed to look closely at a small number of individual
classrooms.   Our approach presupposed a case study
rather than a survey research format, since we wanted to
explore what was distinctive within classrooms, as well as
what might be common between them.

THE SCHOOLS INVOLVED

For these reasons, we chose to limit our investigation to
four classrooms, within two schools.   It was crucial, for
examining collaborative learning modes, that both schools
should be inner city, mixed and multi-ethnic, and that
both should be committed to mixed ability teaching.
Beyond this, however, it seemed appropriate to embody some

diversity, and we therefore selected two schools which differed considerably in their resources.   Although direct comparison of the two schools was not likely to prove helpful, it seemed important to examine the different meaning which a collaborative learning approach might have in two rather different institutional contexts.   We have called the two schools Newlands and Claremont;   the following descriptions define in outline some of their most important features.

Newlands Comprehensive

Newlands Comprehensive is a striking glass and concrete building in the inner city.   Formed roughly twelve years ago by the amalgamation of five local schools (two of which had been single sex grammar schools), from the start it attracted a reasonable proportion of academically able pupils.

Its reputation was boosted soon after its opening by the introduction of a special music course, for which 15 pupils each year are selected by audition, to follow a curriculum which largely overlaps with the mainstream, but also gives special emphasis to instrumental work.

Newlands has also been used for piloting a great deal of the Authority's experimental work, namely in Science, Maths, French and Spanish.   Special projects designed by other bodies (such as the Royal College of Arts) have also been launched in the school.

The intake has always been very mixed.   For London, its multi-ethnic intake is not unusual.   What is more noticeable is the broad spread across social class lines. Because of its position, the school serves run-down working class estates, and high status middle class inner city areas alike.   The music course attracts children from relatively far afield.

Though oversubscribed on Band 1 (partly because of its high reputation for art and music and its sixth from academic results), it also has its share of problems, social and academic.

The school is used by the community after hours, and its policy is to encourage children to stay on to 'End On Clubs' after school.

Pupils all have opportunities to use the country annexe which the school owns, to extend their curriculum, or for intensive courses.

Claremont School

Claremont School came into being in 1976 following reor- ganization from a four-form entry, all boys secondary modern. The original intake, now at the top of the school, was not only single sex, but academically unbalan- ced, predominantly black and working class - a reflection of selection procedures. By 1979, when we became assoc- iated with the school, the lower school had of course become socially and ethnically more mixed and academically more balanced; but the two halves seemed to sit uneasily together. New low-level buildings in a landscaped site had been built to accommodate the enlarged reorganized school, but many classes continued to operate out of the old Victorian buildings on the same site, which was not totally helpful to forging a new identity.

Like Newlands, Claremont serves quite a wide catchment area though it is sited in a less central and socially more homogeneous part of the city.   It has a far larger Asian intake than Newlands, a reflection of the local com- munity.   When we were working in the school, only a very small number of children came from the middle class, though, as its 'boys secondary mod' reputation fades, the school has been able to build a more positive image, widen its curriculum and the range of exam subjects which are offered, and taken up.

The school has a Youth Club on the premises, which, while we were there, seemed mostly to be used by the older boys in the school.   Mother tongue classes for Asian women are run in the school, by a community group.

Claremont has been working hard to improve its image and the curriculum it can offer.   However, it did not appear to benefit from special status as a pilot school for the Authority, as did Newlands.

THE FOUR TEACHERS AND THEIR CLASSROOMS

To allow some breadth in our examination of collaborative modes, it was important to study more than one curriculum area.   After a good deal of preliminary exploration of

possibilities and a number of false starts in classrooms
where collaboration between pupils turned out to be rather
limited, we settled on four classrooms, two in Claremont
and two in Newlands.   In every case, the decision to
study the class concerned developed out of the teacher's
interest in the research.   Because our concern, in each
classroom we studied, was to define our questions in terms
of the particular teacher's goals and perceptions, each
teacher was involved in moulding the form which the investigation took within her or his class.

Mac's class

The first class was Mac's second year Design and Technology class in Claremont School.   We first encountered him
early in 1979, and studied his class during the school
year 1979-80.   As in two of the other classrooms, we
chose to focus on second year pupils because they seemed
to offer greater scope for an investigation than younger
or older age groups might have done.   By this stage, the
children would no longer be strangers in their school context.   Ability groupings would be less salient than later
in secondary schooling.   The teacher would have greater
freedom for innovative methods than at later stages, when
exam constraints might limit teaching possibilities.
Finally, at this age, when most children are not yet feeling disaffected from school, they themselves might feel
more positively about taking part in a project such as
ours, and engage themselves in it more fully.

    Mac himself endorsed these judgments, and saw his
second year group as well suited to research study.   As a
teacher who was trying to innovate a new approach to his
subject in a somewhat traditional institutional context,
he was enthusiastic about our involvement, and felt that
it might be professionaly helpful.   In establishing with
us the specific focuses for our investigation of his
classroom group, Mac particularly emphasized the significance of pupil evaluation - something we incorporated as
the major feature of our assessments of his class.
He also set up two specific projects for class work, which
it was agreed we should monitor.   During the course of
the year of our study, Mac was generous in allowing access
to his class, not merely to Phil and Hilary, but also to
Brenda, and to Sally, a student temporarily attached to
the project.   He gave time also to discussion, before,
during and after the year, of his own frame of reference,
his experience of the group's progress, and our own perceptions.

Islay's class

Unlike the other three classes we studied, Islay's Social
Studies class, also in Claremont School, was a fifth year,
all boys, group.   The boys in this group had all experienced traditional methods and low streaming throughout
their secondary schooling.   Now, as they approached
school leaving age, the likely difficulties of finding
work in a time of high unemployment seemed to contribute
further to very instrumental views on the value of education.

We were aware from the start that the boys' attitudes
and experience might well vitiate Islay's efforts to work
collaboratively with them, or to get them to collaborate
with each other.   However, we still thought it worthwhile
to pay some attention to a group which illuminated the
constraints which can work against the viability of collaborative modes.

Islay, whom we also met early in 1979, was personally
very committed to, and experienced in collaborative modes,
which she saw as essential for her subject.   She welcomed
our involvement with this particular class group.   On the
one hand, she endorsed our perception that the group represented a critical test for the viability of collabora-.
tive methods, given the social and educational disadvan-
tages of the boys concerned.   But Islay, who liked and
cared about these pupils, also thought our association
with them, with the prestige it carried, might do something to mitigate their low status within the school.

Because our major commitment was to the three second
year groups, we had a relatively occasional contact with
Islay and her class during the school year of 1979-80.
However, she herself made this involvement maximally productive, by integrating our assessment of the group with
the exam curriculum she taught.   In this way, the boys'
discussion of our questions about school and out-of-school
experiences formed part of the material submitted for the
Mode 3 examination syllabus.   Islay also shared fully
with us her own goals and perceptions, and helped us for-
mulate the meaning of collaborative methods for her curriculum area and for this pupil group.

Terry's class

The third group was in Newlands School, Terry's second
year Humanities class.   Our involvement with Terry was
negotiated gradually.   Early in 1979, we asked him, as a
teacher experienced in using collaborative modes, to act
as a consultant for us, so that we could develop our own
understanding of good practice.   At that stage, we envisaged using his work as a general source of ideas about the
kinds of project and task which lend themselves to pupil
collaboration.   However, our observation of his second
year classroom work so revolutionalized our own concepts
of what classroom collaboration could mean, that we decided to ask Terry whether we might focus explicitly in our
investigation on his own class, during the 1979-80 school
year.

Terry, who was happy to accept our research involvement with his second year group, directed our attention
particularly to questions about how pupils perceived
school learning, and specifically about the perceptions of
working class boys.   These questions governed the kinds
of assessment we made of the children, while Terry's concern with the kinds of tasks in which collaboration is
most feasible, and the composition of particular pupil
pairs who work well together, defined the continuing
focuses of our classroom observation.   Terry himself gave
fully of his time to discussions of the research throughout, and after the year, and, by his involvement, helped
us set up an investigation which genuinely embodied his
own concerns.   This investigation continued, informally,
into the following year, during which we pursued some
further questions that had arisen during our main study of
his class; however, this aspect is not reported here.

Rachel's class

When we met Rachel in the summer term of 1979, it was
quickly apparent that her own concerns, and her sense of
the possibilities of collaborative learning modes, very
much echoed and extended our own.   It was agreed that we
should study the second year Humanities (Drama) class that
she would be taking on in September 1979.   As it happened,
the class group involved was, for various reasons, very
disorganized and chaotic at the beginning of Rachel's contact with it.   For us, this was fortunate, since it
became clear that collaboration between pupils could not
begin to happen until an atmosphere of mutual trust and

mutual respect had been established.   This necessarily
involved us in focussing on a basic level of class group
functioning, and using our observations to look at how
Rachel herself developed a relationship with her pupils,
and then, through this, fostered their capacity to work
together.

At the end of the 1979-80 school year, the class group
would normally have left Rachel, and the Humanities curriculum, taught by her, would have been replaced by
English, History and RE, taught by three other teachers.
However, because, after their turbulent early history,
this group of pupils was obviously benefitting from their
contact with Rachel, it was decided that she should retain
teaching continuity with them by taking them for English
in the school year 1980-1.   This gave us the opportunity
to follow on our study of her class group for a two-year
period.   During this second year, we observed the class
less often, but tried to monitor any changes and general
progress.   Given this longer time period, we viewed our
study of Rachel's class somewhat differently from our
study of the other three classes, in that it seemed appropriate to attempt some assessment of change in the feelings and perceptions of the children.

Our contact with Rachel's class allowed us to explore
the meaning of collaborative modes within a curriculum
which, as well as involving a good deal of drama, was very
open-ended, and accessible to the children's construction.
Rachel tailored her curriculum, in Humanities, and still
more in English, to the experience and interests of the
children in her class.   This enabled us to focus on maximally personal, and inter-personal, kinds of collaborative
working.

Partly because of the length of our working partnership
with her, we spent more time with Rachel than with any
other teacher, meeting her socially, as well as in her
classroom and the school staffroom.   In our collaboration,
there was much mutual exchange of ideas, and interactive
influence.   What took place in Rachel's classroom was the
outcome, at least partly, of our talk together, just as
what became written about that classroom embodied interpretations and insights jointly arrived at with Rachel.

OUR METHODOLOGY

As will be evident, we saw a need for research into classroom collaboration to be conducted in ways which were
themselves collaborative.   In order to come to understand
the ways teachers saw their classrooms, their pupils,
their goals, we needed to meet them personally - to
acknowledge and respect their individuality, and to be
accessible ourselves as particular human beings.   If the
research was to incorporate these teachers' concerns, then
it was essential that they should contribute to the form
that the study took, and to the interpretations that were
made of what had been investigated.   These considerations
governed the kinds of methods which we set out to use in
our investigation.

Observation

Our methodology had two strands: observation and assessment.   In both we tried to combine personal informality,
on the one hand, with clarity of focus on the other.
Observation, if it was to enable access to the intimate,
subtle, shifting meanings of social interaction, was
necessarily participant.   Only if we entered classrooms
as persons, became personally familiar to pupils and
achieved some measure of personal trust, could we hope to
engage with what was happening, moment-to-moment, among
them.   The attempt to be flies on the wall seemed entirely inappropriate; without knowing how children view
classroom events, one cannot know the meaning of those
events.   Similarly, a closed, pre-determined observational schedule was likely to preclude the unforeseen, and
cast the richness of social interaction into a standard
and limiting form.   This seemed particularly at variance
with the needs of an investigation into collaborative
learning methods, which, by definition, involve an open-
ended curriculum, and invite the construction of new possibilities.   Finally, since we were concerned to tailor
our observations to the current concerns of particular
teachers, we needed to focus on different aspects for different classrooms, and at different times within the same
classrooms.   This meant, in general, defining the focuses
of our research in each classroom, in terms of central
concerns within the teacher's frame of reference.   But
since particular circumstances change over a year, and
teachers' concerns themselves develop, we also modified
our observations through regular - if often hurried -
consultations with the teacher concerned.

In practice, this meant that both the focus and the
time scale of our observations were different within the
four classrooms we studied.   In Mac's class, we maintained near-weekly observations in the first two terms,
when, with notes and tape-recordings, we were monitoring
two mini-projects he had set up for collaborative working.
In these observations, we focussed intensively on pairs or
small groups working together, usually covering about half
the pupils in each lesson.   During the third term, our
contact was much less frequent, and we used our observations to monitor progress for the whole class group.
With Islay's group, our contact was more occasional;   it
involved sitting in on the class - sometimes, taking part
in group discussion - for three or four lessons each term.
We did not attempt to record events, but aimed at a general impression of group functioning.   However, our role
in this group also involved presenting the material which
later formed part of the Mode 3 examination syllabus;   and
to this extent, we stepped briefly out of the observer
role into a more active intervention.   Where Terry's
class was concerned, our observation was done in major
chunks rather than continuously.   To monitor the mini-
project he had set up, we observed the whole class for the
six weeks that the project lasted, moving round the group,
and using notes and tape-recordings.   Subsequently, in
visits every other week, we focussed on particular pairs
of children in whom Terry was specially interested;   again
we used notes, and, when we could, tape-recordings.   In
observing Rachel's group, we used notes to record events
as fully as possible.   We tended to alternate between
observations of the whole group and close monitoring of
individual pairs, using tape-recordings where these seemed
of particular interest.   Our contact with the class was
mainly weekly during the first year, but much less frequent during the second year, when we sat in on three or
four lessons each term.

The pupils' response

Setting up and maintaining classroom observation entails a
good deal of negotiation with pupils, particularly at the
beginning.   One aspect of this is the clear establishment
of an observer role which is seen to be different to the
role of a teacher.   To help this, we introduced ourselves
as people who were writing a book about the school, and
needed to find out how pupils learned, and what they
thought about their learning.   In all the classroom
groups concerned, this explanation obviously aroused

interest, although some children were disappointed by our inability to say what the book would be called, by the fact that the schools would not be identified, and by the long time schedule of publication. But the prospect of being in a book, and talking to us, as writers, was exciting to most children, and on this basis we were generally welcomed into the class.

Hilary decided not to tell pupils that she was a trained teacher as she reckoned this could affect the children's attitudes to her.   Instead, like Phil, she established gently, at the beginning of our involvement in each class, that she was not an alternative teacher, and referred children back to each other, or to the teacher, when they asked for help.   So, within the classroom, we tried to maintain an attitude of sympathetic attention and interest, without actually entering into what was happening.   Another strategy in establishing ourselves as observers, was to ask pupil pairs for their permission to sit with them during the lessons, and to be sensitive to any reluctance they might feel to have their conversation overheard.   Thus on one or two occasions, Hilary moved away from a pair where she felt intrusive, though such occasions were actually very rare, as we became increasingly familiar presences in the classrooms.   It is true that few children used our first names - a practice we had suggested as a symbol of our non-teaching roles.   Like other female adults in the school we were typically addressed as 'Miss'.   But when teachers occasionally left the classroom, or arrived late, so that we were the only adult present, it was clear that we were not regarded as part of the authority system of the school.   We deliberately encouraged this by not attempting to exert any adult authority over children who were flouting usual classroom rules.

In all four classrooms, we managed to establish a relationship of friendliness and trust with the children, some of whom were, of course, more forthcoming than others. The general warmth and interest which they showed us must have been at least partly the product of the collaborative classroom atmosphere, and the easy and positive relationship which the children typically had with the teacher concerned.   One index of the quality of pupil response to us as researchers is represented by their reaction to our request late in the year, that we should accompany them around the school for one whole morning.   We wanted to make these across-the-curriculum observations mainly on pupils who were socially marginal.   The fact that in

every case they readily agreed to this request suggests
that even for the less confident, more isolated children,
we had become people who were generally trusted.

Assessments

Like our observations, the assessments we made, of
teachers as of pupils, were designed to be informal rather
than systematic, and idiosyncratic rather than standardi-
zed.   We hoped to set up the kinds of assessment which
would reflect the concerns and focuses prevailing, in
each particular classroom.   In assessing the frames of
reference of the four teachers, we relied entirely on conversational methods.   We interviewed each teacher at
least twice, for these assessments, using a few prompting
questions, and inviting the teacher to talk as fully as
possible about her or his work.   We tried to cover the
meaning which the curriculum had for the teacher, the
functions which collaborative modes of learning were felt
to have, the way pupils were perceived, the teacher's
plans, hopes and expectations, and the sense of pressures
and constraints within and outside the institution.
After the first interview, we drew up a draft scheme to
represent the teacher's frame of reference, as we had
understood it.   We then asked the teacher to modify or
elaborate this, and we re-drafted the scheme, until the
teacher was satisfied that it did justice to her or his
standpoint.

It was from each teacher's frame of reference that we
selected the focuses for assessing pupils.   Because of
this, our pupil assessments were ad hoc, and to a large
extent were different across the four different classrooms.   Again, these assessments were generally informal.
Mostly they involved talk, in pairs, small groups, or
individually with us.   Only two were individualized,
paper-and-pencil tasks;   and in one of these, we used the
pupils' response as a baseline for comparison with small
group discussion of the same material.

Something needs to be said about the way we treated the
data we gathered in this study.   We saw this material,
not as representing generalizable evidence of a quantitative sort, but rather as providing potentially illuminative slants upon certain highly specific focuses.   These
focuses, arising out of the particular teacher's frame of
reference, were themselves differentiated across our four
classrooms.   The number of subjects involved was there-

fore always small.   The assessments we made were generally qualitative, and did not lend themselves to statistical
treatment.   Where we obtained quantitative rather than
qualitative data - as in the case of judgments about curriculum areas - we decided to present this as simply as
possible, in the form of frequency counts, or, sometimes,
of rank orders.   There was, however, one exception to the
non-statistical character of our assessments.   This was
the Idex Grid, which we used with Rachel's class to assess
changes in construing.   Here, the data was essentially of
a statistical kind, and we processed it accordingly.
However, for the sake of clarity and coherence in presentation, we decided not to provide the statistical analysis
of this measure here, but merely to describe the results
verbally.   Any reader who wishes to look at the Idex Grid
data, and our analysis of it, is welcome to do so (contact
Phil at the Institute of Education).

Being informal, these assessments depended, for their
viability, on openness and trust on the part of pupils.
Again, our experience with the children concerned was very
positive.   Both in small groups and individually, pupils
typically took our questions seriously, and offered a full
response.   For some of them, the prestige of being in a
book seemed to play a part in this.

OUR ROLES IN THE INVESTIGATION

The roles which we, as members of the research team,
played in the investigation, were partly differentiated
and partly not.   Phil and Hilary brought quite similar
concerns to the project, but viewed these from somewhat
different perspectives.   Both of us were aware of the
disjunction for many children between freer, more participant primary methods and more formal, atomized secondary
schooling.   We were interested in whether it is possible
to build confidence and autonomy within secondary classrooms using the collaborative methods that are practised
in some progressive primary schools.   We were also interested in how far the practice of secondary schooling could
forestall social divisiveness on race, class and gender
lines, that more traditional structures either endorse, or
do nothing to counteract.

For Hilary, these concerns arose out of her commitment
to the goals of collaborative learning, her own work as a
teacher and from the experience of her own two children
and their peers, as they moved on from primary school.

Phil's perspective on these questions had been shaped by
her experience as a clinical psychologist, in contexts
where many situations parallel those operating in schools.
Just as Kelly's personal construct theory had proved
liberating, within psychiatric contexts, it seemed to
promise both an endorsement of the value of collaborative
learning methods, and a number of avenues for exploring
what such methods mean.

Our own rather different professional experience meant
that we brought different insights and skills to the
study.   Where Phil lacked familiarity with secondary
schools and classrooms, Hilary contributed much first-hand
knowledge and understanding, and a wealth of contacts and
information.   As far as the conceptual framework of the
research was concerned, this arose out of Phil's long-
standing orientation to personal construct theory.   Phil
also had a background in psychological assessment, and her
familiarity with the limitations of psychometrics was one
reason for our reliance on unstandardized and ad hoc
forms.   Brenda, on her side, developed an interest in the
concerns of the project, and was willing to play an occasional part in classroom observation, and help with the
analysis of material.

In our participation in the work which the investigation entailed, both Phil and Hilary took some part in
every aspect.   However, Hilary carried the lion's share
of classroom observation, except in Islay's class, where
Phil was the main contact.   In the other three classes,
we thought it appropriate that, though Hilary was the regular observer, Phil, as a relative stranger, should occasionally also make observations.   Similarly, where Phil
carried out most of the assessments, Hilary, as someone
less familiar with these forms, was able to take a different perspective towards the tasks.   We worked together,
both in deciding how to treat the material we were gather-
ing, and in analysing this.

The writing up of the work was also collaborative.
Phil and Hilary discussed, in some detail, both the content of the book and the format it should take.   Because
Hilary had taken up another post by the time the writing
got under way, inevitably Phil did most of the actual composition, incorporating modifications which Hilary suggested.   We also involved the four teachers, at this, as at
other stages.   We outlined the general shape and content
of the book, and showed them what we had written about
their class, asking for any amendments needed.   Unfortu-

nately, Rachel was unable, because of concurrent pressures,
to respond at this stage; but the other three teachers
endorsed the general line we had taken, and contributed
some quite substantial elaborations.

Chapter 3

Mac's second year Design and Technology class

(a) MAC'S FRAME OF REFERENCE

When we began work with Mac and his second year class
group, he had been Head of Design and Technology in Claremont School for five years.   As a young, ebullient man,
active in promoting a new approach to his subject both
within and outside his school, Mac contrasted quite
strongly with the older, more conservative staff who
worked in his department.   Mac himself formed part of the
vanguard in schools and colleges working to change the
image of D and T from a low-status, craft subject, to an
intellectually demanding subject, deserving as much academic respect as any other area of the curriculum.   In
this capacity, he had produced a number of teaching and
resource materials for D and T teachers.   Quite often, in
his talk with us, Mac referred to these materials, with
their somewhat abstract and idealized discussion of D and
T.   However, in relating these aims and methods to the
work he did with his second year class, he often emphasized the compromises which it was necessary to make.
For example, he described setting up an observational project.

> 'I wanted them to go and find out things - an outside
> project, it was observational.   The kids just see it
> as something Sir asks you to do.   You do what you're
> asked.   They don't extend beyond the work given ...
> they don't do something for the sake of doing it - they
> don't go out and look for things.'

Because of his sense that D and T meant much more than
merely learning practical skills, Mac was concerned to
emphasize the imaginative and ideational goals towards
which he tried to work.   To quote one of his Department

curriculum documents, a central aim was: ' to culture
design awareness, the solving of problems, and the ability
to overcome obstacles by the use of imagination, logic and
conscious use of resource material.'   Helping children to
adopt a problem-solving approach, by drawing on their own
intellectual resources, was a theme to which Mac often re-
turned.   He spoke of 'sorting a question out - searching
in their own experience'.   He saw himself as encouraging
his pupils to take initiatives themselves, rather than
being merely imitative, and habitually resorting to copying.   This covered evaluation as well as design;   for
Mac, it was important that children should develop their
own criteria for assessing the work they did, rather than
just following the teacher's evaluation.   'It's a pathway.   The pathway goes from identifying a design problem,
researching the problem, producing a specification and
materials selection, then the construction, and then evaluation.'   Mac also commented about the breadth of the
subject, 'There are many methods of designing, and not all
of them are just paper and pencil work.'   This involved
quite broad considerations;   for instance, 'The possible
effects of designing can be both positive and negative -
it depends on who's designing.'

   For Mac, what he termed design awareness was an essential foundation for the independent approach he tried to
cultivate.   He often mentioned how important it was for
pupils to be conscious of what was involved in D and T
Work.   As Mac saw it, this awareness was developed
through communications with others: 'It's important that
children express to other people what they're doing....
In sorting questions out, children come to be able to express ideas verbally as well as physically.'   As we shall
see, this was one of the main reasons why Mac valued collaboration.

   Mac also emphasized the importance of pupils being personally involved in the work they did in his D and T classroom.   Children should experience excitement in what they
were doing.   He saw this involvement as underpinning
independent work.   'Involvement, obviously in a real
sense, rather than just follow the teacher.'   This could
only be brought about, Mac thought, by the experience of
success: 'If they can do something successful, you can
build on that success.'   In turn, confidence in themselves could lead to children putting more into their work,
and produce an upward spiral: 'Children are happy in
reaching a level - doing better than they thought.   Increased self-esteem may lead to a person doing better.'

For Mac, it was particularly important that the less able
children should experience success; again, collaborative
work could help ensure this.

If children developed these kinds of understanding
through their D and T work, then this subject contributed
to their performance in other curriculum areas. Mac also
thought D and T entailed other subjects more directly:
'There's a spin-off for other subjects of doing well in D
and T - encouraging skills, say, in literacy, via their
interest in D and T. You actually do practise other
skills.' The numeracy and drawing skills needed for D
and T work were also, as Mac saw it, likely to help children in their Maths and Art work. This needed to be accepted in the school system, which tended to put knowledge
into separate compartments.

For many years, D and T had been a boys' rather than a
girls' subject. This was something which Mac referred to
quite often. He thought it very important, in the context
of a mixed school, to break down sexist attitudes. 'If
you're going to have boys and girls you've got to develop
this, give this, just a little bit broadish attitude
towards making them do it. And that transposes the kinds
of things that were done in the 1950s and 1960s. Otherwise we get the girls turning it down wholesale.' The
key, as Mac saw it, lay in the choice of what he called
'neuter artifacts', rather than the traditionally 'male'
products of D and T workshops. Mac thought his own non-
sexist approach had paid off, at least with this age-group.
He said that he had never heard anyone in the first three
years say 'This isn't for girls.' 'They do well, eleven
to fourteen - no problem.' He felt the girls in this
group were well assimilated into the workshops, with no
sense of being intimidated by their craft content.

Later things might be different. 'At fourteen to sixteen it becomes more difficult to choose the subject.
Both parental pressures and the other subjects available
for the girls to choose - like Fabric Craft or Commerce -
are along more traditional lines.'

Collaborative learning

For Mac, the meaning of workshop collaboration lay in its
capacity to develop pupils' confidence and independence in
their D and T work. He thought that, through working
together, children could come to realize the resources they

already possessed.   This was partly because in pupil-
pupil talk, unlike pupil-teacher talk, children were able
to draw on the rich field of out-of-school knowledge.
'Pupils can share with each other in different ways from
sharing with the teacher ... across a very wide range of
daily experiences, including telly sharing.... Kids have
thousands of experiences outside school.'   Mac believed
that potentially, classroom work could be stimulated and
enriched through this kind of talk, and classroom knowledge could become personalized.   Children could also
gain a sense of confirmation: 'They validate each other's
experience, instead of the pupil always being wrong.'

Talk between pupils, Mac believed, was also capable of
facilitating thought in a way that could not happen when
they talked with a teacher, because 'You're using a different language from kids ... there's greater freedom
between kids.'   Without the pressures of the teacher's
evaluation, children were free to communicate about many
aspects of the work they were doing, to 'articulate non-
verbal relationships and processes', and to 'try ideas out
on each other, spark each other off - the Design method
known as brain-storming'.

Mac believed that an appropriate evaluation of D and T
work was ultimately achieved only through a collaborative
approach.   Whereas traditional, individualized methods
were essentially aimed at the assessment of craftsmanship
qualities in the finished product, collaborative working
methods were essentially aimed at understanding.   This
meant, on the one hand, a grasp of the relation between
plan and method - measuring, tools, sequence, problems -
and on the other, a capacity for critical evaluation, in
terms of alternative and revised designs and the functional effectiveness of the product.

Mac also thought collaborative work had an important
part to play in developing pupils' self-esteem.   This was
partly because, where problems arose, it was less humiliat-
ing to ask other children: 'It's face-saving not to go
back to Sir.'   But collaboration was also likely to
bolster the self-confidence of children, particularly less
able children.   If pupils shared their work together,
everybody was eventually likely to take the role of expert.
'Even weak children have strengths, not just strong children, in inverted commas.   I think all children have
strengths.'

When he talked about making learning collaborative, Mac

often referred to the function it served for him personally.   He felt it fundamentally altered his relationship
with the children in his class.   Although the greater
knowledge, skill, and general expertise of the teacher
could not be denied, nevertheless collaborative methods
enabled him to move out of a heavily authoritarian role
into an essentially personal relationship.   'You may
share personal details with your pupils, discovering <u>their</u>
interests and dislikes, and communicating some of yours.
You're more than just a teacher in authority - you're
someone to go to when you don't know.'   One aspect of
this was the freedom to acknowledge personal limits:
'You're fallible ... human and vulnerable - you can say
you're not sure.'   Mac thought, ultimately, children
could learn D and T work only through a non-authoritarian
relationship with the teacher.

> 'You must have your traditional authoritarian point of
> view as a teacher.   Being a teacher, you can't get
> away from that, it's always one of the underlying
> things.   But at the same time, if you can merge your-
> self in with your class, you become more than "Yes Sir
> and no Sir."   And if you're going to design success-
> fully - because designing is ultimately highly personal,
> and the skills that are covered by designing methods
> are in a way highly personal - you've got to be more
> than the authority, because otherwise you can't reach
> the inner child.'

Mac also believed that teachers communicated their own
ethos and perspective on life through the teacher-pupil
relationship that developed in collaborative work.   He
thought this was particularly the case where the teacher
was a charismatic person, and that he had personally influenced the children in his class by the atmosphere he
created, which he described as consistent, firm and knowledgeable, on the one hand, and on the other, as kind,
understanding, tolerant and compassionate.   Mac saw himself as representing for his pupils 'a basic Christian
belief';   his message was 'You share things, you accept
one another', though he did not 'overdo the churchy bit'.
He believed this message had got through: 'When you're
talking to some pupils ... your central view can be picked
up by those pupils.'

It was very important, Mac thought, that collaborative
work should be set up carefully.   The most crucial aspect
was the graduated structuring of tasks.

'Many people make the mistake and try to get children
to design by letting them loose like a ship off a moor-
ing, so the kids drift.   That is dangerous.   I think
you have to start off your designing and practical experience little by little, and build up on it.... I
think many people have made the mistake of thinking
designing is throwing a whole lot into a big kind of
bucket, and digging, and stirring well, and dipping in
the bucket, and telling children go here, there and
everywhere.   You know the nice thing about designing
is that you can set things with perimeters but you can
still get answers you don't expect out of it.   Setting
those perimeters is the skill of the teacher.'

Mac described the skilful teacher as delineating what he
wants, without defining things too tightly, and then inviting children to try it out.   'You start with ideas and
let the children have their part in it.'   This frees the
teacher to monitor the pupils, and to do more than just
teach: 'You don't want all your energy going into organizing.'   Sometimes this meant encouraging a brain-storming approach.   'You say, "here's a problem, let's talk
about it".'   The teacher was, in this role, 'able to
listen, as well as be listened to.'   It was important to
help children relate the problem to their own experience:
'You don't put pupils out on a limb.'   When things got
difficult, 'you help children circumnavigate the problem.'

   Children also needed to be helped to see each other as
resources.   Mac believed this was achieved partly by the
teacher simply withdrawing, after encouraging pupils to
ask other pupils if they got stuck.   Mac himself did not
just encourage the children - 'ask each other, help each
other' - to work together.   Within the context of an open
plan workshop, he would move out of the area for short
periods.   To make pupil communication as easy as possible,
he invariably rearranged the classroom furniture, often
putting the benches into a square.   Sometimes it was possible to engineer collaboration.   Joint work could be of
quite a humble kind or at a high level: 'You can share
small things without setting up pair work.   You just get
kids to help each other.'   Once pupils began to work
together, collaboration usually maintained itself: 'It
takes care of itself once you get it going.'

   However, Mac believed there were limits to the use of
collaboration in D and T work.   Children greatly varied in
their wish to work with others.   'Some children at eleven
design for themselves, others again share ... I think that

some children will quite happily get on with the task in
hand, and solve the problem without any word to their
neighbour or me.   But ... the two Georges ... they just
couldn't survive one without the other.'   More basically,
Mac himself believed that design was in the last resort a
matter of indiviudal effort: 'Sooner or later you have to
go solo.'   One reason for this was the desire for personal achievement: 'Personal desire, trying to conquer
things.   Collaboration can't help here - you must do it
for yourself.'

Other constraints

Although Mac thought there were ultimately certain built-
in limits to how far collaboration could reach in pupils'
classroom work, it was nevertheless to external obstacles
and constraints that he referred most often.   He described his own situation as typical of D and T head teachers
- 'At times frustrated, with traditionally less able children, behaviour problems, and a low status subject.'

    Many of the problems Mac experienced related to his
particular school context.   He felt that the attitude of
the headmaster was sympathetic to both his subject and his
methods, but that D and T held low status among the school
staff.   Mac also described difficulties in his own
department.   Although he had succeeded in involving students in his approach, this had not happened with his own
staff, who tended to 'retreat into things they've done
before' and 'felt it was safer just to teach skill'.   His
own methods were, additionally, less easy to communicate,
or even to work out, than traditional methods because the
latter 'had easily identifiable parameters that had been
established for some 20 or 30 years'.   This was, Mac
felt, because of a lack of central guidance about how to
operationalize the new D and T philosophy: 'There has
been a wide range of information explaining attitudinal
change explicitly.   There now is a need to help teachers
work out the nuts and bolts in everyday experience for
their pupils.'

    Mac also thought pupil attitudes were in the main high-
ly traditional.   In trying to encourage children to work
together, he was swimming against the tide.   A comment
reveals how narrow he felt his limits to be: 'This one
teacher, in one subject, can, in his own domain, change
their approach - slightly.'

As a footnote, it is worth saying that we talked to Mac
in the autumn of 1982 - two years after the end of our
study of his workshop.   At that stage, he seemed much
happier.   He had had a change in staffing, new teaching
material had become available, and the department had
'really begun to gel'.   There were now pupils following
courses to A level.   Many more girls were following both
Design and Graphic-based courses, and active discussion
was taking place about inter-disciplinary study.   As for
Mac's use of collaborative working methods, 'Collaboration
still continues to be one of our main themes in Design
studies and in the practical completion of work.'

(b)   THE PUPILS' FRAMES OF REFERENCE

Mac's class group (Form 2E)

Mac's class group consisted for most of the year of twelve
pupils.   Two boys - David and Jason - left in the first
term, and one girl - Fiona M. - joined the class.   We included Fiona M., but not David or Jason, in our study.
In addition, there were six other girls, and five boys.
Two of the girls - Maria and Suzanne - were quite often
absent through truancy.

(i)   Perceptions of Design and Technology

About half way through the year, we asked the children in
both Mac's Design and Technology class groups (10 from 2E
and 12 from 2T) to rate his subject, together with other
school subjects.   We used the same format, for this
assessment, as the one we adopted in Terry's and in
Rachel's class.   It involved the children in rating six
curriculum areas, including D and T, on five scales: enjoyable, not boring, useful, I'm good at, and easy.   The
children were asked to add any comments about D and T.
We wanted to find out how the children saw this particular
subject, in relation to other school subjects.   But as
well as obtaining this general portrait, we also hoped to
explore the relationship between the ratings made at this
half-way point by the children and Mac's own judgments, at
the end of the year, of their commitment, skill and intellectual capacity.

<u>The results</u>   Table 3.1 sets out the rankings, for the two
class groups together, for the six subjects on each of the
five dimensions.   From this, it can be seen that D and T
is a moderately popular school subject for these children
as a whole.   D and T is rated as relatively enjoyable and
not particularly boring, though it is not seen as very
useful.   The children generally view themselves as relatively competent in it and see it as a moderately easy
subject.

TABLE 3.1

	Enjoyable	Not boring	Useful	Good at	Easy
Design and Technology	2	3	4	2	3
Maths	5	5.5	2.5	4	4.5
Games	4	4	6	6	4.5
Home Econo- mics	3	2	2.5	4	1.5
Science	6	5.5	5	4	6
English	1	1	1	1	1.5

Table 3.2 shows the numbers of positive ratings by 13
boys and 9 girls of six curriculum areas on the first
three scales combined.

TABLE 3.2

D and T			Maths			Games		
Boys	31	8	Boys	23	16	Boys	20	19
Girls	10	17	Girls	17	10	Girls	10	17
Home Economics			Science			English		
Boys	21	18	Boys	21	18	Boys	22	17
Girls	19	8	Girls	11	16	Girls	18	9

As can be seen, boys have a very much more favourable
image of D and T than do girls, in terms of the first
three scales.   What makes this difference all the more
salient is that it applies only to D and T;   for none of
the other subjects do boys and girls produce noticeably
different ratings.   This evidence certainly does not bear
out Mac's expressed belief that no gender differences

exist in the children's attitude to his curriculum area, although it does accord with the bias in his own ratings of relative commitment. However, there is no clear difference in the ratings which boys and girls make of their own competence in the subject, nor in its level of difficulty, and to this extent the results are more encouraging.

In terms of gender difference, the additional comments offered by 13 of the 22 children seem to point the same way. Nine boys made comments, and of these, 7 are clearly favourable; whereas 3 out of 4 girls expressed some negative feeling. The content of the two gender groups is also not quite the same. The boys tend, as a group, to refer to the intrinsic enjoyability and interest of the subject: five boys mention this. Lenworth's comment is much more personal, and expresses his sense of playing an entirely different role in this setting: 'I like Design and tequnoloji it helps me to find a new caractor in myselph.'

Lenworth's very personal slant, though not typical of the boys, is more characteristic of the four comments made by the girls. Of these, only Christine is unreservedly positive: 'I think that design and technology is a very useful and enjoyable subject. I feel that it helps me a lot.' In contrast, Suzanne and Barbara both refer to Mac in personally critical ways.

We can now look at how these children's ratings relate to their commitment to the subject, their practical skill and their intellectual capacity for design, as these are judged at the end of the year by Mac. It seems appropriate to look at different aspects of the ratings for commitment, as against those for skill and intellectual capacity. We could expect commitment to be reflected in positive ratings of enjoyment, interest and usefulness. Skill and intellectual capacity, on the other hand, might be associated with perceived competence and easiness, although one could perhaps equally argue that the more able children might be more keenly aware of the challenges and difficulties of the subject, and of their own limitations. At any rate, we looked at all three sorts of relationship.

Table 3.3 shows ratings on the first three scales combined, for boys and girls, in relation to their rated commitment.

TABLE 3.3

Boys				Girls			
		Rated Commitment				Rated Commitment	
		high	low			high	low
Ratings	high	11	12	Ratings	high	1	6
on				on			
first				first			
three				three			
scales	low	1	15	scales	low	8	9

There is again a striking difference, as between boys and girls, in the degree to which Mac's judgments of commitment are reflected in positive ratings of D and T. For boys, the association is a strong one.   Boys whom Mac sees as highly committed do indeed seem so from their highly favourable ratings of D and T, as against the relatively unfavourable ratings of those whom Mac judges to be relatively uncommitted.   This close association is not, however, evident where the girls are concerned;   here, though most ratings are relatively unfavourable, it is the girls whom Mac judges most committed who express the most negative feelings.   There seem to be two possible interpretations of this.   Either Mac is much more accurate in judging the level of commitment to his subject where boys, rather than girls, are concerned.   Alternatively, the commitment of the boys remained relatively constant across the time period, while that of the girls changed over time.

Table 3.4 shows ratings on the last two scales combined, for boys and girls, in relation to their rated skill.   Here again, while Mac's judgments and the child-

TABLE 3.4

Boys				Girls			
		Rated Skill				Rated Skill	
		high	low			high	low
Ratings	high	8	5	Ratings	high	3	3
on				on			
last				last			
two				two			
scales	low	4	9	scales	low	7	3

ren's ratings are positively related for the boys,
they have a slightly negative relationship for the girls.
This situation is reversed, however, when it comes to
Mac's judgments of intellectual capacity, as can be seen
from the next table.

  Table 3.5 shows ratings on the last two scales combined, for boys and girls, in relation to their rated
intellectual capacity.   In this case, though there is no

TABLE 3.5

Boys			Girls		
	Rated Intellec-tual Capacity			Rated Intellec-tual Capacity	
	high	low		high	low
Ratings on last two scales	high 2	4	Ratings on last two scales	high 5	3
	low 2	5		low 1	7

relationship for the boys, the girls' ratings of competence and easiness tend to be positively associated with
Mac's ratings of their intellectual capacity for design.
As far as this evidence goes, it suggests that rather different factors may be operating in feelings of confidence,
for boys and girls, with practical aspects being relatively more important for boys, and ideational aspects, for
girls.

  Taking all this together, the strongest theme to emerge
is that of difference between boys and girls in relation
to D and T.   The bias which Mac himself shows, in favour
of boys, in his ratings of their commitment to the subject,
is strikingly borne out in the boys' much more favourable
ratings of the subject - and this subject alone, out of all
six curriculum areas.   This positive attitude is also evident in the boys' personal comments, which contrast with
the more critical remarks of the girls.   There is also a
gender difference in the way Mac's judgments of commitment
to the subject relate to the children's ratings of it.
The close relationship where the boys are concerned suggests that Mac has an accurate sense of their level of
commitment, particularly of highly committed boys.   This
is in contrast with the relative lack of association, among
the girls, between his ratings and their own.   Finally, it

may perhaps be that different factors make for a sense of confidence towards the subject among boys and girls, with skill critical for boys, and ideational aspects for girls.

(ii)   Construing other children

Among his concerns with the children he taught, Mac put a strong emphasis on fostering Christian values.   Quite often he referred to the encouragement he tried to give pupils to act unselfishly towards each other, to share things together, to help others, and to show compassion for weaker children.   In the classroom situation, this implied, for Mac, a non-competitive approach, and a preparedness to see potential strengths even in the least able children.   It seemed relevant to explore how far the particular children in the class we were studying shared these values, or were operating another kind of ethos.

   For this purpose, we decided to elicit, half way through the year, from the sample of pupils from the total group, interpretations of other children, and of everyday life situations.   We used different materials for these two aspects.   In eliciting views of peers we presented the children with eight school photographs of same age, same gender children, and asked them to pick out some who seemed alike in some way, as persons, and say what this likeness was.   Similarly, we asked them to group together a number of everyday situations in and out of school, as depicted in sixteen specially prepared drawings;   these included, for instance, a disco, a fight, a family meal, two friends talking, a classroom, an older child helping a younger one dress, and so on.   We picked 9 pupils on a random basis (3 girls and 6 boys);   they were seen individually by Phil or Hilary.   Two of these - George K and Vincent - are members of our target class; the remaining seven are from the parallel class which Mac taught for half the year (2T).   We will summarize the judgments for the group as a whole, only presenting in detail those made by George K. and Vincent.

George K.   The main focus in George's constructs is that of peer group relationships;   seven of his judgments refer to these.   In four cases, there is a reference to trouble, particularly in terms of the support given by friends: 'Good friend, stick up for you, play out with you', 'Will help you out in all circumstances.'   George seems to speak from the perspective of the victim rather than the

aggressor: 'Vicious - pick on you - get you into
trouble.'   He also expresses some ambivalence about
depending on the support of others: 'Stick up for themselves, don't rely on someone else.'   Another of his constructs also refers, perhaps a little contemptuously, to
lack of aggression: 'Kind-hearted, harmless, gentle.'
Two other constructs refer positively to togetherness
among friends: 'Being together happily.'   'Playing
together happily, things in common, agreeing with each
other.'

    Another concern, implied in George's constructs, is
with family, especially parent-child relationships.
Again, there is the possibility of trouble: 'Disagreement
with parents', 'Goody-goody at home, don't argue with
parents and brothers, do homework.'   That parents may
perhaps do the wrong thing is also suggested, implicitly,
in another construct: 'Parents being helpful, doing the
right thing.'

    Of the three remaining constructs, two refer to rela-
tive competence in school.   George seems, perhaps, to
align himself with the more able group in the way he words
things: 'OK, clever - in a higher group', 'A bit backward
- in a lower group.'   The last construct is rather general: 'Wrong things to happen.'

Vincent   Bad relationships with adults, especially
teachers, represent the major theme in Vincent's constructs.   Two of his references describe deliberately
disruptive or rejecting behaviour: 'Smash window.   Throw
things, play about in class' and 'Hopping the rag, getting
into trouble.'   But much more often Vincent suggests that
bad relationships develop regardless of children's inten-
tions.   Two constructs refer to the effects of academic
difficulties: 'Sort of dopey - can't manage, and teachers
don't understand,' 'Thick kid, never concentrates.'   In
another construct Vincent describes another, involuntary
source of problems with adults: 'Little brothers and sisters get them in trouble, they feel angry and they've been
bad.'   Two further constructs imply a polarization
between adult and peer group relationships: 'Act flash to
friends, but good to teachers' and 'Make jokes and get in
trouble, but they're really good sorts, they don't think.'
Vincent does refer, in one construct, to positive motiva-
tion in school work: 'Hard worker and helper.'   But he
also implies how difficult this is by his phrasing of the
construct 'Try to get on working.'   His description of

successful relationships with teachers also suggests the possibility of contempt for docility: 'Don't argue with brothers and sisters, get on with teachers, don't muck about.'

Of the remaining three constructs, two refer to relationships: 'Cowards, pick on weaker, smaller people', 'People getting on with each other.'   The last construct is matter-of-fact: 'Everyday happenings.'

The group as a whole   In the most general sense, these nine children can be said, from the evidence of the constructs they offered, to share Mac's concern with human relationships.   Throughout the whole set of constructs runs the theme that relations with other people matter, and that good relationships are valued.   Beyond this, however, some differences in perspective clearly exist, particularly where boys are concerned.

If we look at the constructs of girls and boys separately, two rather different standpoints seem to emerge. For the three girls, the pleasure of social encounters seems salient.   This is seen as a function of temperament: being lively, happy, carefree means being able to enter into and enjoy relationships with other people. Mac's central concern with sharing, helping, giving, is reflected only marginally in some of the girls' constructs.

The six boys seem to speak from a distinctive position. Though good relationships with others are implicitly valued, these boys place central emphasis on the likelihood of conflict and strife between people.   There are differences in the perspectives taken towards such people, some apparently speaking from the standpoint of victim, and others adopting the perspective of instigators of trouble.   In these boys' constructs, quite unlike those of the girls, there is a strong consciousness of disharmony and friction, of persecution, vulnerability and misunderstanding.   While bullying is condemned, the need to withstand aggression is emphasized by several boys, with some contempt for weakness.   The implicit assumption in these boys' interpretations - that mistrust and hostility are endemic in certain kinds of human encounter - sits at variance with the ideal of universal tolerance and caring.

Mac's own values held implications, for him, of a collaborative approach to classroom work in which sharing, and the absence of competitiveness, were evident.   How

far does this approach seem to underlie these children's
judgments?   Very few references are made to classroom
work;   but where they are, they suggest a very different
ambience.   Classrooms do not seem, from these constructs,
to represent an arena where all children are valued, and
where people help each other and share things together.
On the contrary, relationships with teachers are construed
negatively rather than positively, and school work is
apparently seen as a source of anxiety, difficulty and
boredom.   In terms of attitudes towards different ability
levels, these seem to be construed as very much a divide
between children: all those who refer to them, except
George K., speak from the standpoint of the less able.
To this extent, these children do not seem, half way
through their year in Mac's class, to have assimilated his
personal ethos towards classroom relationships.

(iii)   How the children assessed themselves

In his teaching of Design and Technology, Mac was concerned to develop in the children the capacity for evaluating
their own work.   For him, it was important that pupils
should not merely rely on the teacher for a sense of their
standing in the subject, but should have available an
appropriate frame of reference in terms of which they
could make judgments about their own progress.   For this
reason, we set out to assess, in at least some of the
children in his class, how they construed this particular
subject, and how they saw their development, and potential
development, within it.   This involved an ad hoc rating
scale, together with questions about the judgments made in
relation to it.

   Since we wanted to explore how far, by the end of the
year, the children had assimilated Mac's own evaluative
standpoint, we made this assessment towards the end of the
third term.   We saw all nine children who were then
present - four boys and five girls.   The children were
seen individually.   We asked them to rate themselves
somewhere along a 7-point scale representing ability in D
and T.   They were then asked to rate themselves as they
were when they began the year, and as they expected to be
in the future.   We asked the children to talk about what
the scale points represented and about the basis for their
judgments: in most cases, this involved quite a long discussion.

   Three major aspects of these children's views seem par-

ticularly important in relation to Mac's standpoint, as a
teacher of Design and Technology committed to collaborative learning.   First, Mac hoped that, through their experience of his classroom context, all the children would
come to have positive feelings towards their work.   It is
therefore important to see how far such positive attitudes
do emerge from the way children talked about the subject.

Mac cared, too, that the children in his workshop group
should come to have an appropriate view about the work
which D and T entails.   This meant moving beyond the
common stereotypes: that D and T is merely a craft subject, that it is set apart from academic areas of the curriculum, or that it is not suitable for girls.   For Mac,
the ideational, imaginative aspects of D and T were particularly important;   and he tried to ensure that the
children he taught came to an awareness, and a respect,
for these aspects.   From the children's comments, we can
see how far they had achieved a sense of the D and T curriculum which was consonant with Mac's own sense.

Finally, we need to look at the way these children saw
the learning process in this part of the curriculum.   For
the success of Mac's collaborative learning modes, it was
important that the children viewed themselves, and each
other, as resources in D and T work.   One aspect of this
is a sense of some potential independence from the teacher.
It is also important to look at how the children had experienced their own learning so far, and how they saw
future possibilities for themselves in D and T work.

1 Positive involvement in D and T   From what they say
about their work in D and T, most children evidently have
positive rather than negative feelings towards the subject.
Five children express such feelings unambiguously.   Gary,
George K., Lenworth, Fiona M. and Sarah all comment on their
work in clearly favourable, and sometimes enthusiastic,
terms.   Gary declares his intention to take the subject
to O level and CSE if he could, while George K. hopes 'to
maybe learn it in college or something'.   Lenworth is enthusiastic about Mac's approach: 'I really gone to the
way of how Sir makes things.'   Fiona comments 'I like D
and T, it's quite good.   I think I'll go on with it for
quite - like, till I get to my fourth year.'   Sarah expresses still greater commitment: 'It's one of my best
subjects, this is.   If it's allowed, I would like to
teach Design and Technology.'   Vincent's feelings seem
rather more mixed;   he says: 'I'm not really interested,

but I like to do it.'   Only three children, Barbera,
Maria and Suzanne, express clearly negative feelings.
Barbera's dislike is strongly stated; she says she would
drop D and T as soon as she can because 'I don't really
care about this lesson.'   Her negative feelings are well
known in the group, and both Sarah and Maria refer to
them.   Speaking about her own feelings, Maria also says,
'I'll drop it as soon as I got the chance to.'   Suzanne
also expresses dislike: 'I don't like it much - it's
boring.'

Another index of positive involvement in the subject is
perhaps a sense of being at least reasonably competent in
it.   As far as this index goes, it seems significant, and
encouraging, that not a single child gives self-ratings of
below average competence.   Even those who, like Barbera,
express strong dislike for D and T, nevertheless see themselves as being at least average in ability.   Fiona,
Maria and Suzanne also put themselves at the mid-point of
the scale, while Gary, George K., Vincent and Sarah rate
themselves as above average ability, and Lenworth judges
himself as nearly at the top of the scale.

2 Defining the D and T curriculum   In their talk about
D and T work, these children have a good deal to say about
what it involves.   How far does their sense of the work
they did reflect Mac's own definition of the subject?

Mac strongly stressed the dual character of D and T,
which he saw as entailing ideational as well as practical
aspects.   For most of these children, it is the practical
side of the work which seems to be most immediately
salient.   However, many of them are also aware of its
imaginative, intellectual side.   Eight out of the nine
children refer to the practical demands, and the practical
skills, which D and T work entails; only Sarah dwells entirely on its ideational character.   The children mention
many aspects.   Several of these are encompassed within
the general concept of accuracy in D and T work: exact
measurements, cutting straight and at precisely the right
points, steady hands, making a tidy piece of work, with a
smooth finish.   Sometimes the children elaborate the idea
of accuracy by relating skill, and difficulty level, to
the kind of object involved: for instance, producing the
right angles in a complex piece of work, or getting the
measurements exact where curves are involved.   A number
of children, in talking about practical aspects, refer to
equipment and materials.   Several times tools are por-

trayed an an essential factor in D and T work;   understanding their functions, and using them correctly are
seen as crucial.   For Lenworth, the availability of good
equipment actually governs the level of work possible in
D and T.   A few children also refer to the kinds of
material involved as a factor in the work done, in relation to its interest or its difficulty;   for George K.,
working in balsa wood has been a less demanding preliminary to D and T.

For Mac, the intellectual demands intrinsic to D and T
were one of its most important, but also one of its most
under-estimated aspects.   He saw these as, ultimately,
entailing the complex ability to produce designs for products that will function as they are meant to, and that
possess, additionally, the best aesthetic, human and
social character that is possible.   Five out of these
nine children refer spontaneously to the intellectual, as
opposed to the merely practical, demands of work in D and
T.   Several times, the capacity to evolve one's own
design is mentioned.   Often this is seen as governing the
difference between high and low level D and T work.
Several children talk about the need to think out a pattern, to figure out a design, to have a plan.   This is
seen as involving imagination, since in the process of
evolving a design, several possible forms have to be considered, compared and analysed.   For most of those who
discuss these aspects, the link with function is clearly
important;   several children comment that things cannot
work if they are not properly planned and thought out, and
that knowing how things would work out in practice is
essential.   It is interesting that, whereas it is in general the four boys who have most to say about the practical aspects of D and T work, it is two girls - Fiona and
Sarah - who talk most fully about its ideational aspects.
Fiona refers to the importance of imagination and to
having to 'Think of your own pattern and analyse it.'
Sarah, who thinks making is the easiest part, and designing the hardest, tries to describe why: 'You've got a
picture of how it's going to be, and if it's something
that you gotta, that it works, you've gotta kind of, how
it works and that.   If it's not designed right and all
that, it won't work.'

In the light of Mac's concern that D and T has some
continuity with more academic areas of the curriculum and
is not just out on a technical limb, it is worth looking
to see how these children see the subject in relation to
other subjects they do at school.   Very few comments are

made about this; only Fiona and Sarah relate D and T to
other areas of the curriculum.   Fiona thinks D and T is
differentiated from English, but aligned with Maths,
because of the calculations involved in measurement.
Sarah, on the other hand, contrasts D and T with both
Maths and English, on the grounds that it offers freedom
and autonomy to pupils, whereas Maths and English require
strict teacher direction.

One of Mac's most strongly felt concerns was that, as a
curriculum area, D and T was as relevant for girls as for
boys.   He felt that not only did his own teaching counteract any sexist divisions in his classrooms, but that,
within this group, there was not even a sense of the existence of such divisions.   Unfortunately, the children's
own comments do not bear out this judgment.   Although
none of the boys refer to gender in talking about D and T,
four out of five girls do so.   For Maria and Suzanne, a
strong sense of the gender-inappropriateness, for them, of
the subject forms the basis of their rejection of it.
With rare fluency, Maria comments:

'Because boys more enjoy doing the woodwork, because
when they grow up they could become woodcutter or something like that.   Girls, they get bored.   A girl said
just now, outside, why do we have to do this rubbishy
exam with woodwork.   It doesn't do anything to girls.'

Suzanne, similarly, judges that 'It's for boys really,
isn't it.   They should do cooking or something for the
girls.'   Fiona and Sarah, highly motivated though they
are, nevertheless express a clear awareness of prevailing
sexist attitudes which could cast doubt on their own involvement.   In this situation, Fiona takes a fighting
stance towards possible sexism;

'I asked a question to my little brother, Do you think
girls should have D and T, and he said Yeh.   I think
it helps because I think that when you leave home, if
you want to put up some pictures or anything, when you
get your own flat or anything, what sort of nails to
use for your walls and everything like that.   That's
when I think it's helpful.'

Sarah fears that social barriers might forestall her own
intended career as a D and T teacher: 'You know, it's men
mostly do these jobs rather than ladies.'

In talking about his curriculum, Mac rather under-

emphasized the particular products made in his D and T
classrooms.   For these children, however, this was clearly an important factor.   Surprisingly, several children
express the sense that the difficulty of D and T work is
related to the size of what is being made.   Tables and
chairs are seen, because they are larger, as more difficult than mazes, model towns or cheeseboards, larger
shelves as more difficult than smaller ones.   More appro-
priately, perhaps, George K. relates difficulty to whether
the product is 'for real', as against what he calls 'mess-
about work'.   For many of these children, particularly
the girls, however, it is the character of the product
which seems to govern their own feelings towards D and T
work.   Several stress the personal, or potentially personal, character of what they make in their D and T lessons.
Gary, Fiona, Maria and Suzanne all mention the possibility
of using D and T products as gifts for members of the
family.   Sarah sees D and T as involving a continuity
with earlier family activities;   'Children, when little
children were small, they liked family things with toys,
and making things and all that.'   Several children refer
with some feeling to their preference for making some
kinds of things rather than others.   Making a model village is evidently popular; but preferences do not always
go the same way - Suzanne, for instance, likes making game
boards, whereas Vincent does not.   More fundamentally, as
Sarah describes in relation to Barbera, the product involved can, through its personal relevance or lack of relevance, govern a pupil's whole attitude to D and T classroom work:

   'Last week, we had a choice of what we could make.
   And we all decided to make a little model village.
   And Barbera thought, Oh, that'd be nice.   And she
   goes, I'll take part in that.   But with things like
   shelves and all that, she doesn't have the time to do
   it.'

3 Attitudes to learning   How far, from their discussion
of D and T, do these children seem to have assimilated a
sense of the validity, and the possibilities, of learning
through collaboration?   A factor which seems very important here concerns their sense of the accessibility of the
subject to their own learning.   If D and T is seen as an
area where ability is governed purely by natural talents,
this would militate against the active engagement in
learning which collaborative work demands.

One approach to this question is via the children's account of their own progress so far in D and T. Here, things seem on the whole encouraging.   Seven of the nine children say that they have definitely improved in competence from the start of the year; and several think their progress has been very marked.   Only Barbera and Suzanne see their abilities as having declined during the year's work.   In terms of the whole group's development, Lenworth volunteers the comment that the class as a whole has come a long way through their work in Mac's class: 'They have climbed, most of them, pretty high for their age.' From this evidence, it seems that in general these children have found that Mac's collaborative methods facilitated their own learning.

What do these nine children actually say about the process of learning and how far do they see it as a collaborative enterprise?   Several lines of analysis seem relevant here.   First, what do the children see as underlying the development of competence in D and T?   What view do they take of their peers in the D and T learning situation?   How do they see the role of the teacher?   Finally, to what extent do they view themselves as possessing resources for learning the work of D and T?

If we look at the comments the children make about what makes for competence in D and T, some difference of emphasis emerges in the comments of boys and girls.   Gary, George K. and Vincent all stress the importance of effort and application, while Lenworth says nothing specifically about the process of learning.   Among the girls, Maria says nothing clearly relevant.   Suzanne implies that competence is a function of the level of task difficulty; it arises from how hard the work is.   Fiona suggests that competence is largely a function of natural gifts: 'Some people are naturally better at it.'   Barbera and Sarah, however, both emphasize the critical importance of attitudes, though from opposite personal positions towards D and T.   Both these girls see competence as essentially developing out of a personal interest in the subject. Sarah's account, in relation to Barbera's motives, has already been quoted.   On her side, Barbera makes the approving comment, about a previous D and T teacher:

'Well, the things he was telling us about it, and what he was saying, like, um, if we was doing a shelf, he'd make it himself before us, to see how it's done.   And he would show us places like where we could put it up. And he would tell us what sort of wood it's made out,

bring out all the tools that we needed to do, and sort
of tell us how interesting it is to do, and things like
that.'

When it comes to the position of peers in the D and T
learning situation, four out of the nine children mention
their relevance, but in opposite terms.   Again, boys
differ from girls.   Gary and Lenworth portray other
children in the classroom as a source of distraction,
through talking in class, or just mucking about.   Gary
adds that sometimes they can help, however, by passing on
what the teacher has said.   By contrast, for Barbera and
Maria, peers are a potential resource.   Barbera describes
her sister Sarah as helping her in this, as in other areas,
while Maria refers to Fiona G. as having helped her, so
that she is now able to help Suzanne.

On the question of the role of the teacher in D and T
classroom learning, several comments are significant.
The view taken by most of the children seems broadly consonant with the role which Mac saw as appropriate to a
collaborative learning approach.   Only Vincent and Gary
imply a sense of learning as entirely teacher-dependent.
Other children clearly see the teacher's role in much less
authoritarian terms.   George K. seems to view Mac as an
exemplar of high-level competence, rather than a direct
transmitter of skill;   Mac 'has gone to a higher stage ...
the things he does, they're actually for-real things,
making tables.   They're for-real, making them perfect....
Ours is only mess-about work, if you know what I mean.'
Lenworth, though he sees the need for the teacher to control pupils, also expresses appreciation for Mac's way of
teaching, which offers pupils some guidance while also
allowing them a good deal of responsibility.   This is
also Sarah's theme.   Barbera, despite her personal alienation, puts forward the view that good teachers are those
who make work interesting, and help pupils understand.
Maria defines pupil competence in terms of autonomy,
seeing more able children as those able to work independently without having constantly to resort to the teacher.

Finally, in terms of the resources which these children
seem to feel they possess for learning the work of D and T,
there is again a contrast between boys and girls.   Whereas Gary, George K. and Lenworth all mention out-of-school
resources of some kind, none of the girls does so for
themselves, although Barbera makes a reference in relation
to Sarah, who she describes as having gone with her Dad,
when he used to do building.   Gary refers to his own

study, out of school, of designs in shops, which he sometimes buys, to study still more closely.   George K. mentions his previous experience in fixing windows, and to
the relevance of D and T to mending furniture at home.
Lenworth describes the kind of help his father gives him,
in similar terms to those in which he describes Mac's
teaching, 'He said that I should think, that I should
figure it out for myself.'   In the girls' talk, no such
references are made to out-of-school resources and support
on their part.   On the contrary, Maria poignantly describes the potential contempt at home for her D and T
work.   'If it's bad, I just chuck it in the bin when I
get in.   I don't bother to show it to my Mum or Dad,
because they'd say, what you do is a load of rubbish.'

Gender differences   The recurring differences in emphasis
in these children's discussions seem to point to a very
different significance, for boys and for girls, in the
work that they do in Mac's D and T workshop.   The most
obvious difference is that, where the boys are unaware of,
or unconcerned about, the existence of sexist divisions in
D and T, these divisions are centrally salient for the
girls.   For some girls, the power of sexist stereotypes
is reflected in their lack of involvement in D and T,
even, sometimes, in a declining involvement.   For these
girls, D and T lessons have little connection with their
out-of-school lives and their envisaged future lives.
This may be why the slant they take towards D and T -
whether they like or dislike the subject - is different
from the boys' perspective.   It seems that, for these
girls, skills in themselves are not specially valued.
Their involvement in the subject, if it is to occur at
all, seemed to be of a kind which is both more intellectual and more personal.   Perhaps this is why the role of
the teacher, in making the subject interesting and understandable, is so important to these girls.   It may also
be why the product to be made is not, for them, an inci-
dental feature of the lesson, but has significance, potentially, in relating the work to their personal life and
personal interests.

(iv)   Collaborative assessment of work

One aspect of collaborative learning is the willingness,
and the ability, to work with others in evaluating what
has been learned.   This was something which Mac specially
emphasized.   In his view, children were generally unused

to taking responsibility for assessing their own school
work; but a careful personal appraisal of their own progress represented a crucial phase in the learning process.
Arriving at an assessment jointly with a working partner
was, as Mac saw it, just as important a part of collaborative learning as working together in making a product.

Towards the end of the third term, we set up, jointly
with Mac, a project for two of his lessons which was
designed to explore the children's use of an opportunity
for collaborative assessment. We asked the children to
work, with a partner they chose, in evaluating the shelf
which was the last piece of work each had produced. This
evaluation included grading the work from D- to A+ and
then explaining why they had decided on that grading.
For this, we asked the children to fill out a form, with
the grades at the top, and three sections for a written
response, entitled Why we have decided on this grade.   In
what ways would this work have needed to be different to
get a higher grade?   In what ways would this work have
needed to be different to get a lower grade?   We also
gave each pair of children a list of suggestions for the
sorts of things they might think about in awarding grades.
These were: How useful is the shelf?   How well will it
work?   Should anything have been done differently or
changed?   Has the person thought how it will be put up?
How well is it made?   In addition to the written evaluations we asked for, we tape-recorded, with the children's
permission, the conversation they had in arriving at their
assessments.

Five pairs of children took part in this assessment.
They were Barbera with Lenworth, Gary with George W.,
George K. with George W. (the following week) Christine
with Sarah, and Fiona M. with Suzanne.

The children's use of joint assessment   Two aspects of
this exercise in collaborative evaluation seem important.
First, how far did the children take the opportunity
really to work together, and to produce their evaluation
out of genuinely co-operative thought?   On this aspect,
the outcome seems disappointing.   In the case of two
pairs - neither regular partners - there is little real
co-operation, often one over-ruling the other.   This is
so for Gary and George W., and, largely, for Fiona M. and
Suzanne.   When George W. works with George K., his part
in the assessment is obviously different; though the
relationship is not symmetrical, judgments are genuinely

shared and jointly agreed.   There is much mutual empathy, and genuine mutual listening, in talk between Barbera and Lenworth; but the two children do not negotiate their judgments with each other.   It is only Christine and Sarah whose assessments seem to arise out of an equal, joint effort.   Here, not only is mutual respect evident; the two girls consistently listen to each other, modify their judgments and arrive at a negotiated evaluation.

As an exercise in collaboration at the end of a year in Mac's classroom context, this task did not seem to elicit a high level of joint work.   A number of factors may have affected this.   Some partnerships were formed by neces- sity rather than choice; and several children may have found it difficult to work with those who were not special friends or regular working partners.   George W. certainly took a more genuinely collaborative part in the assessment with his friend George K. than in his previous work with Gary.   It also seems that the task was not one which readily engaged the children's interest.   Even Barbera and Lenworth, who took the task seriously and worked through it conscientiously, operated in a self-conscious, stilted way quite unlike their classroom conversation. Several pairs carried out the exercise in a rather per- functory way, seemed to be concerned to get through the task as quickly as possible, and paid little attention to the details of what we were asking them to do.   Since this was the first time that Mac had asked them formally to evaluate their own work, it might have been better to devise a much simpler assessment task than the one we actually set up.

This task also served, like the individual assessment task, to elicit the kinds of judgments which these child- ren made about the work they did in D and T.   To what extent did their criteria reflect those which Mac himself saw as relevant?   Most of the judgments which these child- ren make as they talk about their D and T products refer to practical, technical aspects.   Over and over again, good work is defined in terms of a smooth finish, while poor quality work is defined by rough edges, scratches, marks and dents.   Less often, accuracy of measurements is referred to, in terms of closely fitting sections, or sym- metry of parts.   These references to technical aspects greatly outnumber references to design.   However, where design is mentioned, this is usually with reference to function - something which Mac himself saw as central. Some children refer to the need for a product to be stable rather than unstable, and to be usable in practice.   Only

one pair - Christine and Sarah - mention, in passing,
aesthetic aspects.   One other, additudinal, factor in D
and T work is mentioned by some children, who see good
work as the outcome of close attention and care.

These findings are all the more striking because four
out of the five factors which we listed for the children
to consider - usefulness, function, design, and context -
all refer to non-immediate aspects of the products.
Their own stress, on largely technical features of D and T
work, suggests that when actually considering the products
they have made, these children do not readily think in
terms of their less immediately tangible, concrete
features - features so crucial in Mac's own sense of D and
T.   However, it may also be that the design aspects of D
and T work were difficult for the children to put into
words.

(v) Views of collaboration

Aware that his encouragement of pupils to talk together
went against most of their daily classroom experience, Mac
was particularly concerned that these children should
develop positive attitudes towards collaborative work.
For him, this meant a sense of their own, and each
others', resources for D and T work, including an awareness of the relevance of their out-of-school knowledge.
It meant, too, being prepared to use each other to spark
off ideas, and to operate in linguistic and social modes
that did not have the constraints of teacher-pupil interchange.   This school context, in which these children
already experienced streaming in some subjects, might be
expected to promote an awareness of differences in ability.
For Mac, it was of central importance that children respected each other as learning resources, regardless of
academic ability level.   Mutual esteem across differential school competence was, from his point of view, a crucial aspect of collaborative work within a mixed ability
classroom.

For this part of the study, Sally Davies, an undergrad-
uate student with a six-month attachment to the project,
interviewed eleven of the twelve children individually,
using as starting points our questions about school and
out-of-school experience (see Appendix).   Sally was interested in the significance of educational banding for attitudes to collaboration; and for this purpose she ascer-
tained the bandings for each child on transfer from primary school.

1 Attitudes to school and school learning   The children's
attitudes can be defined in terms of what they said about
three areas: personal identity in and out of school,
relationships in the peer group, and the significance of
school learning.   Talking about whether or not most
people were different in and out of school, all except
three children think they are.   The general theme, among
those who stress difference, is that school constrains
freedom and inhibits behaviour (for instance, Christine:
'In school you've got to be quiet and can't do what you
want.')   Some children talk in germs of 'good' and 'bad'
behaviour.   (Gary: 'In school they're concentrating,
outside they're mucking around and jumping on buses.')
If we look at ability differences, as represented by secondary transfer banding, we find that whereas both the two
band 3 children - Maria and Suzanne - endorse the view
that differences exist, Vincent - one of the two band 1
children - says people are the same.

Another aspect relevant here is the children's perception of peer group relationships, particularly of how
these relate to school.   Asked about friendship groupings,
the children put forward a variety of bases, ranging from
going around in gangs to Zodiac sign attraction.   Here
again, some relationship exists with ability differences.
Of the two band 1 pupils, Fiona G., in a frankly snobbish
speech, refers to intelligence and social class:

'Intelligence - it's very difficult to get on with
someone who is stupid.   It's almost a strain, you
have to correct your language, and it really gets me
down.... The same way of living - the same amount of
money coming in.   People can't afford to have a boat,
cottage or pony sometimes ... there's a girl in another
class who has no money to live, to be ... I'd hate to
be poor.'

Two of the four relatively low band pupils also refer to
intellectual differences, but from a standpoint of lesser
competence (for instance, Lenworth: 'Most people don't
really know how to do the work, so they still try at it,
and they hang round together').   From this evidence, it
seems that ability differences are seen to be a factor in
friendship groupings, by those who themselves are rated
both high and low in ability, though not for those in the
middle range.

Another aspect of peer group relationships in school
has to do with conflict and trouble.   Here again, there

seems to be some association between the children's attitudes and their ability.   Whereas 8 out of the 11 children think children are unable to sort trouble out for
themselves, and need teachers to intervene, it is 3 children in the lowest banding quartile - Maria, Suzanne and
George W. - who believe children can sort things out for
themselves.   George W. for instance: 'If there's a fight
going on, you might be sensible and stop the fight.'
From this, it seems that peer group relationships may be
more independent of official school life for the less able
children.

The last aspect relevant to perception of school and
school learning relates to how the children see their work
at school.   Talking about particular aspects of the curriculum that are important to themselves and their parents,
all these children place great stress on getting qualifications for employment.   Christine's comment is typical:
'English and Maths.   That's what you need to go to work.
Most parents don't care if you do no good at Science or RE,
or things like that.'   There is no difference in terms of
ability level, in this emphasis, though the slant the
children give it is not quite the same.   For instance,
Vincent says that if you do Maths, English and foreign
languages 'You can go abroad ... and get a good grade in
life', whereas George W. comments that Maths and English
'are the most important things for jobs in a supermarket'.
Perhaps because of this general emphasis on school work in
relation to job qualifications, few children even mention
D and T as a subject that they or their parents value.
The three who do are all boys: Gary, George K. and
Lenworth.

Employment prospects are also seen by these children as
the reason why exams are important.   Banding level makes
no difference to this perception.   However, again, the
personal standpoint from which the children discuss this
is somewhat different.   Vincent, one of the two highest
rated children, says: 'They give you grades and you can
get up to the top.'   Suzanne, in contrast, remarks: 'You
have to do well in them to get a good report.'

Attitudes to attainment   The children are almost equally
divided about streaming, with five children favouring it,
and six disapproving.   What is striking is that it is the
two band 1 children, and three out of four lower banded
ones, who make up the approving group.   Again, however,
the personal slant is very different.   Characteristically,

Fiona G. remarks: 'If I was in with dumb ones all the
time I'd get fed up.'   Vincent takes a similar stance and
tone, saying: 'You should leave all the clever people
together, and all the dummies on their own.'   George W.,
Lenworth and Maria also believe that streaming is a good
idea; the general theme of their comments is that low
ability pupils disturb brighter ones and waste their time.
Maria even equates low ability with badness: 'If you put
good with bad, the bad will annoy the good workers and
disturb and try and copy off them.'   By contrast, among
the average ability children in this group, there is a
general feeling that less able children can learn from
more competent ones.   Suzanne, the only band 3 pupil who
disapproves of streaming, speaks personally and feelingly
about the stigma of a low stream: 'Mixing them all up,
then no one takes the mickey out of you, and calls you a
dunce or anything like that.'

    The children also talked about school attainment.   For
most of them, doing well in school is equated with good
behaviour in class.   Behaving well towards the teacher,
getting on with work, not mucking about, are frequently
mentioned by children in all categories of ability.   It
seems that being generally conforming and docile rather
than troublesome in the classroom is viewed as the crucial
factor making for success in the world of school.   The
children take a similar position towards the question of
why pupils learn better in some classes than in others.
Again, pupils' behaviour is seen by most as governing how
much is learned.   Here, there is some emphasis among
the boys on other pupils as negative influences on behaviour and concentration - Vincent, Gary, George K. and
Lenworth all mention the problems caused by peers talking or distracting you.   For instance, Lenworth says:
'Because if you're in one class, and some people influence
you so you neglect your work.'

<u>Attitudes to collaborative learning modes</u>   Crucial to the
success of a collaborative approach to learning is the
sense that talk among pupils can be valuable.   Asked
whether talking with other pupils could ever help with
learning, eight of the eleven children think it can, at
least sometimes.   The reservations are concerned with the
direction that talk takes: several children comment that
merely chatting is not helpful.   Two children, Christine
and George K., see peers as playing a specially valuable
role in learning.   Christine says 'Most times I have
trouble understanding the work and questions and my friend

will explain it to me.'   George K. comments: 'Yes,
because they exchange thoughts - "yes that's a good idea"
- and if you think it's a bad idea you tell him.'   The
three children who think pupil talk never helps are in
lower bands.   George W. explains: 'No.   If a clever
person is distracted by a not so clever person, the other
person wouldn't learn that way.'   Maria thinks talk would
never be learning-directed: 'Because when they talk they
don't about work.   They talk about the pictures and
discos.'   Lenworth clearly dismisses the idea that talk
could help: 'No, because if they're talking, how can they
get on with their work?'

However, nearly all these children are prepared to
allow that, in some cases, friends could explain things
better than teachers.   For instance, Vincent: 'Sometimes
friends are easier to understand.'   Fiona G. relates this
capacity to the familiarity and sympathy of friendship:
'[Teachers] don't understand exactly what you're asking,
but a friend, especially if you know them well, can understand what you're asking and explain.'   Gary, in his reference to talking with friends, mentions their out-of-
school knowledge: 'Kids may know something from elsewhere.'   In some children's comments, the sense of frustration in talking with teachers is as strong a theme as
the ease of communication among friends.   For instance,
Sarah says: 'Teachers talk about what they know, and
sometimes children don't know what they're [i.e. teachers]
talking about.'   Suzanne remarks 'Teachers don't know
what they're saying sometimes and make you get it wrong.'
Maria emphasizes the lack of help from some teachers:
'Teachers sometimes say, try and figure it out yourself,
but friends tell you all the details.'   For Fiona G.,
there is potential humiliation in asking teachers: 'If
there's things you don't totally understand and don't want
to ask the teacher because you feel silly.'

Finally, the use which these children are likely to be
able to make of collaborative learning opportunities must
relate to how, in this particular workshop group, they see
each other.   Sally asked them who they would nominate as
resources when they got stuck in their work.   In saying
who they would turn to for help, although six children
mentioned the teacher, five chose other children: George
W., Vincent, Barbera, Fiona G. and Sarah.   These five
represent mainly high bandings;   only George W. is below
average.   However, it is interesting that those chosen as
resources in difficulty are not those of the highest bandings in academic subjects.   Neither Fiona G. nor Vincent

are nominated, while Christine, Sarah and George K. are
all average banding, and Lenworth - chosen twice - is
banded relatively low.   It seems that children seen as
doing well in D and T are not those whom teachers judge to
be academically able.

   What of the choices made by those who are themselves
seen as resources by other children?   Except for Sarah,
they all nominate the teacher as their own source of help.
This attitude is clearly borne out by the remarks these
children make.   Christine sees friends as lacking knowledge of an academic kind: she says she would go to the
teacher 'because friends might have the wrong answer
because it's a subject'.   George K. thinks other children
have little to offer him: 'Other kids probably know less
or the same as me.'   He also clearly feels uneasy about
his own role as a resource in classroom work: 'Sometimes
I don't like it.   It's best if people put what they
think, not take everything I say down and get it wrong.'
This standpoint is also taken by Lenworth, who says, about
being asked for help, 'I'd probably tell them to go and
ask the teacher as I wouldn't want them to copy my mistakes.'   Like Christine and George K., Lenworth does not
have much faith in other pupils as resources: 'If I ask
someone in the class, I might do their mistakes as well.'

General comments   In all this material, there are a few
encouraging straws in the wind which suggest at least the
possibility of these children making use of collaboration
in their classroom work.   Certainly, as a group, they
believe that friends can act to facilitate understanding
and that peers can be experienced as a resource in classroom learning.   Against this, however, have to be set
certain attitudes towards school learning which seem extremely hostile towards collaboration.   The keen awareness of academic banding differences and the large significance given them, emerges in many ways.   The children
speak from a clear sense of their own labelled position on
the ability continuum, and what is more depressing, speak
with a contempt for low ability, whether or not they identify themselves as able or less able.   Ability is seen by
high and low ability children as governing friendship
patterns; and to some extent this seems borne out by the
pattern of choices made of working partner - choices which
perhaps have a social rather than a work base.   Finally,
nearly half the children do not believe in mixed ability
classrooms.

Another depressing feature is that school learning, for
these children, is equated with certification for employment. This means not only that D and T, as a subject,
holds a low status in their valuation of the work they do
at school. It also suggests that the more personal
aspects of school learning, those which could potentially
link school with life outside and draw the pupils into
real involvement and participation in their school work -
these aspects barely exist for this group of children.
Although it is the lowest banded children for whom a
school-life disjunction seems strongest, references to
school are largely unenthusiastic, conformity rather than
initiative is seen as the key to learning, and there is a
sense of difficulty and frustration in relationships with
teachers.

(c) THE DYNAMICS OF INTERACTION

Throughout the year of our study, Mac encouraged the
children in this class to work together. He did not,
however, actually intervene in what groups or partnerships
they should form, nor did he specifically structure the
ways in which they were to collaborate. For us, it is
important to look to the material we have for the basis of
commonality in the working groupings which these children
came to form. What was this basis? How did it affect
the way the children functioned in class? How far was it
facilitative of Mac's teaching goals?

The material we gathered during the year was designed
to illuminate relatively broad aspects of children's
orientation - aspects which we did not expect to alter
very quickly. In this part of the project, we were not
concerned to assess change, but to elicit perceptions,
attitudes and feelings which had a bearing on Mac's classroom goals. We made seven kinds of assessment. Mid-
year, we assessed attitude to D and T, obtained some
children's comments on a particular D and T project, and
elicited constructs about children in general. At the
end of the year we obtained general self-evaluations, and
joint evaluations of work from pairs of children, and we
assessed attitudes to collaborative learning. Throughout
the year we observed some of the children in their D and T
workshop setting, and in the last term, in some other
lessons too. Because these kinds of material represent
particular angles on a number of attitudinal themes, it
seems appropriate to draw upon them as they illuminate
these themes, rather than treating them as separate kinds
of data.

In examining what groupings actually formed in Mac's
workshop during the year, it is striking that a number of
groups established themselves quite quickly and remained
relatively stable across this whole time period.   This
was most obviously the case with that almost unseparable
pair - the two Georges.   Fiona M., after her arrival in
class, also formed a regular grouping with Maria and
Suzanne.   Until the very end of the year, Christine and
Sarah constantly sat together.   After Jason had left,
Gary regularly joined Lenworth and Barbera - already regular working companions.   Only Fiona G. and Vincent were
not regularly attached to particular groups, although
Fiona G. was sometimes on the fringe of Fiona M.'s group,
while Vincent was a marginal member of Lenworth's group.
It seems from this evidence that, left to themselves as to
what associations to form, most of these children readily
established groupings which they continued to find satisfying.   What common basis did these groupings have?

George K. and George W.

If we consider the two Georges first, as the stablest
partnership of all, the most obvious feature is the large
discrepancy in competence at D and T between the two boys.
From the material we have, it seems that an awareness of
this imbalance was probably quite salient in both boys'
perceptions.   In jointly assessing their products, they
agreed that George K.'s should be awarded an A- and George
W.'s a B.   In talking about other children, George W.
mentioned 'less brainy children'; his reference to the
future was to having a job in a supermarket.   Explaining
why he would choose George K. as a work partner, George W.
said: 'He does well at school, he concentrates, he's not
easily distracted. He's clever, he knows what to do.   I
go to him if I can't do the work.'   Conversely, George K.,
describing why he would pick his friend as a work partner,
mentioned that 'Sometimes he doesn't understand things',
and that 'Sometimes he gets out of hand, and asks too many
questions'; however, George W. was 'a good friend to exchange ideas'.

This essentially sympathetic mutual appreciation,
between two boys of unequal ability, did, from what we
observed of them, define the nature of their classroom
collaboration.   George W. clearly looked to his friend
with trust and respect, unreservedly accepting both his
suggestions and his criticisms; while, on his side,
George K. not only found his less able partner 'a good

friend to exchange ideas' - an audience for his own ideas - but was also able to understand and anticipate, in an empathic way, the difficulties George W. might be meeting.

The Georges' working partnership was also marked by a quite unusual dedication to classroom work. Unfortunately, we have very little material relating to George W.'s feelings and perceptions. All that we have from George K., however, suggests that he was serious in his commitment to D and T. He gave D and T the highest ratings of all subjects and spoke of his plans to take it beyond O level, into college level if he could. George K.'s strongly stated respect for this part of the curriculum was based on its usefulness, and, concomitantly, he valued 'for real' artefacts over other kinds of design. The sense of continuity with ordinary life, of which making real furniture in the workshop was a part, obviously contributed to George K.'s respect for the subject. Finally, his judgments of his own competence were clearly made within a frame of reference embodying very high standards, in terms of which he could be critical of his own work. Given that George K. had such strong positive feelings towards D and T, and given that he played an essentially dominant role towards George W., it does not seem surprising that the working relationship between the two boys reflected this commitment to classroom work.

What part did this partnership play within the total group? Several children were clearly aware of its exclusive nature. During the year, we saw Barbera, Gary, and, several times, Vincent attempt unsuccessfully to break into the two boys' interactions. From what evidence we have, it also seems that other children were well aware of the competence differential between these two boys. Invariably, it was George K., not George W. who was sought out as consultant; and Lenworth, himself a highly competent class member, cited George K. as someone he would choose to work with, remarking 'I'd ask him for help. I'd work with him. He's got a different approach.' The difference in competence was also, not surprisingly, endorsed by Mac himself.

If other children may not always have welcomed this exclusive partnership, it clearly performed very important personal functions for both George K. and George W. More obviously, George W., as the less able pupil, was enabled to get by in class work, and thereby avoid all the problems of total failure. His friend's presence also protected him from the potential ridicule and bullying of

which we saw occasional signs.   In working with George K.,
he regularly experienced genuine personal support and
attention, as against the rough-shod treatment he got, for
example, in the joint evaluation with Gary.   But George K.
too, clearly gained.   Not only must the role of master-
to-apprentice have helped him to articulate the problems
and processes of designing and making, and in so doing,
develop his own understanding.   As well as this, George
K.'s absorption with his weaker friend probably helped him
avoid other, more problematic, interactions.   In construing other children, George K. referred more than once to
trouble and friction.   Another theme was hostility to
adults, and we saw for ourselves problems with teachers in
a classroom context which did not endorse his special
friendship with George W.   Even his ability in D and T -
which he turned to such good account in helping his friend
- might have proved problematic for him in other relationships.   George K. was clearly uneasy in the role of a
general consultant in the classroom.   He thought people
should go to the teacher, because 'other children know the
same, or less', and that he did not like others asking him
'because I might tell them my mistakes, and they'd go
wrong'.   From this point of view, the comfort which
George K. evidently felt in his unambiguous role towards
George W. was all the greater for not embodying any anxiety
about being in a false position.

Fiona M., Maria and Suzanne

These three girls made up a subgroup which was nearly as
stable as that of the two Georges, and just as self-con-
tained.   The variability in the group's composition was a
consequence of these girls' quite frequent absence from
school - never the result of their choosing other classroom partners.   Their high level of social cohesiveness
was evident not only in their consistently choosing to
work alongside each other in their 'own' part of the workshop, and sitting together, where possible, in other
lessons.   It was also clearly endorsed by what they said
about each other.   Maria and Suzanne, asked about preferred working partners, chose each other and Fiona M., making
no reference to anyone else in their classroom group.
Suzanne, who mentioned knowing Fiona M. before starting at
her present school, remarked that both Maria and Fiona M.
lived nearby, and the three of them went round together.
Maria also referred to the out-of-school context of the
group friendship, but expressed some ambivalent feelings
towards the two other girls: 'Suzanne and Fiona in school

are kind, but outside they're mean and tell men I fancy
them, and show off.' Even so, for Maria, as for Suzanne,
these friends were clearly very important in their school
lives.   Both girls said they would like to sit by these
friends in all their lessons, and both said they would
allow them, but no one else, to see their school work.
It is a pity that we do not have the same kind of interview material for Fiona M., but from what we saw of her in
the classroom, it seems likely that she would have expressed reciprocal feelings towards her two friends.

One common denominator which these three girls shared
was probably some degree of felt incompetence in D and T.
Mac judged all three to be relatively lacking in both
technical skill and intellectual understanding of design,
although he rated Fiona M. a little more competent than
Maria and Suzanne.   When we saw them in his workshop,
these girls usually seemed to be struggling with whatever
they were making, or actually to have given up altogether.
Fiona M., who more often took the initiative, sometimes
tried to direct the others, or take over from their unsuccessful attempts;   but from what we saw, things usually
proved too difficult for her also.

Although we do not have records for Fiona M., both
Maria and Suzanne had experienced a global categorization
of relative incompetence in school.   Both these girls
were banded uniformly low by their junior school teachers
in verbal reasoning, English and Maths.   This categorization formed a clearly painful theme in some of what they
said.   Maria actually equated low ability with being
'bad'; while Suzanne, arguing against streaming, commented 'Then no one takes the mickey out of you and calls you
a dunce.'

In this little subgroup Fiona seems to have been experienced as the most able member.   Certainly neither she
nor Suzanne, in jointly assessing their shelves, hesitated
to award her own work a much higher grade.   Fiona also
stood apart from the other two girls in her general feelings about D and T.   She said she liked the subject, and
hoped to go on with it, and she defended its relevance to
girls.   This is in marked contrast to what Maria and
Suzanne said.   Both girls expressed strong dislike for D
and T; both said it was a boring subject and not for
girls, and both added that it was irrelevant for later employment, unlike English and Maths, which really mattered.
Another feeling shared by Maria and Suzanne was the sense
that the artefacts they took home from D and T were not

valued;   their general disaffection from the subject was
also clear in what they said about a particular D and T
project.   Questioned about what they had learned, neither
girl could suggest anything, nor were they able to describe anything they had really enjoyed doing.

Still more fundamentally, both Maria and Suzanne seemed
to share a sense of alienation from Mac.   Each of them
described teachers as a crucial resource in learning,
although Maria envisaged the possibility of mutual pupil
help in some circumstances.   However, she referred to
teachers not helping when they could do so.   Suzanne,
more bitterly, remarked that teachers, so far from helping,
could actually 'make you get it wrong'.   For Suzanne, D
and T lessons seemed to be experienced as places where
her own incompetence aroused the teacher's hostility.
She spoke of Mac as getting angry, and as shouting at
pupils who could not do the hard work he set.   Relationships with teachers evidently mattered a good deal to
Suzanne, who mentioned liking English and Maths because
she liked the teachers, and who remarked 'You got to like
the teacher to get on well.'

Fiona M. was, in this subgroup of girls, the most dominant member.   She was probably experienced as the ablest
of the three, seemed to be the social leader, and, in the
joint assessment task which we recorded, took a strongly
dominant role towards Suzanne.   Nevertheless, in the part
this subgroup played in Mac's workshop, it was the attitudes of Maria and Suzanne which prevailed over those of
Fiona.   It was disaffection from their work which characterized these girls' functioning in their D and T lessons.
This may have come about partly because Fiona M., Maria
and Suzanne were virtually ignored both by Mac and by the
other children except Fiona G.   This invisibility was
certainly largely self-chosen, and must have served a
self-protecting function, particularly to Suzanne, who had
experienced the humiliation of her lack of competence
being exposed to public ridicule.   Nevertheless, it meant
that, where their own limited ideas and skills were inadequate for the work set, these girls had no access to help
from others.   The fact that Mac himself had little to do
with this group also deprived them of the kind of teacher
guidance and encouragement which, for Maria and Suzanne at
least, might have enabled them to feel positively towards
their lessons.   Their triadic relationship certainly provided these three girls with much needed social support.
However, its encapsulation of them also cut them off from
other resources, and ensured that they regularly experienced failure.

Fiona G.

In a number of ways, Fiona G. stood apart in Mac's workshop group.   Her affluent and socially prestigious family
background was in marked contrast to the social and economic situation of the other children.   She was also accus-
tomed to being labelled an academic high flier.   Her
junior school banding had been consistently high, she was
currently in the high ability Maths group, and, as she remarked, her parents expected her to come first in all her
school exams.

    What is still more striking is that Fiona G., on her
own account, was at pains to dissociate herself from the
other pupils in this class.   She did so in both social
and academic terms.   Talking about children's friendships,
she remarked that this was usually a function of 'The same
way of living - the same amount of money coming in.   Some
people can't afford to have a boat, cottage or pony sometimes.... There's a girl ... who has no money to live, to
be.   I could afford cherries - I love cherries - every
two days if I wanted to.   I'd hate to be poor.'   Fiona G.
also commented that, in relating to other children, intelligence was very important to her.   'It's very difficult
to get on with someone who is stupid - it's almost a
strain.   You have to correct your language, and it really
gets me down.'   She thought streaming was right, 'because
if I was in with dumb ones all the time I'd get fed up.'

    As we saw from our observations of the group, Fiona G.
usually sat in the part of the workshop 'belonging' to
Fiona M.'s subgroup, and she occasionally joined in with
their work.   However, she explained to Campbell that her
membership of this group had come about accidentally.
Fiona G. was clearly ill-at-ease in being witnessed in
this setting; once, she gestured to Phil that she found
the other girls stupid and exasperating.   Her comments
about the class group were in kind.   After mentioning
Christine, Barbera and Sarah, she dismissed the other
pupils: 'All the other lot are hardly ever here, and are
boring, and are parasites - they watch and copy everything
you do.   It's really awful, I look up and see copies of
my work.'   How was it that Fiona G., socially and academically striving as she was, came to associate herself
with such an unlikely subgroup?

    A more probable association for Fiona G., on the face of
of it, would have been with Christine, who was also a
member of the upper Maths group.   Fiona G. did in fact

nominate Christine as her choice of working partner in D
and T lessons, saying that Christine was nice to talk to,
and got on with her work.   Christine herself reciprocated
this choice, and commented that Fiona was 'interesting and
brainy - she talks about all kinds of things'.   Despite
this, the two girls never, from what we saw, actually col-
laborated in their D and T work.

   There are probably several reasons why this particular
partnership did not come about.   Fiona herself was, in
her approach to school work, highly competitive.   Her
contempt for less able pupils, her resentment of 'parasites' together with the pressures she felt to be top of
the class - all these things must have militated against a
free-and-easy sharing of school work.   When we saw her
briefly combining forces with Fiona M. and her friends,
collaboration was not apparently very productive.

   In order to work with Christine, Fiona would have
needed to establish a positive role towards Sarah, Christine's regular D and T partner.   However, as Fiona herself was aware, Sarah did not like her.   Fiona commented:
'She doesn't really want to know me ... she's least accepted me in this class.'   Fiona was, in fact, conscious
that she had difficulties in relating to others.   'I
don't get along with people very well, I quarrel a lot.
I get angry at too many jokes.   Maybe I'm like a spoilt
child.'

   Both Fiona's competitive approach to school work and
her difficulties in personal relationships are likely to
have created problems for her in a collaborative setting.
An additional factor, which may also underlie the part she
played in this workshop group, was her strong dislike of
the lesson.   When she spoke to Campbell of a particular
D and T project, she conveyed a sense of floundering out
of her depth in the work - an impression endorsed by what
we saw of her efforts in the workshop.   Fiona was also
very critical of Mac and his teaching.   In what she said,
there were undertones of anxiety and possible humiliation.
Talking about being stuck in D and T work, she commented,
'In the end, I'd go to the teacher.   But if he's in a bad
mood, I'd put it off as long as possible.'   She said she
found it difficult 'if there's things you don't totally
understand, and don't want to ask the teacher, because you
feel silly, or they don't understand exactly what you're
asking.'   From this point of view, Fiona - though at the
other end of the social and academic spectrum from Maria
and Suzanne - nevertheless shared with these girls a sense

of alienation and mistrust towards the lesson and the
teacher.   It seems to have been this negative common
denominator which underlay such association as they had.
All in all, however, Fiona remained an essentially marginal member of the group who, for all the intensity of her
views, had little impact on the other children.

Christine and Sarah

Until the third term, Christine and Sarah formed a regular
working partnership in Mac's lessons.   At that stage,
however, they seemed to be moving out of it, both in D and
T and other classrooms.

    From the evidence we have, these two girls were rather
different in their outlook.   Sarah, in what she said to
us, expressed generally positive, often enthusiastic,
feelings towards her school experience.   She praised the
school itself.   'It's a good school because they mix boys
and girls together.   The coloured girls here do no teasing, and there's no fights against each other.   My sister
[Barbera] in another school used to be teased by black
girls.'   She hoped, herself, to be a teacher.   Towards
D and T, Sarah declared a whole-hearted commitment.   She
described it as one of her best subjects, felt she had
made great progress in Mac's classes, and envisaged a possible future career within it.   Mac echoed this judgment,
in rating Sarah highly committed to the subject.

    On her side, Christine referred to generally less posi-
tive experiences in school.   She remarked: 'In school
you've got to be quiet, and can't do what you want.'   Her
comments on school learning conveyed a sense of personal
difficulty.   She said, 'Most times I have trouble understanding the work and questions.'   Though banded high in
Maths, it seemed that Christine did not feel at ease in
the classroom context.   Another comment suggests some
feeling of alienation from boys in school: 'In classes
like sex education, boys laugh at it, and it's not funny.'
In talking about D and T, Christine described it as a
useful subject; but she obviously valued other subjects a
lot more - 'English and Maths.   That's what you need to
go to work.   Most parents don't care if you do no good at
Science or RE or things like that.'   Mac, in his rating,
judged Christine to be uncommitted to D and T.

    Sarah and Christine also differed in their feelings
about Mac's particular concerns.   We unfortunately were

not able to interview Christine about the curriculum.
For her part, Sarah's sense of D and T as curriculum was
remarkably close to Mac's own.   She saw design as its
crucial feature, and imagination as critical to learning.
She understood Mac's aims in allowing his pupils responsibility, and appreciated the opportunities he gave: 'He
tells you what he would like you to make.   And then he
goes, design it for yourself, and then make it for yourself.... You really like it, because you can make things
for yourself.'   Like Mac, Sarah vehemently denied the inevitably of sexist barriers.   On questions of collaboration in D and T, Sarah was clear that other pupils were
resources.   Asked who she would go to if she got stuck in
D and T, she cited Lenworth, and said she would go to him
before asking the teacher.   Christine thought otherwise:
'The teacher, because friends might have the wrong answer,
because it's a subject.'

The two girls were probably different, too, in their
level of competence.   In Mac's judgment, Christine lacked
technical skill, though possessing potential intellectual
competence.   He judged Sarah to be highly competent intellectually, and also technically skilled.   These relative positions were endorsed by the two girls themselves
in the grades they agreed to award each other for the
shelves they had made, when they gave Christine's a B,
and Sarah's a B+.

Finally, Christine and Sarah had contrasting relationships with Mac.   Sarah's close sympathy with Mac's
approach has already been described.   Christine, from
what we saw, had a very distant relationship with Mac,
and, indeed, seemed virtually invisible to him when she
sought his help in a lesson.

How did this partnership actually work out, between
able, confident, committed Sarah, and the more ambivalent,
doubting, less competent, Christine?   Not surprisingly,
Sarah, from what we saw, usually took the dominant role in
their interactions.   Hers was generally the initiative.
She took it upon herself to criticize Christine's work.
She seemed generally acknowledged the greater expert.
Nevertheless, in the set piece collaboration we recorded,
there was genuine mutuality.   The two girls listened to
each other, showed respect for the other's views, and, to
a large extent, jointly negotiated their judgments.

In terms of the quality of work done together, on the
whole this partnership was not very impressive.   As often

as not, the two girls' talk was unrelated to what they
were supposed to be doing.   Their involvement in the
lesson was patchy.   We noticed that what they produced
was sometimes slapdash.   Once, they confessed to being
totally at a loss: 'We don't know what we're supposed to
be doing.'   In the third term, when the two girls seemed
to withdraw from their association, we witnessed a rather
different quality of work on Sarah's part.   Moving
amongst the looser grouping of boys - notably Lenworth,
Gary and Vincent - she seemed more involved and attentive
to the work she was doing and, concomitantly, her interactions with these boys was more clearly work-related.

How did this particular partnership come to be established?   Christine and Sarah, from what we saw, did not
seem to be special friends, outside Mac's workshop.   This
was confirmed by what they said.   Christine cited Fiona G.
as a preferred work partner, while Sarah said it was
Lenworth - for whom she expressed great admiration - that
she would choose to consult if she were stuck in her D and
T work.   It seems that it was largely a matter of chance
that Christine and Sarah came to establish their regular
association.   They chose each other as work partners on
the first occasion and, for some time afterwards, evidently did not consider making a change.   The partnership
itself obviously served a function.   For Christine -
needing the support of others, anxious about school work
and somewhat passive in her approach - the regular presence of Sarah was obviously personally reassuring and
maintaining.   For Sarah, too, the freedom to share the
work and talk with a partner must have been important; we
saw her rebel openly in a lesson where pupil talk was dis-
allowed.

However, her association with Christine was probably
ultimately much less productive for Sarah than other partnerships she might have formed.   Sarah herself had wider
relationships in Mac's group than Christine, particularly
among the boys.   Had she regularly joined forces with
Lenworth, Gary or Vincent, who shared her liking for D and
T, her work might have developed much more fully.   In
turn, her own appreciation of Mac's goals, her generous
attitude to other children, and her capacity for give-and-
take might have done much to sustain their sometimes fluc-
tuating efforts in D and T work.

Barbera, Gary and Lenworth

Throughout the year, Barbera and Lenworth sat near each
other in Mac's workshop, chatting together from time to
time.   For the last two terms after his friend Jason left
the class, Gary usually sat alongside Barbera and Lenworth,
and joined in the chat.   The association was not an exclusive one;   all three children interacted with others in
the class.   Essentially, this grouping seemed to be
focused on social concerns.   The three children hardly
ever seemed to talk about the work they were doing.
Sometimes they were concerned with what were clearly personally important questions, such as violent and abusive
fathers.   Sometimes their talk was more gossipy.
Towards the end of the year, Gary and Barbera conducted an
enjoyable flirtation together.

The social functions, and the social pay-offs, of this
triadic relationship, were quite clear.   All three children had bad reputations in school generally, and, as we
saw, all three were currently living out these reputations
in other classroom contexts.   Barbera was openly disruptive in a number of non-D and T lessons.   Gary, defined
as a 'scallywag', also played the part of naughty boy in
several lessons, on one occasion bringing down the
teacher's sanctions on his head.   Lenworth, also labelled
a 'scallywag' was, as we witnessed, involved in an angry
confrontation with a teacher.

The potential for anti-school, anti-teacher feeling
formed one theme in what both Barbera and Gary said.
Barbera commented: 'Sometimes you get teachers who talk
to you, and others don't.   Some don't like blacks, like
Mr. ..., he clips Lenworth sometimes for nothing.'   She
thought teachers were quite likely to be unhelpful in
cases of difficulty: 'He might say, I've told you once,
and you weren't listening.'   Barbera was also highly
critical of Mac himself, saying that he did not really
care how pupils got on in his lessons, and that as a
result, she felt habitually lost in the work.   Gary, for
his part, spoke feelingly about the whole institution of
school: 'Some kids don't like school because they feel
trapped, and they feel it's a punishment, so they skip
school.'

Yet, despite the familiarity of all three children with
the experience of being at odds with school and teachers,
their behaviour in Mac's workshop was consistently positive
rather than negative.   Lenworth was the most obviously

absorbed in his D and T projects, and he spoke warmly of
the 'new character' he found for himself in Mac's lessons.
Gary was also generally work-oriented.   Even Barbera,
though she did not always give much attention to the official business of the lesson, made no attempt to disrupt
the class, or disturb the work of other children.   With
Mac, of whom she was so critical, we witnessed a brief
contretemps; but we also saw a prolonged tutorial interaction which Barbera obviously found satisfying.   From
this point of view, it seems that Mac's workshop context
offered these three ebullient personalities a safety valve
for personal expression and social interests which might
otherwise have erupted into class-disruptive behaviour.

   What did this association do for the class work of
these three children? As far as Barbera is concerned, the
benefits are obvious.   Barbera consistently expressed the
strongest possible dislike for D and T.   These feelings
were well known to her classmates.   Fiona G. described
Barbera as slapdash, not caring about the work, not getting on with it.   Maria said Barbera thought D and T was
'a load of rubbish', while Sarah commented that Barbera
disliked the subject, and felt herself to be no good at it.
Barbera's association with Gary, and, still more, with
Lenworth, clearly did much to forestall her hostility to
the lesson and also to mitigate her feelings of dislike.
Despite what she said about D and T, Barbera obviously
admired those who were competent in it.   Explaining her
partnership with Gary, she said, 'Boys are good at woodwork.   That's why I went with Gary, because some of the
girls don't know what to do.'   Barbera was openly admir-
ing of Lenworth's D and T skills, and she seemed to set a
high value on these because she personally respected
Lenworth.   Barbera also gave serious commitment, in working with Lenworth, to their collaborative assessment of
the shelves they had made.

   For Gary and Lenworth, the benefits of this partnership
to their work are not so clear.   Both boys brought to
their D and T lessons a strong commitment, recognized by
Mac.   Both saw D and T as a useful, interesting and
important subject, and both hoped to take it on to a high
level.   For both, this aspect of the curriculum was continuous with their everyday lives.   From what we saw of
them, both boys, particularly Lenworth, usually worked
hard and with interest in their D and T lessons during the
year.   But their association with each other, and with
Barbera, seems to have accompanied their work rather than
actually facilitating it.

Neither Gary nor Lenworth apparently saw much potential
for real collaboration in their workshop association.
Both boys mentioned someone else as a preferred work partner - Gary citing Vincent, and Lenworth citing George K.
More fundamentally, they both saw the teacher as the only
real resource in case of difficulty.   For Gary, dependence
on teachers was a strong theme, while he saw peers as a
potential distraction in classroom work: 'If you put
people in with a group who never concentrate, that stops
you.'   Lenworth put this point still more emphatically,
seeing other children as undermining concentration, and
talk as inevitably work-disruptive: 'If they're talking,
how can they get on with their work?'   To Lenworth, the
idea of mutual pupil consultation was itself dubious.   He
commented that if he asked someone else in the class he
might make their mistakes, and conversely, that he would
not want anyone to consult him: 'I'd tell them to go and
ask the teacher, as I wouldn't want them to copy my mistakes.'   Although Lenworth was highly appreciate of Mac's
workshop ethos, this was not because of the collaborative
opportunities it offered, but because it allowed him to
work things out for himself.   Getting on with the work on
his own was something he valued, and, as we saw, something
for which his capacity was generally much admired.

Gary, however, was not like Lenworth in this respect.
Despite his reservations about the resources of pupils,
Gary was, as we saw, able to make good use of collaborative opportunities.   This was particularly the case with
Jason; both boys seemed genuinely to help and support
each other in the work they were doing.   In many ways
Gary seemed to be a 'natural' for collaboration with
others.   He also had an obvious need for quite frequent
advice and help in his classroom work - a need which often
went unmet.   Gary spoke often, and with emphasis, about
how hard he found the work in his D and T lessons.
Barbera's role of apprentice effectively precluded her
from acting as a resource for him, while Lenworth's preference for independent work, and general reluctance to act
as consultant, tended to block this source of guidance.
George K., absorbed in his relationship with George W.,
gave scant attention to Gary's appeals.   In this situation, Gary, though he certainly gained in terms of his
general experience, did not actually find in his relationships there the resources which might have helped him
overcome his difficulties in the work.

Vincent

Like Fiona G., Vincent, when we saw him, was usually
hovering on the fringes of a subgroup in the classroom.
In Vincent's case, it was that of Barbera, Gary and
Lenworth, although we also saw him occasionally with the
two Georges. Socially, Gary was his particular friend;
both boys referred to their friendship out of school, and
Gary described Vincent as 'a good mate, not bossy - I
always go round with him.'

How did this marginal position in the group fit with
Vincent's attitudes to Mac's classroom? What did he feel
about school learning, D and T, and Mac's collaborative
modes? Towards school generally, Vincent seemed to have
quite complicated attitudes. On the one hand, he was
evidently ambitious for academic success. He spoke about
'getting to the top', in order to have 'a good grade in
life'. Vincent had been banded high at junior school and
was currently in the upper Maths group. Ability differentials were apparently salient for him; for instance, he
supported streaming, saying that 'You should leave all the
clever people together, and all the dummies on their own.'

However, Vincent seemed to see academic success as
dependent on a withdrawal from relationships with other
children. More than once, he polarized good relations
with teachers, and good relations with peers. He spoke
from the inside about getting into trouble at school, and
was clearly familiar with the role of disruptive pupil.

This conflict was also apparent in Vincent's stance
towards Mac's lessons. Mac judged him to be exceptionally highly committed to D and T, and this was very much
borne out by what Vincent said about the subject. Not
only did he give D and T the highest possible ratings; he
also conveyed the sense that Mac's part of the curriculum
could be genuinely enjoyable, and have real personal significance. But, again, Vincent saw progress in D and T
lessons as depending on keeping apart from other children.
He often referred to 'being with people who talk a lot,
and so you don't learn', and said of himself that he would
prefer to have no partner in D and T: 'If I get on on my
own I do my work - otherwise I talk.' Vincent saw Gary
as a particularly tempting distraction: 'I prefer talking
to Gary best ... Gary is no good because he talks too
much.'

To this extent, rather than welcoming Mac's collabora-

tive mode of learning, Vincent actually fought against it.
We need to ask whether, in fact, his work was facilitated
by his independent stance, and undermined by his association with other pupils.   When he sat with Gary, his
closest friend in the group, Vincent did actually seem to
exemplify his own belief in the distracting effect of
other children.   Their conversation seemed generally non-
work-related, and occasionally, the two boys were, though
briefly, quite disorderly.   To a lesser degree, their
association in Mac's class recapitulated their joint disruption which we saw in other classes where teachers were
actively concerned to separate them.   But if Vincent
sometimes got into minor trouble through his association
with Gary, this was certainly not the case when he sat
with Lenworth and with George K.   We saw him devote careful attention to the work which he shared with both these
boys, and in their collaboration, contribute to their own
understanding, as well as gaining, himself.

Vincent certainly needed help from time to time in his
D and T class work.   He expressed anxiety about his own
position, saying that he worried about the problems he
met.   In general, Vincent seemed to have great difficulties in pacing himself - difficulties he was probably
aware of.   In talking about what made for success in D
and T work, over and over again he stressed the need to
take time - being careful, not rushing things, doing the
work slowly and accurately.   When we actually saw Vincent
working, we noticed him doing things rapidly and impres-
sionistically.   Not surprisingly, this often led him into
difficulty.   Meeting problems, Vincent did seek out
others for guidance - notably George K. - but frequently
met with only a perfunctory response.   Given his enthusiastic, ambitious approach, it is not surprising that in
this situation he sometimes expressed a sense of frustration, at the 'fucking hard work'.   In Vincent's case, the
guidance and support he clearly needed - and was himself
able to give - were, for social reasons, not available to
him.

Conclusions

Taking all this evidence together, it seems that the
children in Mac's class demonstrated a high level of
sociality in the way they interacted together during the
year.   Even with groupings whose common denominator was
dislike of the lesson, mutual social support was generally
high.   Within their partnerships and small groupings,

these boys and girls typically treated each other as particular persons whose interests and feelings were known
and respected. This mutual acknowledgment and support
must certainly have acted to maintain individual children,
who might otherwise have disrupted the class, or withdrawn
from it altogether.   Feeling across subgroups was also
clearly positive rather than negative.   Except for
Fiona M.'s subgroup, which remained very isolated, a
friendly mutual interest was maintained amongst the children generally, and there were seldom any hostile
encounters.

What is particularly encouraging is that, to a large
extent, this positive group feeling cut across potential
barriers of gender, race and academic ability.   It is
true that Fiona M.'s subgroup remained an island within
the class, seeing themselves apart from other children,
and largely ignored by them.   Gender seemed to play some
part in this sense of apartness in Mac's class, which, at
least for Maria and Susanne, was felt to be unsuited to
girls.   But Sarah and Christine - the other girls' grouping - did not separate themselves from the boys, either in
their interactions within the class group, or in what they
said about their experience.   Lack of alienation is most
striking, however, for Barbera, whose dislike of D and T -
emphatically stated, known throughout the group - might
have polarized her position in the workshop, where boys
were acknowledged to be the enthusiasts.   Instead,
through her lively interest in Gary, and her genuine
admiration for Lenworth, Barbera willingly submerged her
negative feelings, and participated in supporting the work
of the class.

The children's social relationships in Mac's classroom
did not embody, either, any racial antagonisms.   In this
group, two children - George W. and Lenworth - were West
Indian in origin, while two - George K. and Maria - were
of Greek origin.   Within the school generally, racist
comments and racial conflicts were commonplace, and several of these children spoke about them.   As far as attitudes in this group were concerned, none of the children
referred to racial antagonisms in talking about each
other, and we saw no evidence of any racial barriers
between them.   It was Lenworth who seemed to hold the
highest social prestige in the group, while he and George
K. were generally respected as the ablest members of the
class.

Interactions among these children also transcended

ability differentials.   This was true where academic
ability was concerned.   It might well not have been so.
By this stage the children were very familiar with banded
class groups, and with their own position in the bandings.
Some of them clearly carried this consciousness with them.
Fiona G. and Vincent both spoke from a sense of academic
superiority, while Maria and Suzanne expressed an equally
clear sense of a low place in the academic hierarchy.   At
least half the children agreed with streaming in schools.
Yet their relationships with each other cut across such
differences; in Mac's workshop there was no segregation
of subgroups by academic ability.   Nor was it the case
that the children grouped themselves by their ability in
D and T.   Despite a clear realization within the group of
who were the more and less competent members, the partnerships the children formed cut across such differences -
George K. working with George W., and Lenworth with
Barbera, for instance.

How far did this generally favourable social set-up
actually forward Mac's teaching goals?   We have seen that
its capacity to facilitate the children's classroom work
was quite variable.   While certain children very obviously benefited greatly from their contact with others, this
was not always the case - either because social relationships did not cover those who had the necessary resources,
or because they served merely to endorse negative feelings
towards the lesson.   But Mac also looked to classroom
collaboration to bring about other, more subtle, benefits.
One of his concerns was that weaker pupils might, through
working with peers rather than with the teacher, gain the
experience of success.   Here again, their collaboration
did more for some children than for others.   Because of
their social isolation, Fiona M.'s subgroup had little
access to more resourceful pupils, and paid for their
mutual social support and protection with regular experience of failure.   Barbera, on the other hand, obviously
benefited from her contact with the expertise of Lenworth,
and, in discussing the shelf she had made, expressed some
pride in what she had achieved.   Still more strikingly,
George W., who was probably the least competent of all the
children, was regularly helped by George K. to manage the
task set - something he could almost certainly not have
achieved in a straight teacher-directed lesson.   More
subtly, their social relationships in class may well have
helped the children to experience themselves more positively, in the face of potentially damaging criticism, we
saw Jason draw on Gary's support to laugh off some sharp
comments from Mac, and thereby re-establish self-esteem.

Mac hoped that working amongst themselves might also enable the children to overcome the sense of disjunction between their school learning and their everyday lives. In this sphere, there was a marked difference between the boys and girls in his group.   Gary, Lenworth and Vincent all spoke of out-of-school resources as facilitating their D and T work; while George K., referring to artefacts that were 'for real', emphasized its practical application.   All these boys also spoke of personally enjoying D and T lessons.   It is difficult to know whether their sense of D and T as integrated with personal concerns and everyday experience was part of their existing orientation or had actually been brought about by sharing their lesson work.   Certainly Mac's collaborative opportunities did not seem to achieve any personal integration for the five girls.   Only for Sarah did D and T seem to be continuous with her out-of-school life.   In some cases, even the possibility of integration was precluded by a sense of its irrelevance to their gender roles.   This sense also extended, for several girls, to the kinds of artefacts that were the product of D and T lessons - artefacts which they felt to be uninteresting, and un-valued at home.

For the girls in Mac's workshop group, teachers were highly salient.   Mac himself believed that collaborative modes enabled the teacher to adopt a more human, less unequal relationship with pupils.   However, in the workshop, it was with boys that Mac most often interacted, while girls who sought his attention were sometimes not noticed.   It was boys whose orientation to D and T he seemed to understand most closely, and conversely, it was boys who most often adopted his own approach to the subject.   Mac's relative distance from the girls in his group was reflected, on his side, in the fact that he did not appreciate the gender barriers that stood between some of them and his part of the school curriculum.   On their side, several of the girls felt some sense of alienation towards him.   Nevertheless, we saw even Barbera - most emphatic of all in her expressed dislike - engage with Mac in a prolonged one-to-one encounter which she visibly found satisfying.   Perhaps over time, greater mutuality might have developed between Mac and the girls in this group, though this might not have reached the high level of sociality we saw between him and the boys.

Chapter 4

Islay's fifth year Social Studies class

(a) ISLAY'S CLASS GROUP

We chose to study Islay's class because, with its distinctive ethos, composition and history, it offered the chance
to explore how far collaborative strategies for learning
could be viable in apparently very unfavourable circumstances.   This part of the study was rather less intensive and rather more impressionistic than our study of the
other three classes.

   The fourth year Social Studies option group was all
male.   Initially there were sixteen pupils, but over the
two-year period during which we saw them, four boys
dropped out for one reason or another.   This group represented part of a fourth year class who, four years earlier,
as 11-plus failures, had entered an all-boys secondary
modern school.   The following year, the school had been
incorporated into a purpose-built co-educational comprehensive.   The vintage double-decker Victorian building
which had been their old school now stood as an annexe to
the modern metal and glass structure which housed most of
the integrated lower forms.

   The 'secondary modern' boys were very visible in the
co-educational setting of younger pupils.   Whereas the
new intake of boys and girls to Claremont Comprehensive
involved an increasingly even balance of racial groups,
the upper school classes were mainly Asian and West
Indian in origin.   By the end of their fifth year (when
we assessed the group) the class contained 6 West Indians,
4 Asians, 1 Anglo-Asian and 1 white (Italian).   These
boys had been designated bottom stream from their first
year of secondary school, and had remained in this stream
since that time.   In general, the lower stream groups had

a poor reputation in the staff room, and this particular
group were regarded as very immature.

The pupils involved in our study were: Abdul (Asian),
Bertie (West Indian), Eric (West Indian), Jawaid (Asian),
Jeffrey (West Indian), Joseph (Anglo-Asian), Lenny (West
Indian), Paul (Italian), Rajesh (Asian), Roy (West Indian),
Seeven (Asian), Trevor (West Indian).

Throughout their secondary schooling, these boys had
received mainly traditional kinds of learning experience.
Though less authoritarian than its predecessor, Claremont
School remained essentially a conventional school, operating teacher-dominated educational methods.   A strong
message conveyed by the school was that written work and
exam grades alone constitute real work.   To a large
extent, classroom activities consisted of structured tasks:
for this group, finding the right answers and filling in
words in worksheets were typical.   There were not many
opportunities for pupils to use their own initiative, or
discuss the work they were doing.   For this group, as a
bottom stream class, low expectations held by most of
their teachers further limited opportunities for active
participation.

The Social Studies option

Islay's Social Studies class represented a two-year course,
consisting of two double lessons a week, each of one hour,
twenty minutes.   The course was aimed at CSE Mode 3 examinations.   This involved four parts: a written paper
representing 50 per cent of the marks, a project, 20 per
cent, course work, 15 per cent, and an oral, 15 per cent.
The syllabus, for the first year, covered such topics as:
child upbringing and family relationships (including
family conflict, battered women), social inequalities
(sex, race, class), childhood in other countries and the
social conditioning of behaviour, law courts and the
police (including sus, and the rights of young people),
the mass media and the images they present (including
images of women and black people).   During the first part
of the second year, the syllabus consisted of a large
scheme concerned with the situation of North American
Indians; this was from the standpoint of the gradual des-
truction of North American Indian culture, and the conse-
quent problems faced by North American Indians today.
Some of the coursework submitted for the exam was derived
from this part of the syllabus.   In the last part of the

second year, lessons were devoted to project work, to revision, and to preparation for the oral.

Islay herself saw this kind of syllabus as holding out
many possibilities for personal learning, and as particularly relevant to a group such as this. She considered
that the heavy cost in teacher time - needed for preparation and marking - was more than outweighed by the possible
gains for pupils. As she saw it, the content of the
course was much more stimulating intellectually than most
syllabuses, and the examination was far more relevant.
Pupils were given scope to undertake their own research,
through coursework and projects, rather than simply having
to receive facts to be regurgitated at the end of the
year. In the examination, the slant of questions required pupils to take an analytic approach towards themselves and their own experience, and to show understanding
rather than simply factual knowledge. This derived from
the assumption underlying the syllabus, that facts are
themselves selected. In Islay's words, this kind of
course 'draws on the things people have learnt through
living, rather than just reading them from a book'.

The philosophy implicit in this course of study, and in
Islay's personal approach to teaching, was essentially a
collaborative one. It emphasized the personal resources
for learning inherent in young people, assumed that knowledge is created rather than given, and offered learning
modes in which pupils could participate actively. The
traditional image of teacher transmission of knowledge was
clearly rejected; instead, informal modes of exploration
and discovery were emphasized. Talk itself was explicitly endorsed as valuable, by being given a place in the
final assessment.

Against the background of this group's educational history, and their current learning experiences, this attempt
to implement a collaborative approach to learning stood
out as a significant experiment. On the one hand, we saw
it as an opportunity to test the outcome of collaborative
methods, in terms of the progress actually made by this
group. On the other, we hoped to explore how far the experience of collaborative work might alter the way these
boys saw learning, and themselves as learners. Could
that experience reverse the message they were otherwise
likely to have received from their schooling? It seemed
likely that being in the bottom stream would produce a
negative attitude towards school work, and a sense of personal incompetence. In a largely traditional school, it

was probable that these boys would equate learning with
being taught, see writing as the only real school work,
and marks as the only real index of progress. The social
composition of the group also seemed likely to influence
their perceptions, in ways running counter to Islay's
approach. Did these working class boys feel alienated
from school, with a disjunction between school and out-of-
school knowledge? Did awareness of racial conflict and
discrimination enter their perception of their school
status? As young people facing the probability of unemployment, how did they evaluate the relevance of school
learning? To try to answer these questions, we asked the
boys to write and talk about a number of issues at the end
of their second year in Islay's class.

Our involvement

In this part of the project, our own direct involvement
was relatively occasional, and essentially informal. The
aim was to maintain friendly contact with the boys and
with Islay, and to get a general feel of the way things
were progressing, rather than attempting systematic observation.

On the whole, the effect of our involvement on the
class group was a positive one. They received the
request for such involvement with some pleasure; according to Islay, the message of being chosen as research subjects was flattering, and ran counter to their general
school status. Although, at first, Phil's presence produced some showing off, later on, Islay felt, it led to
the boys behaving in rather more mature ways. This was
partly because the presence of two adults in the classroom
broke down the usual sense of teacher-versus-us, and enabled a feeling of greater equality.

Our involvement with this class group also had implications for the work done for the exam. The questionnaires
and discussion in small groups of the same questions, were
submitted as part of the course work requirements. The
boys clearly took this task seriously, and saw it as setting them apart in positive terms within the school.

The group's progress

Before sketching the progress which this group made over
the two years, something should be said about their

general orientation at the beginning of their course.
Unusually for a bottom streamed group, these boys were
very work-oriented.   This meant that they were, in general, prepared to work in class, and wanted to be given
homework.   They were also an unusually cohesive social
group, who had been together from the start of secondary
school, and had achieved quite a high degree of group
solidarity.   There were, however, to begin with, a few
very aggressive and disruptive boys within the group.

During the first year, Islay was concerned to contain
the handful of boys who threatened the stability of the
class;   this necessarily introduced some constraints on
the way she was able to work.   The lesson structure was
in two parts: first discussion, which usually followed a
film or reading, and then written work.   As far as the
curriculum was concerned, involvement was variable;   some
topics were evidently felt to be personally engaging, but
others seemed only to induce boredom.   In terms of the
work of the class, writing, which was always done individually, was treated seriously by the boys, while discussion, seen as a preliminary to this, produced visibly less
commitment.

By the beginning of the second year, all the disruptive
boys had left the class, and there was a much more settled
atmosphere.   The group were at this stage very exam-con-
scious and anxious to do well in work, which was seen as
preparation for exams.   Midway through the year, projects
were introduced.   A great deal of individual effort was
put into these;   no one, despite encouragement to do so,
chose to work jointly, even though two boys chose the same
topic.   During this year, the discussion part of the
lesson was given over to preparation for the CSE oral.
As part of exam preparation, these sessions were taken
seriously.   Several boys were able to speak for three or
four minutes, with only occasional looking at notes;   the
rest of the group were generally attentive and prepared to
respond with relevant comments and questions.

This group of boys saw exam results as the real measure
of their progress.   Unfortunately, the class was paired
for Mode 3 assessment with a group of academically highly
able pupils from another school.   Against this standard,
the boys did relatively poorly.   Of the eleven who took
the exam, though all passed, only Lenny got a grade 2,
with Roy getting grade 5, and the rest, grades 3 or 4.
All the boys except Abdul, Jawaid and Jeffrey did best in
the oral part of the exam.   These results were disappoint-

ing to the boys themselves, and, in Islay's view, did not
properly reflect the effort they had put into their preparation for the exam.

Social relationships

Crucial, from our own point of view, is the use these boys
made of opportunities during the two years to work
together collaboratively.   In considering this, it is
important to look at the social relationships which came
to be established in the class group.   In this group,
pupil-pupil relations were already good at the start of
the Social Studies class.   Apart from the few disruptive
boys, the group maintained an atmosphere of good-humoured
tolerance towards each other.   This was expressed in a
steady barrage of friendly teasing and banter, in which
established nicknames formed part of the group culture.
Increasingly, the social subgroups in the class came to
reflect ethnic groupings; but there were no signs of
racial tensions within the group, and Islay commented that
she had never seen an incident of inter-racial hostility.
Group solidarity was also enhanced, it seemed, by the experience of Islay's collaborative learning context.   One
of her goals, in class discussion, was to get the boys to
operate as a group - to listen to each other, and to take
others seriously rather than putting them down.   From the
growing interest which the boys showed in each other's
work, in the oral preparation, it seemed that this did
happen.

   This pupil group, nevertheless, did eventually divide
into three distinct subgroups.   Two of these were made up of
West Indian boys; Eric, Bertie and Jeffrey in one grouping,
Lenny, Roy and Trevor in the other.   In the first grouping, Eric and Jeffrey were long-standing friends, with
Bertie, who usually sat with them, not much involved in
their interchanges.   All three boys seemed unenthusiastic
towards academic work.   Eric, probably the dominant member of the class, and a witty, sardonic speaker, clearly
disliked writing, and generally put little effort into
formal classroom work.   Jeffrey, also very quick-witted
in talk, was extremely slow in written work.   Bertie,
though quite competent in academic tasks, usually appeared
apathetic towards writing assignments which Islay set.

   Unlike these boys, Lenny, Roy and Trevor were apparently very work-oriented.   Although Roy evidently found
writing difficult, he was strikingly keen.   On their

side, Lenny and Trevor both had considerable academic
skills, and showed some initiative and independence in the
way they tackled classroom work.   From what we saw of
their relationship in class, these two boys expressed
their close friendship in terms of good-humoured competitiveness, and a constant, friendly banter, which often
included Roy, and, more occasionally, Eric and Jeffrey.

   At the other end of the classroom sat a group, which, as
the two years progressed, came to represent an ethnically
distinct clique.   Abdul and Jawaid, close friends who sat
together throughout the year, appeared to use their relationship as a defensive wall against others in the group,
with whom they remained shy and reserved.   Towards class
work, both boys seemed consistently unconfident.   A third
Asian boy, Rajesh, who had sat near Eric and Jeffrey at
the start of the year, soon moved to sit with Abdul and
Jawaid, although he tended to be excluded from their private interchanges.   Initially somewhat disruptive in class,
Rajesh became increasingly work-oriented during the two
years, and in particular put much effort into the project
he was doing.   The last member of this subgroup was
Seeven;   like Rajesh, he sat at the 'Asian' table, but was
not socially integrated with the other boys.   Towards
class work, Seeven was serious and hard-working.

   The remaining two members of the class did not form
part of any regular social grouping.   In the case of
Paul, this was an aspect of his marginality within the
class;   he seldom participated in group talk, and increasingly dropped out of school, having ceased to attend
Islay's class by the stage of exams.   Joseph, on the
other hand, had generally friendly relationships with the
other boys.   He did not, however, establish a regular
membership of any social groupings, sitting sometimes with
Eric and Jeffrey, sometimes with Paul, and sometimes with
the Asian boys.   Joseph took class work seriously and
seemed to set high standards for himself;   he was also
notably oriented to Islay, and to adults generally.

   Pupil-teacher relations were similarly good.   From the
beginning of her contact with them, Islay liked the group,
and enjoyed taking the class.   This liking was evidently,
and increasingly, reciprocated by the boys.   It was
striking that the equality which Islay offered in her relationship to pupils was quite readily accepted by this
group.   For example, Islay was always prepared to talk
about her own personal situation and feelings.   While
eager to elicit personal reactions from her, and percep-

tive of her feelings, the boys themselves set certain
limits beyond which they were unwilling to intrude further
into her privacy.   Another aspect of their response to
Islay's openness was a readiness, among some boys at
least, to reveal something of their own personal feelings
and experience.

The work done

Despite the fact that the group's social context should
have facilitated collaboration, the extent to which this
occurred was very limited.   Written work - the 'real'
work of the class for these boys - remained an individualized activity throughout the two years.   Despite encouragement to work together on the projects, and the coinci-
dence of one topic chosen, project work was similarly
tackled alone.   Most crucially, group discussion never
really came to be used for collaboration between the boys.
During the first year, when discussion was followed by
written work, the boys clearly saw it as preparation for
this, rather than as work itself.   As such, it was not
accorded much respect, as can be inferred from Eric's
remark, early on in the second year, 'No, carry on talking, Miss, so we don't have to begin work yet.'   This imposed narrow limits on the way that Islay was able to use
this part of the lesson.   She remarked that she would
have liked sometimes to take the whole double period for
discussion, but felt unable to do so because the boys
would have regarded it as wasting time.   During the
second year, there were perhaps even fewer opportunities
for genuinely collaborative talk, since the group were
concerned to use talk for practising the highly formalised,
rule-bound talking called for in the oral exam.

   At no point during their two years' work, therefore,
did this group use talk for sustained exploration of the
curriculum.   In group discussions, the initiative was
always from Islay;   the boys characteristically followed
her lead rather than introducing their own concerns, or
directing the course that serious discussion took.   Despite the fact that many of the boys were able and witty
talkers, these group discussions never took off as conversations;   they remained somewhat artificial and highly
teacher-dominated activities.   For Islay, group talk
should have afforded the opportunity for pupils to draw
freely on their own personal material, and to adopt a
critical and analytic stance towards the material they
were considering.   At best, this could have meant pupils

themselves taking responsibility for organising discussions among themselves in small groups, with a report back
to the larger groups; it could have entailed pupils in
taking the initiative about the content of discussion, and
in themselves exercising a large measure of control as to
how topics were to be explored.   While these kinds of
possibilities were successfully taken up by some of the
later generation of mixed ability class groups in Islay's
Social Studies course, this particular group was clearly
unable to make use of them.

(b)   COMMONALITY AND SOCIALITY

How is the relative failure of these boys to learn collaboratively to be explained?   Part of the reason must lie
in the salience of exams, for a 'low ability' group about
to leave school at a time of very high unemployment.   To
some extent, even a Mode 3 syllabus imposes its own constraints on what can be done within the class.   But perhaps the fundamental reasons go deeper than this.
Throughout their experience of secondary schooling, these
boys had received consistent messages both about what con-
stitutes real learning, and about their own potentialities
as learners.   On both levels, these messages must have
implicitly contradicted the expectations carried in
Islay's approach.   In the great proportion of their classroom learning experience, work was equated with writing,
and the value of schooling, with exam grades.   The
pupil's role was typically a passive one - certainly not a
role to encompass the autonomy, initiative, and analytic
powers which, in Islay's class, collaborative learning
called for.   Even more important may have been the image
which these boys held in school.   Of all pupils, they
were least expected to make their own demands in class, to
play some part in directing the course of events in lessons, or to take part in school decisions.   On the contrary, their image at school as immature, incompetent and
unsophisticated people was likely to have strongly reinfor-
ced their sense of needing to be taught.   It seemed,
therefore, that institutional factors in these boys' personal history might have led to firmly held expectations
on their part towards classroom learning - expectations
which finally undermined the possibilities for active participation, and responsibility for their own learning,
available in Islay's class.   In our elicitation of attitudes to school and out of school experiences, we hoped to
see whether they did indeed have such an approach to
learning, and themselves as learners.

We asked the boys to respond in two ways to our questions about their experience in and out of school (see
Appendix).   First, we asked them to provide individual
written answers.   Two weeks later - as part of their Mode
3 course work - we invited them to consider the same questions in a tape-recorded discussion within small friendship groups.   We hoped that this two-fold response would
tell us something about the way the boys used an informal,
collaborative mode, as against a traditional individualized one.   The discussions might also throw some light on
the particular subcultures within the class group.

Unfortunately, because of absences, the pupils involved
in the two forms were not totally comparable.   On the
first occasion Roy was absent from the class, and on the
second, Paul and Seeven were absent.   The three subgroups
involved in the discussion were as follows:

    Group 1: Bertie, Eric, Jeffrey
    Group 2: Lenny, Roy, Trevor
    Croup 3: Abdul, Jawaid, Joseph, Rajesh.

Of these groups, the first two represent natural friendship groupings, whereas the third is more arbitrary, including, with the three Asian boys, Joseph, who did not
regularly sit with them.

If we look at the written answers and the discussions
in small groups, how far does the content of what was said
seem to be a function of the context it was said in?   A
close examination of the two kinds of responses suggests
that the effect was quite a complex one.   Let us first
see how the task of discussing set questions was managed
by the three groups, each of whom conducted things rather
differently.

Group 1

Of all three groups, Group 1 talks in a way which seems
closest to real conversation.   On the surface, their discussion is often light-hearted and good-humoured;   there
is a lot of laughter, jokes and sexual innuendo.   The
boys move easily from one topic to another, often straying
a long way from the official topic;   they frequently
switch to dialect.   However, the impression of gaiety is
clearly contradicted by the content of what these boys
actually say.   Throughout their talk, there is a pervad-
ing sense of bitterness.   Discontent with school and

teachers is matched by strong anti-parent feeling: and
there is also a frequent denigration of themselves, which
sometimes takes the form of contemptuous comments on their
own talk; for instance 'How can you say a stupid thing
like that?' 'Ours is going to be the worst, with stupid
things on there.'

How does this conversational context alter the way
these three boys talk about the questions we asked?   On
one level, it provides a much fuller response than was
available by asking them to write.   Jeffrey, who speaks
freely and at length in the discussion, has some difficulty in writing; he answered only six out of the eleven
questions, often very briefly.   Eric and Bertie both
answered all the questions, often at some length; but the
content of their replies tended to be generally milder and
less negative than when they talk together.   In the context of discussion, all three boys express strong dissat-
isfaction with the school system.   When they talk about
mixed schooling, it is with reference to this being too
late for them ('stupid school').   In discussing teacher
intervention in pupils' fights, they depict teachers as
using the opportunity for punitive action against pupils:
'They just get suspended, or expelled or something.   Or
detention, stupid old detention.'   A consideration of
homework similarly leads to talk of caning, where they
feel singled out for its use: 'It's banned for the
others, but not for us - we still get caned.'   These boys
also portray school, in the way they talk about it, as
operating highly coercive pressures on pupils.   Despite
the bitterness with which these are mentioned, there is
clearly ambivalence towards them.   On the question of
different identities in and out of school, the comment is
made that people 'start acting stupid' if there are no
teachers to worry about.   This note is repeated when the
three boys talk about changes that have taken place in
school since their first year in it, when someone comments
'Don't forget, if you got plenty of liberties, so you mess
about.'   Similarly, whereas no strongly anti-parent feeling comes across in their written replies, this is clearly
evident in their talk together.   It emerges from their
discussion of doing well at school, when parents are described as harshly coercive, from their talk of parents'
understanding, when parents are dismissed as 'Stone Age
people', and from the picture of some fathers: 'He might
just be an old drunk, goes round the pub, spend all the
money ... he comes in drunk and beats the kids, beat the
wife.'   Finally, though it does not emerge clearly from
their written replies, the generally low image of them-

selves in school and in the labour market is very evident
from what these boys said.   When they talk about people
who do well at school, there is a clear dissociation of
themselves from such people: 'they got posh parents',
'brainy boy'.   Their hopelessness about their own prospects in terms of employment is also obvious, from their
account of the various culs-de-sac that open out before
them, ending in a 'British Rail buffet car, with a five-
year-old sausage.'

What can be said about this group of boys, in terms of
the commonality of their experience, and the sociality of
their relationships?   From what these three boys say
about their experience in and out of school, they have an
exceptionally close accord in construing their life situations.   This shared view is, however, very much at variance with the positive philosophy implicit in their
teacher's expectations.   Generally pessimistic about
their life chances, Eric, Jeffrey and Bertie clearly are
particularly at odds with school, whose potential for enhancing their prospects has passed them by.

No doubt their close agreement in making sense of their
experience contributes to the very high level of sociality
which these boys demonstrate in their talk together.   The
particular friendship between Eric and Jeffrey does not
act to exclude Bertie from discussion;   all three boys
take an active part in talking.   They speak with obvious
mutual trust, expressing their ideas far more freely in
this conversational context, and going further in the
views they put.   They show a ready empathy with each
other, communicating easily, and often falling into dialect and shorthand ways of talking.   They are mutually
appreciative, particularly of wit.   This discussion shows
how lively, inventive and enjoyable is the relationship
between the three boys;   in encouraging it to flourish in
her classroom, Islay must have affirmed its value for them,
even though she did not succeed in linking it with school
learning.

Group 2

Group 2 conduct their discussion very differently.   The
talk is rather more a managed interview than a spontaneously developing conversation.   One person - nearly always
Roy - reads out each question, and, acting like a chairman,
asks the others their opinion.   Unfortunately this means
that Roy's voice was seldom heard.   It also means that

the boys stick closely to the topic of the question,
giving their opinions in turn, so that dissent among them
is not explored.   Nevertheless, within this somewhat unnatural kind of talk, the boys offer quite full responses.
Usually, each contribution is fairly long, and, typically,
involves reference to personal experience;   the relatively
self-exposing remarks which these boys make imply a
sense of mutual trust.

The most obvious difference between written and discussion responses for this group is that Roy was not present
form, while Trevor, who arrived late for the session,
answered only three questions.   As a group, despite the
somewhat stilted nature of this discussion, these boys express themselves much more freely in small group talk.
There is one exception to this;   on the question of
streaming, where, in writing, he had placed his eloquent
indictment within his own experience, Trevor back-pedals,
taking care to point out that he has not personally undergone humiliation.   This was what he wrote:

> In the first year I was streamed into the lowest form
> in my year.   By putting us into this form people
> started criticising us for what they feel we dumb, dim
> witted and have an handicape or mentally ill.   The
> whole school puts you down and you feel that it's not
> worth going on in school.

In group discussion, he refers more briefly to the experience of discrimination, but maintains he has not
undergone it personally.   On other questions, however,
there is a much greater freedom in the context of talking;
and this is true even of Lenny's contributions, as compared with his written answers.   One aspect of this
greater freedom is that references are made in talk to
racial strife and racial discrimination.   For instance,
in writing his response to the question about pupil
friendships, Lenny had not mentioned race (Trevor did not
answer this question).   In talking about it, however,
these boys locate friendships firmly in the context of
racial conflict and bullying.   It is interesting that in
doing so, they put forward different stereotypes for the
three racial groups they talk about, with their own,
black, group, alone being seen as achieving solidarity
through sport, not through bullying or defensive gangs.

> 'The black kids in our school, they stick together, you
> know, go round together and play football.   The Paki
> kids, Asian, they go round together in a bunch because

they feel that if they went round with white kids, that
they might get led into trouble, because the white
kids, they mostly go into trouble in our school.... You
know why people bully the Indian kids, it's because
they just stick to themselves, they don't mix with
other people.   That's why people usually pick on
them.'

Race is also a strong theme when it comes to the question
of parents' understanding, although, again, it had not
come up in these boys' written answers.   Police discrimination is talked about, too, as a taken-for-granted aspect
of the experience of young blacks.   Later, Lenny intro-
duces his own experience of being beaten up at school -
something he did not mention in his written answer.   The
theme of violence also comes up spontaneously, when the
boys are invited to suggest a topic; here it seems that
all three boys, though not agreeing with each other, see
caning as an important issue.   A further theme that
emerges from this group's talk, though not from their
written replies, is that of the school system as creating
conflicting pressures which makes it impossible to fulfil
its official demands.   'Sometimes people are silly at
school, but they act grown up, more their age, when they
go out in the street.   The reason is because at school
everybody mucks about, everybody.'   Throughout their discussion, these boys convey a sense of respect for learning, and a wish to take advantage of educational opportunities.   Yet they also express the view that school
reduces people to childish and silly behaviour, and that
friends, who are needed to counteract the boredom of
school, inevitably distract from learning, and lead to
mucking about.

In terms of sociality, Lenny, Roy and Trevor are less
successful in their use of small group discussion than are
Bertie, Eric and Jeffrey.   Unlike the boys in Group 1,
these boys do not take up and develop each other's ideas;
the presence of the tape recorder leads them into a rather
formal presentation of individual views, in which Roy,
acting as interviewer, seldom features.   The discussion
sounds much more constrained than the free-and-easy interchanges Phil had seen in the classroom among this group.
Nevertheless, these boys' sense of ease and trust in each
other's presence is apparent in the way they talk.   Lenny
and Trevor regularly speak at some length, and are prepared to be personal, often expressing strong feelings.

Their discussion of issues also suggests that these

boys, like those in Group 1, have a high level of commonality in the way they experience their lives.   Their
shared stance towards school learning is clearly positive
rather than negative; but alongside this seems to be a
sense of frustration and resentment towards aspects of the
school system.   A further common theme in what these boys
say is the salience of race in their experience: race as
the basis of victimization and discrimination both inside
and outside school.

   Again, Islay's encouragement of classroom collaboration
did not engage these boys in any real joint learning endeavour.   Yet it must have made room for a mutual relationship which supported an apparently largely shared view
of life and been itself a source of much-needed social
solidarity.

Group 3

If Group 2's discussion is somewhat unnatural, Group 3's
is still more so.   Throughout these boys' talk, there is
the sense of an invisible teacher to whom answers are
being addressed.   Not much is said in response to most
questions; typically, two or three boys offer an opinion,
and the group then go on to the next question.   The context is typically generalized and impersonal.   It seems
likely that, whereas the close friendship between the two
other groups leads to greater freedom of personal expression, the lack of real social integration in this group
produces a much greater guardedness than when the boys had
been writing.   In effect, these boys do not collaborate
at all.

   Alone among the three discussion groups, Group 3 was
composed arbitrarily, so far as existing friendships were
concerned, in that Rajesh was marginal to Abdul and Jawaid,
while Joseph did not form a regular member of the group at
all.   It is therefore not very surprising that these four
boys, in their tape-recorded discussion, show a low level
of sociality.   The phrasing and tone of voice they use to
each other are highly formal and distant; impersonality
also marks what they actually say, their comments being
mainly bland and emotionally neutral statements.   The fact
that these boys are more, rather than less guarded in
their expression of feeling than they had been in compos-
ing individual written replies, suggests that they have a
low level of mutual trust.   Things might have been very
different, of course, if Abdul and Jawaid had been able -
and willing - to talk together without the other two boys.

All the same, some commonality among these boys does
emerge from what they say, either individually or in discussion.   The experience of victimization - introduced in
discussion by Joseph, and, for once, endorsed with obvious
feeling by the others - seems to be a common denominator.
However, this experience is apparently not quite the same
for Joseph as for the three Asian boys, all of whom talk
as members of a persecuted minority group.   There is also
an apparent lack of commonality among these four boys in
their stance towards schooling.   Whereas Joseph conveys
some quite positive feelings towards school learning and
teachers, all three Asian boys speak much more negatively,
expressing dislike of school and mistrust of teachers.
This difference must have been particularly significant in
preventing a close social integration within Islay's
classroom.   But, again, her endorsement of the relationship which existed between Abdul and Jawaid, and more marginally, between them and Rajesh and Seeven must have
allowed these boys to maintain a sense of security within
the larger classroom group.

The tendency to give 'safe' answers within this context
can be seen in relation to several questions.   Whereas in
writing about people who do well in school, Rajesh had
mentioned racial discrimination: 'Lots of black people go
for interviews and they don't get a job - because he's
black, so black people work hard at O level or A level so
they can get a job but some just give up.'   Talking in a
mixed race group, he does not raise this possibility, but
endorses the generally bland comments made about this
topic.   On the question of mixed schooling, where several
members of this group had referred to personal feelings
(making friends, getting to know each other, being influenced by girls' greater maturity), in talk only the neutral topic of curriculum choice is mentioned.   The contrast is particularly striking when these boys discuss
changes in school.   Jawaid wrote that people learned more
in the first year.   Joseph and Rajesh referred to disappointed hopes.   Having wanted, he wrote, to study
French and Spanish in his first year, Joseph now saw these
as unattainable, while Rajesh had abandoned his plan to
become a pilot: 'I am not that clever.'   In talking
about the question, the boys content themselves with a
simple list of changes.   The spoken comments are characteristically made in a detached tone, and often expressed
in the third person.   On two areas, however, this small
group context does seem to have elicited perceptions which
had not been expressed in writing.   It is noticeable that
in talking about trouble in school, this mainly Asian

group speaks from the viewpoint of the victim.   These
boys also reveal a preoccupation with teachers as caring
or uncaring, and as sometimes using written work as an
easy option ('in some forms they give you homework like if
they're bored ... at least they can sit down and do some
written work').

Commonality with Islay

We saw these questions as opening up areas of perception
that have a bearing on collaborative learning.   We asked
the boys to respond to them at a stage when they had been
in Islay's class for almost two full school years.   How
far did their answers suggest that they had assimilated
her collaborative approach to classroom learning - an
approach which, as we have described, represented a very
small and highly atypical island within their whole school
week?   Five broad areas seem critical for the success of
Islay's collaborative learning methods.

Attitude to school   The first area is that of general
attitude towards school.   If pupils are to participate
fully in their own learning, this must predicate generally
positive feelings about school, and a sense of school as
playing a meaningful part in their personal lives.   The
reaction of these boys to questions about school suggested
that for them, things were quite otherwise.   As an institution, school was clearly viewed by this group as a
source of qualifications for jobs.   However, there was a
recurring theme of personal experience of restricted
opportunities to gain educational qualifications, through
lack of access to relevant, interesting or difficult areas
of the curriculum, through poor attainment as a result of
low streaming, or simply through not being made to work.
For some boys, even qualifications obtained could be nulli-
fied by racial prejudices.   It seemed, therefore, that in
terms of what was felt to be its central function, school
was experienced as having largely failed these boys.

   On a more personal level, these boys also seemed mainly
alienated rather than identified with the institution of
school.   There were occasional comments about hating
school.   More generally, school was portrayed as a place
which was socially very impoverished.   Sex-segregated
classrooms forestalled possibilities of exciting and personally enriching relationships.   The boredom and mono-
tony of school activities could only be countered by con-

tact with friends; but this was seen as necessarily
undermining the purposes of the school system.   Finally,
these boys depicted the school institution as creating its
own kind of identity for pupils - an identity in which
pupils took little responsibility for their own behaviour,
and might often act in ways that were far less mature than
in their out-of-school lives.

Perception of teachers   The second area which seems relevant to collaborative learning is that of teachers and how
they are perceived.   Collaborative methods depend on generally positive attitudes towards the teacher, and on a
sense of the teacher as a working partner rather than a
distant and impersonal authority.   Despite the fact that
in an aside, Group 1 - the most negative and alienated of
the three boys' groups - endorsed the idea that Islay herself was 'a very good teacher', teachers generally come
over from the responses either as non-persons, or as coercive and punitive agents of school.   It was striking that
very few references were made to teachers, and fewer still,
to personal relationships with teachers.   Where teachers
were referred to, it was negative features that were most
often mentioned.   Many boys commented on teachers' use of
sanctions against pupils, and arbitrary and extreme sanctions were often instanced, particularly against their own
group.   Some teachers were seen as not caring about
pupils, and again, this was felt to be specially true of
low ability pupils.   Here too, these boys' comments suggested that their approach was not one which would easily
accommodate collaborative classroom methods.

Perception of peers   Collaborative learning also means
viewing other pupils as resources in the development of
one's own understanding.   How did these boys see their
peers?   A strong sense emerged from their responses that
other boys were a source of solidarity, and that peer
group relationships were important.   However, themes of
racial strife and inter-racial violence clearly coloured
this group's experience; and several boys spoke as victims of such violence.   In the context of school, which
was seen as imposing a relatively irresponsible role on
pupils, other boys were depicted as generally stirring
things up, and fanning the flames of personal conflict.
When it came to classroom activities, this group clearly
saw peer interaction as incompatible with learning.
Talking with friends was necessary for surviving the boredom of school; but even work-related talk might get out

of hand, and the presence of friends was inevitably distracting from work.

Attitude to classroom learning   The fourth area which
seems important for the success of collaborative methods
is that of perception of classroom learning.   To learn in
collaboration involves taking a high level of responsibility for one's own work.   It was important, therefore, to
see how far this group's feelings about classroom learning
incorporated this sense of responsibility.   Here again,
the responses were discouraging.   On one level, many comments implied that learning was the responsibility of
others, particularly teachers, and that people learned
only if they were made to work.   At another level, school
learning seemed to be viewed as extraneous and mechanical,
rather than as personal and creative.   One aspect of this
was that whereas talk was viewed as mainly counter-produc-
tive to work, there was clearly a great respect for set
tasks, written work, and work that could be marked.
(Implicit in this was the assumption that learning was an
individualized activity;   and some boys even commented
that classrooms were poor learning contexts, as against
the privacy of home.)   Perhaps most ominous of all, for
the possibility of responsibility for one's own learning,
was that difficulties and failures in learning, rather
than any positive learning experiences, represented the
main theme in these boys' references to classroom work.

Self-image as learners   Finally, leading on from this,
there is the question of how these boys saw themselves as
learners.   Collaborative methods of learning to some
extent throw pupils back on their own resources.   This
calls for quite a high level of self-esteem as a learner
on the part of pupils.   Did this seem to exist for these
boys?   The responses provide multiple evidence that, on
the contrary, they had a very poor sense of themselves as
learners.   Their comments on their experience of secondary schooling consistently emphasized restricted opportunities, closed options, and the failure of school to live
up to their personal expectations.   In particular, their
experience of learning seemed to be dominated by their low-
stream categorization.   The effects of this were portrayed
not just in terms of a duller curriculum.   These boys also
documented, with considerable bitterness, the personal
stigma which low streaming carried, and the self-fulfilling
prophecy which turned them into 'dim people'.

All in all, this was a depressing picture.   It seemed
that these boys had a generally negative perception of
school, and saw it as having failed to provide them with
qualifications they urgently needed.   They also seemed to
feel considerable personal distance from teachers.   Their
peers, though evidently a source of social support, were
not felt to contribute to classroom learning.   Classroom
learning itself was seen as imposed rather than under-
taken.   Finally, this group of boys seemed to have assimilated, from their particular educational history, a very
low image of themselves as school learners.   In the light
of these attitudes, it does not seem surprising that take-
up, by this group, of Islay's collaborative learning
opportunities was so limited, or that their encounter with
her collaborative teaching philosophy failed to tip the
balance against the accumulated weight of attitudes
derived from five years' experience of traditional teaching.

Islay's classroom approach was undoubtedly valuable
personally for the boys in her group, and it probably enhanced their mutual sociality.   However, the level of
commonality between their views of schooling and Islay's
philosophy was too low to enable them to integrate their
classroom learning with their social relationships.

Chapter 5

Terry's second year Humanities class

(a)   TERRY'S FRAME OF REFERENCE

Terry was the head of the lower school Humanities department in Newlands Comprehensive.   He was in his early
thirties and had taught in two other inner city comprehensive schools before coming to Newlands four years previously.   As head of department, with a talented staff, his
constraints were perhaps pressure of work and lack of time,
and the nature of the institution, rather than a non-sup-
portive system.   From the start he saw his task as building on the pupils' experience of an integrated curriculum
in the primary school, but also to provide continuity in
their relatively fragmented school week.   By the time we
entered his class as researchers, he had established a
very flexible system: work cards selected by pupils
according to ability, a variety of techniques ranging from
the showing of video tape recordings and play acting, to
writing of newspapers, making of posters, poetry, formal
essays, comprehension, stories and long projects to cover
the broad curriculum area designated as 'humanities'

Expressive writing

Defining the criteria by which he judged his own success,
Terry said:

'Humanities has a basically useful purpose behind it,
namely, whatever we're doing, the purpose is to help
the children to express themselves more clearly in
writing, to be able to become more fluent, to handle
all sorts of information, and to be able to express
information in all sorts of different writing styles.'

Expression included being able to adopt different styles
and perspectives in presenting oneself and in interpreting
materials:

> 'I find it very satisfying to look at work which child-
> ren produce, where they've picked up different styles
> of writing and just absorbed them and used them.   I
> like it particularly if at the end of the two years, if
> things have been working very well for particular kids
> (not everybody) if they can slip into any particular
> style they want.'

It also implied an appreciation of the ways in which
styles are used in the outside world:

> 'If they're going to be able to deal with the media and
> the different newspapers, they've got to understand the
> different styles in which things are presented, partic-
> ularly the sensationalistic aspect, bias, partiality,
> etc. - the way they try and persuade people.'

Expression meant, most basically, correct usage of
written forms:

> 'If I taught them for two years and they can't write a
> sentence in the end, that's absolutely dreadful, I mean
> it's just not on, I've not been any use at all ... it's
> absolutely essential that they have a basic level of
> reading and writing.

Terry aimed, ultimately, to help children produce thoughtful, well constructed pieces of written work, in which
they had real personal involvement.   He believed this entailed quite a long process, in which children took account
of the teacher's reactions, and those of other pupils, in
producing improved versions.   In the development of written expression, Terry voiced a strong commitment to the
prior and concomitant need for talk:

> 'To be able to express yourself fluently you really
> need to discuss and to put your ideas to other people.
> I see that as a process rather than something just
> simply put down on paper for a teacher.'

Enjoyment and involvement

The atmosphere in which learning takes place was of equal
importance to Terry, in that he wished his class to be enjoying his lessons and involved with their content:

'The problem obviously in schools, and with anybody, I
suppose, the degree of turn-off ... if there's a method
which is also enjoyable, which makes it more interesting, that's got to be a sound way of approaching
things.... There's absolutely no point in teaching anything absolutely straight, if after five minutes everybody's really not listening, whether you've got them
silent or not.'

Appreciation of the written word was a spin-off of personal involvement and interest: 'If kids are enjoying a
particular piece that is being read out, or they are reading, then that's valid in its own right.'   In written
work he hoped to elicit an emotional response, to draw on
the children's own imaginations, their own experience, and
their involvement in out-of-school activities.   This happened, he felt, in a dynamic atmosphere when children were
sparked off, enjoying themselves and genuinely immersed in
the topic.   He gave a very down-to-earth justification
for fostering interest and enjoyment in children: 'Where
the kids aren't interested, they don't take in the information anyway.'   If they are presented with factual information and no way to get into it personally, 'you can end
up with a very boring set of lessons and stand to lose
everything'.

Terry was, however, concerned to emphasize that having
fun was not - and must not be seen by children - equiva-
lent to mucking around.   It was very important that the
lesson took place in a context of authority control.
This meant an unambiguous structure with clear lines and
boundaries, without which pupils felt insecure; and it
meant making definite demands on children.   Terry
believed children could accept varying structures, at different times, and that they would be prepared to respond
to an occasional 'straight' lesson from a teacher who at
other times allowed them more leeway.

There was in addition a strong cognitive justification
for encouraging pupil involvement at a deep level.   He
was not a supporter of the 'empty vessel' analogy of
children's learning and on the whole doubted whether
children 'got taught' anything.   Rather he saw learning
as an active process carried out by the learner:

'Facts are less important than ideas which can't be
taught - they happen in people's minds.   Ideas are not
taught from outside.   They are formulated inside
people's heads, not simply passed from one person to

another.   They arise in response to inputs and influences from outside.'

Interestingly, however, he did not feel that 'relevance' was the secret to children's involvement in their
lessons.   He considered that content was important, but
that it was impossible to base the whole curriculum on the
concept of relevance.   This was a technique which, he
felt, had been tried and had failed.

Terry's own view was that personal involvement was a
product, not so much of the lesson content, as of the
nature of the task, and the way the teacher introduced
topics and involved his pupils.   In his experience, to
focus constantly on children's own experience, and try to
build out from there, was in the end self-defeating.   Not
only did pupils become bored by the limitations this imposed; but some children actually wanted to escape from
their own lives through what they did in school.   This
was not to say, however, that Terry thought the personal
relevance of the curriculum was unimportant.   He believed
school learning was worthless if it was not shown to have
some implications for present-day life.   So, for example,
he valued the projects he set up on voyages of discovery
because they illuminated the history of imperialism, and
in so doing, had implications about cultural oppression,
and the reasons behind immigration.

Rather than look for direct and obvious relevance to
the pupils' world, Terry's method was deliberately to seek
out material to stimulate their imaginations and sense of
wonder:

'You slip in anecdotes which might be interesting,
trying to find, or come up with strange pieces of information, storytelling.   That's very useful in teaching
history, because the problem with traditional history
teaching has been that it's always been too straight,
too direct, and therefore extremely tedious and boring.'

While this might not be his approach with older children, the impact of material, the opportunity it gave children to feel themselves into a period, get under the skin
of people of other eras, whether fictional or historical,
was a prime concern with younger classes.

Classroom relationships

Basic to Terry's approach was a happy atmosphere and good
relationships in the class as goals in their own right.
For many children, relationships might be more important
than academic orientation:

> 'I think they tend to judge it [the curriculum] much
> more in terms of the teacher than the subject, and what
> they say they like in Humanities is what the teacher's
> pushed at them.   If they like or respect the teacher,
> like the set-up, they then accept what the teacher's
> pushing at them as valid.   If they find the activity's
> redundant and they don't like the set-up, don't like
> the teacher, then they'll come out with ideas that re-
> flect that, and say it's a waste of time, it's a load
> of rubbish, we don't learn anything.'

Such relationships were, however, essentially set
within the context of teacher control.   Terry strongly
emphasized the basic fact of inequality between teacher
and pupils: 'You're not one of them, you are the one
who's directing.'   This made teacher-pupil relationships
- at least within the confines of the school setting -
professional rather than purely personal.   Though
teachers needed to be experienced as persons, not automa-
tons, this did not mean that they were able to indulge in
free expression of feelings in the classroom.   Rather
than meeting anger with anger, for instance, frustration
and annoyance needed to be stage-managed for maximum
effect, and the occasional inevitable boiling-over, when
it occurred, had to be directed at the whole class group
rather than at particular individuals.   Within this context of professionalism, however, it was crucial that
teachers broke through an alienated and distant relationship with pupils, and responded to them in an interested,
genuine and human way.

Terry had clear views on the nature of the relationships between the pupils themselves.   Quite early in our
dealings with him he expressed his concern at doing everybody justice in a mixed ability class.   He saw this as
necessitating a structure in which everyone could work at
his/her own pace, and in a non-competitive atmosphere,
acknowledging that involvement and enjoyment for pupils
could not be provided by the teacher alone.   The pupils
themselves had to generate this largely via their relationships and interactions, not with him, but with each other
in his classroom.   Terry did not believe in manipulating

pupil groups.   As far as possible he respected natural
groupings, without regard for the ability of their members, and only moved children in a negative sense, away
from each other, when their interactions were proving unproductive or disruptive to others:

> 'I'll be controlling from the front and therefore I can
> spot people I feel are not working in the sense that
> they're simply wasting time, and simply from the way I
> conduct myself, the children know that I expect them to
> behave in a certain way.   If things get out of hand,
> then I simply institute a period of silence which is
> just there to focus them on their work.'

Terry thought the reality of collaborative work was
rather different from the idealized picture of 'small
groups of pupils talking quietly and earnestly together,
followed by pens rushing to paper'.   In practice, things
were much more untidy than this, and necessitated a good
deal more teacher direction.   It was crucial that children knew, quite unambiguously, what sort of work the
teacher was asking them to do.   The situation of individualized work, though different from that of collaborative
work, was something children could accept, when teachers
made it plain that this was the order of the day, by
saying, for instance 'I want to know how well you can all
work on your own.'   On the other hand, if collaboration
was to work, children should be told how to use talk to
work out their response to the task.   Inevitably, this
produced a high noise level.   Terry admitted that he
found this quite difficult to handle, and if things
became too noisy, often resorted to more traditional
teacher-pupil relationships;   his imposition of a period
of silence was 'a way out for all of us'.   He described
the balancing act of operating a collaborative classroom
in this way:

> 'In a sense collaborative learning, which is a looser
> situation, requires more control than an ordinary sort
> of class situation.   It doesn't always work, you
> actually need to have a fine degree of control, because
> you're not insisting on certain situations that are un-
> ambiguous for the children.   You create an area of
> ambiguity in your relationship with them because they
> can talk and they can do things, and you're saying,
> well, you can only do it up to this point, and you
> can't go too far there, so therefore you need a fine
> degree of control.'

Black children

Terry felt schools did not adequately respond to black
children.   He recognized that their alienation might well
be part of a general response to society as a whole, not
just to the particular school institution: 'I can't work
out how far it's the school curriculum and how far it's
the whole society, or how far it's the school in society
that they're alienated from.'

   The kind of relationships that teachers had with pupils
was particularly important with black children.   An inability by teachers to respond on a personal level to the
experience of blacks in Britain, or really to key into the
literature of the Caribbean, for example, could mitigate
seriously against the success of well-meant curriculum
innovations:

   'Most people aren't familiar enough with all these
   sorts of areas, or not well enough resourced if you
   like, to carry out the lesson successfully, partly
   because they don't understand, or have any feeling for
   the culture of another place.   I think a lot of white
   teachers teaching the Caribbean can often be a dubious
   activity, unless they really know what they're doing.

      'You can teach black children about black oppression
   and they can be as bored as hell, I mean it depends on
   the actual method you're using.   You know with the
   National Front and so on, you want the sort of lessons
   that are going to hit at this and give some knowledge
   of the Third World and about independence and relationships of power and the movement of goods around the
   world and how we depend on the Third World for raw
   materials ... and to look at the cultures.   But just
   simply doing that isn't enough, because you can end up
   with a very boring set of lessons where the kids aren't
   interested and we lose everything, we lose the contact
   and the interest.'

   Terry also felt that collaboration was important to
black pupils.   He believed talking together might not
necessarily bring about a greater depth in work, since
many such children preferred to work individually.   However, it provided important social support.

Working-class boys

Terry also felt specially empathetic with working-class
boys and their potential alienation from school; as he
said, 'There's a high level of turn-off by the third year.'
His own background was working class, and he felt closely
in touch with its values.   Working-class boys were often
in an anti-school culture which took priority over the
aims of the school and which largely conditioned how they
responded to school:

> 'Working-class boys are the people who really suffer in
> an academic sense because I think that they go along
> with the school norm which is anti-academic and there-
> fore they drop out when they could actually be achiev-
> ing much better results.'

In discussing the disjunction between working-class
children's out-of-school world and the expectations and
rules of school, two themes emerged.   Many children experienced school as a problem, or rather found themselves
in trouble in school, when they had no problems out of
school.   There was something about the institution of
school itself which turned such children into problems.
Partly to blame was the Catch-22 relationship already discussed, between efforts by the school to implement a
'relevant curriculum', and the automatic turn-off which
many children felt to anything that was designated
'school'.   A further dilemma was that along with their
anti-academic stance, these pupils simultaneously expected
school to operate in formal and traditional ways.   Higher
up the school, when pupils could choose their subjects,
'when they've made a decision to be there', their whole
response became less hostile.   However, for the younger
children, the consequence of their expectations was often
that children would abuse freedom if they were given it.
Terry's solution was to give as much freedom as possible,
but to state the parameters very clearly, to be explicit
about his expectations, and consciously build in for the
children the knowledge that he would 'jump on them' if
they overstepped the limits.

Another aspect of the problem was the nature of school
knowledge, in which literacy was valued for its own sake.
Terry thought that an entirely different style of education, in which writing arose out of a context of learning
practical craftsmanship, would be received very differently by working-class boys, with their respect for manual
and technical skills.

(b)   THE PUPILS' FRAMES OF REFERENCE

Terry's class group (Form 27)

Terry himself categorized the 32 pupils in his group according to their social backgrounds. There were five such groupings, together with two unclassified boys - Jose and Rana - whom Terry felt unable to categorize. The largest group was of 9 working-class boys. There were 6 middle-class girls, 5 of whom were Music Scholars. Five boys made up the middle-class boys' grouping. Finally, there were 4 white working-class girls, and 4 working-class girls of Jamaican parentage. Several children were, however, frequently absent from class because of truancy; this was the case for one of the white working-class girls and two of the working-class boys. Additionally, one white working-class girl was withdrawn from the class for special psychological help during the first term; while a working-class boy was regularly absent from lessons because he attended basic skills classes. Effectively, this reduced the white working-class girls' group to 2 and the working-class boys' group to 6 or 7.

(i)   Perceptions of Humanities

In exploring the significance of Terry's collaborative approach for his classroom group, one obvious question was how the children saw his Humanities lessons in relation to other lessons that they did at school. We assessed this in the way already described for Mac's class.

We carried out this assessment during the autumn term, one-third of the way through the year in which we had contact with Terry's class. In fact this class had been taught by Terry throughout the previous year, and in this sense they were in a position to make considered judgments about his approach.

The class group was not entirely complete that day, but the children we assessed represented all the subgroups within the class. They were:

6 working-class boys:	Dave, John R., John T., Kenny, Michael, Simon.
6 middle-class girls:	Eleanor, Esther, Ilana, Katie, Sarah, Victoria.
4 middle-class boys:	Carl, Chinekwu, Timothy, Vincent

3 working-class girls:	Sally, <u>Tina</u>, <u>Tracey</u>.
4 working-class black girls:	<u>Ann</u>, Carol, <u>Sandra</u>, Valerie.
2 unclassified boys:	<u>Jose</u> (Portuguese), <u>Rana</u> (Asian).
1 unclassified girl:	<u>Jayne</u>.

The underlinings show which children added comments.

The ratings

TABLE 5.1

	Enjoyable	Not boring	Useful	Good at	Easy
Humanities	1	1	1	1	3.5
Maths	2	3	2	3.5	5
Games	3	2	6	3.5	2
Home Economics	4	4	3	2	1
Science	5	5	5	5	3.5
Design and Technology	6	6	4	6	6

Table 5.1 shows the rankings of the whole class group
of 26 children. It is clear that Humanities is the most
popular of all the curriculum areas. The children rate
it the most enjoyable and least boring of all the areas,
as well as judging it to be the most useful. They also
rate their competence in Humanities to be higher than in
any other sphere, although it is not judged to be a particularly easy subject.

If we examine subgroup differences in rating the various curriculum areas, these mainly follow gender stereotypes, with girls preferring Humanities and Home Economics,
and boys preferring Design and Technology. However,
stereotypes are challenged by girls' greater preference
for Maths.

There are also some interactions of class and gender.
Terry's special concern was with black and working-class
children, especially working-class boys. There are very
few black children in the group - no boys and only 3 girls
- and generalizations cannot safely be made. The number

of working-class white girls is also small; but there are
six working-class white boys, whose ratings as a group are
quite homogeneous.

Table 5.2 shows the ratings on the first three scales
combined, for 6 middle-class white girls, and 6 working-
class white boys.

TABLE 5.2

	MC girls	WC boys
Humanities	15	7
Maths	8	7
Games	2	16
Home Economics	12	6
Science	7	6
Design and Technology	8	8

If we look at the profile of ratings of the six curriculum areas for two subgroups we can see that they stand in
marked contrast.   The six working-class boys (whose
ratings are quite homogeneous) rate Games as far and away
the most popular area.   For other, academic curriculum
areas, their ratings are relatively low, and barely differentiated.   In marked contrast, the six middle-class
girls (whose ratings also are homogeneous) show a high
degree of differentiation in rating academic subjects, but
give Games a very low value indeed.   For these middle-
class girls, Humanities clearly stands out as highly
rated, while for the working-class boys, it is merged with
other academic subjects.   No such clear trends emerge
from the ratings of other subgroups in the class, which
tend to be rather less homogeneous: an exception is that
the working-class black girls as a group give highly positive ratings to Maths.

Analysis of comments   Cumulatively, the comments volunteered by 15 children read like a paean of praise and enthusiasm.   Superlatives feature in many remarks.   For
instance, Chinekwu: 'Humanities is a brilliant and wonderful lesson', Jose: 'It's fantastic', Katie: 'Humanities
is the lesson I always look forward to most', Tina: 'He's
a great teacher'.   Most comments are unreservedly positive.
Where a critical note is sounded, it is always qualified:

for instance Esther: 'I don't like doing some of the work, but I am glad after I have done it', or Sandra: 'I think [Terry] works really hard for us to being good in writing good English. Altho at times he is quite strict.' It is striking that reference to Terry himself is made quite as often as mention of the curriculum. These references tend to be very positive, and are often highly personal. Many comments express warm appreciation of Terry as a person: for instance Chinekwu: 'We have a brilliant teacher called [Terry]', or Victoria: 'Our teacher is a good one and I like him', or Jayne: 'I think [Terry] is nice and isn't too strict.... He is also frank although he has a changeable temper.' Strictness is quite often mentioned, in terms which express approval of Terry; although where Chinekwu, Sandra and Rana all describe Terry as being fairly strict, Sarah values him for being rather unstrict. Two children mention the fun and laughter in Terry's class: Chinekwu: '[Terry] has a sense of humour', and Esther: 'Humanities is a good laugh sometimes'. The remaining comments refer to Terry's teaching role. Esther: 'I feel better if I have done all my homework and class work and the teacher is quite pleased', and Sandra: 'I think [Terry] works really hard for us to being good in writing good English'. Ilana's comment is about his competence: 'Seeing as Humanities is a mixture of subjects, some of which are not the teacher's speciality, it is well taught.'

Comments about the Humanities curriculum are equally positive. A number of children refer to the general interest and enjoyment of the work; for instance, Sarah: 'I like Humanities a great deal', or John R.: 'I enjoy Humanities but sometimes it becomes a drag'. Others are more specific. Rana: 'Humanities is a very good, useful lesson.' Eleanor: 'It teaches you history, religion, English Literature, geology, and I enjoy all these subjects.'

Ilana takes a similar view, referring to Humanities as 'a mixture of subjects', while Ann writes: 'I think Humanities is a good subject because you can learn two other subjects.' By contrast, Katie defines the current Humanities curriculum as restricted. 'In the first year we did combined geography and history, but now it is just history - I like this as history is really my favourite subject.'

Other remarks about the curriculum are concerned with being able to learn through class work. Both Esther and

Sandra imply an appreciation of Terry's efforts to ensure
that learning occurs.   Esther: 'I feel better if I have
done all my homework and classwork, and the teacher is
quite pleased.   I don't like doing some of the work, but
I am glad after I have done it.'   Sandra: 'I think
[Terry] works really hard for us to being good in writing
good English.'   Eleanor makes a similar point, but from
the viewpoint of a rather more self-motivated learner: 'I
enjoy Humanities very much because you can work at your
own pace.   If you are good at poetry, compositions etc.
you are encouraged to work and perfect the subject.'   Two
children comment on the difficulty level of the work.
Ann writes: 'You learn about in the ancient times and it
is not so hard or easy.   It is just right.'   Tracey, who
has problems in academic work, expresses her appreciation:
'I like Humanities because I find it very easy and nice to
do.'

   The very positive flavour of all these comments confirms the high rating of Humanities, as against other curriculum areas, by the class as a whole.   The comments
also suggest something more about what Terry's class means
to these children than could be seen from the ratings.
It seems that the enthusiasm and involvement in Humanities
derive as much from a very warm and personal response to
Terry himself as from the content of the work.   However,
where the work is concerned, the children's sense that
they are learning in the class is apparently an important
factor;   it is not merely the fun and enjoyment, or the
variety of content, which matter.   Overall, there is no
subgroup for which written comments are not positive in
tone.

(ii)   Construing other children

This part of the study represented a way of exploring one
of Terry's concerns: how far school values mesh in with
personal values for children generally, but particularly
for working-class boys.

   We chose to approach this through a categorization task.
By asking the children to make judgments about other children of the same age and gender, we hoped to obtain material
from which we could infer something of their personal
orientation to their school and out-of-school lives.   The
task was done individually.   First, the children were
asked to study eight school photographs of ethnically
mixed children, of the same age and gender as themselves.

They were then invited to group the photographs, putting together those who seemed in some way alike.   Following this, they were asked what was the basis of the grouping. The children continued doing this until they had produced eight different categorizations.   The material obtained lends itself to qualitative analysis.   Through an examination of the kinds of content involved in children's categorizations, we can learn something of their experiential standpoints.

The children   We were not able to assess all the children in Terry's class.   Those we saw were:

2 middle-class boys: Chinekwu and Stephen.
4 working-class boys: Dave, John R., Simon and Timothy.
2 unclassified boys: Jose and Rana.
3 middle-class girls - Eleanor, Ilana and Katie.
1 white working-class girl: Tina.
2 black working-class girls: Ann and Sandra.

The constructs   All 112 constructs elicited were categorized in terms of the context they referred to.   Three contexts emerged: school, out-of-school, and a nonspecific or general context.   Constructs for each of these areas were then analysed in terms of the kind of dimension they involved.

Constructs which refer to the school context make up about a quarter of all the constructs elicited.   Most of them mention work (John R.: 'Brainy people').   There are also quite a large number of constructs about sport: these are all very similar, except that the five girls who refer to sport talk generally, while the four boys referring to sport are more specific (Chinekwu: 'Good cricketer accurate at hitting').   Some constructs mention teachers, or school in general (Rana: 'They enjoy school').   A few mention peers in the context of school (Timothy: 'The mouths of the class').

There are social class differences in the frequency with which the children refer in their constructs to the school context.   Proportionately, many more middle-class children do so than do working-class or ethnic minority children.   There is also a clear difference in the kind of perspective from which such references are made.   When the middle-class girls or boys refer to school, they imply a generally positive attitude towards it.   They tend to mention the positive features of school work, teachers or classroom relationships, and to adopt an approving tone towards academic ability.   This is not so much the case with the working-class children, who mention negative features as often as positive ones, and tend to adopt a pejorative tone towards academic ability.   For black and other ethnic minority children, school - though apparently not highly salient - is referred to in largely positive terms;   in this, they resemble the middle-class rather than the working-class group.   Overall, it is the five working-class children who seem to speak from a position in which school work is relatively marginal, and does not hold the strong positive ambience it has for the middle-class children.

Constructs referring to an out-of-school context are much less numerous than those which mention school.   Some refer to the family (Dave: 'Their mums cause trouble');   others mention out-of-school interests (Katie: 'Interested in collecting things and things you do at home').

Much the most numerous category among these elicited constructs covers general judgments which involve no specific setting.   This type of construct makes up three-quarters of all those elicited.   Within this category, the majority of constructs refer to qualities of peer group relationship: and among these four specific qualities stand out as frequently mentioned - bullying, quietness, helpfulness and fun.   It is the working-class and non-white children, rather than the middle-class children, who more often refer to relationship qualities.   There are class differences, too, in the dimensions referred to. Whereas middle-class children most often cite quietness, working-class children refer much more often to bullying, helpfulness or being fun.   References to bullying are exclusive to boys, and are particularly frequent among working-class boys.

It is worth looking more closely at these constructs, which suggest something about the social values of this group of children.   Taking the references to bullying first, there is a marked similarity of orientation.   In every case, disapproval is implied.   Dave, for instance: 'Think they're hard', or Simon: 'Hitting everyone, bullying', or Rana: 'Like to boss other people about but don't like to be bossed themselves'.   None of the boys speaks from an identification with bullies, and in the case of Rana and John, the role of potential victim is clearly implied: Rana: 'They fight and call you names', John:

'Don't take the mick out of you'. Conversely, helpfulness is rated positively. For instance, Tina: 'Nice
personality, you could trust in them and confide in them',
or Ann: 'Good to other children'. A largely positive
tone is also taken by the different groups of children who
cite them, towards both quietness and fun. In terms of
quietness, Ilana says: 'Always nice, never shouts', and
Ann says: 'Quiet, I like that'. In referring to fun,
all the children concerned imply approval, both John R.
and Dave: 'Funny, make you laugh', or Jose: 'Cheerful,
you'd have fun with'.

These constructs, and the social class differences in
their use, suggest that there may possibly be some differences of emphasis in the ethos of this classroom group.
It seems that for the seven working-class boys and girls
represented here, there is a premium on social relationships with peers, to a much greater extent than is the
case for the five middle-class children. The major evaluative axis in experiencing such relationships seems to be
one of general regard for others. The positive end of
this is defined in terms of helpfulness and consideration.
The negative end, with which the boys in the group are
much preoccupied, is bullying and violence. There is
also another dimension of evaluating social relations with
peers which is used by the working-class but not the
middle-class children - that of being fun to be with.
This valuing of extrovert qualities stands in contrast
with the mainly positive valuation by middle-class children of the introvert quality of quietness.

The other constructs which make up the category of references to relationship qualities represent a mixture of
dimensions, such as interest in boys (Tina: 'They like to
impress the boys'), attitude towards friends (again Tina:
'A bit choosey with their friends'), or proneness to take
offence (Jose: 'Make trouble out of little things').

Some dimensions refer to individual rather than social
characteristics, and mention aspects of personal orientation or style. Several children talk about temperament
(for instance, Eleanor: 'Moves at her own pace'), others
refer to appearance or dress (Katie: 'Conscious about
dress'), and the remainder cover a variety of aspects, including attitude to life generally (Stephen: 'Bored with
things').

Two further kinds of construct were produced by a
minority of children. In the first of these, mention is

made of the child's relation towards society, or the world
of adults generally.   All four children who refer to this
describe people at odds with the adult world.   For instance, Dave: 'They get blamed for things that are not
really their fault', and Ann: 'They might be bad when
they're out with friends'.   The second type of construct
covers those in which race is either explicitly mentioned
or clearly implied.   Three children make such references.
Rana, himself an Asian boy, did so twice, once without
comment: 'Both coloured', and once referring to race as
governing friendship: 'I'd have as a friend, the same
colour as me'.   Sandra, a black girl, made a more elaborate reference, in which mention is made of non-majority
group membership: 'To do with their being a different
colour from British, same race, Asian, perhaps Greek, both
West Indian.'   Timothy, a white boy, refers by implication to racial 'otherness', defining this in negative
terms: 'Don't speak English properly.'   Few as these
constructs are, they suggest that minority group membership, with its potentially negative connotation, may be
more salient to the non-white children in this group.

   What does all this tell us about the extent to which
school values mesh in with personal values, for this particular group of children?

   Some differences do emerge between working-class and
middle-class children.   First, it seems that the world of
school is more salient for the middle-class children, and
that, for the working-class children, it is not only less
salient, but also has much less positive connotations.
Conversely, the working-class children have a much greater
involvement in social relationships, amongst their peers,
and tend to view others more in relational than in individualistic terms.   When it comes to the standpoint from
which peer group relationships are evaluated, all the
children express appreciation for regarding others;   but
there are some clear differences in emphasis.   The boys,
particularly the working-class and non-white boys, see
things to a large extent in terms of bullying - a dimension which seems irrelevant to girls.   Whereas the working-class children - boys and girls - value their relatively extrovert peers, for middle-class boys and girls it is
relatively introverted personalities who are appreciated.

   For the group with whom Terry is especially concerned,
working-class boys, these findings have suggestive implications.   In so far as the small group here is represen-
tative, it seems that they are indeed potentially at odds

with the school world.   According to these results,
school does not feature largely in their personal land-
scapes, nor have particularly happy connotations.   Their
central concern is with social relationships, and particularly with peer group solidarity.   They also experience
interaction in relatively physical and extrovert terms,
and set a high premium on fun.   Traditional schooling,
with its imposition of silence and passivity, and its exclusion of social interaction among classmates, might be
expected to arouse the antagonism of children such as
these.   However, by the same token, Terry's classroom
approach would be very differently received - as we saw it
was.   Terry, far from excluding friendships, tried continually to build on these in developing classroom work,
and encouraged rather than discouraged interaction among
the children in his class.   His own emphasis on the importance of laughter and fun in lessons might be crucial
in cementing positive attitudes.   All in all, these findings seem entirely consonant with the enthusiasm for
Terry's classes which we witnessed among the working-class
boys in his group.

(iii) Views of life in and out of school

Our aim in asking Terry's class to respond to our questions about experience in and out of school (in Appendix)
was to explore the ways in which these children, at this
stage of their progress within Terry's classroom, saw
school and school work in relation to themselves and their
out-of-school lives.   This seemed likely to illuminate
the standpoint from which these pupils evaluated their
classroom activities, and also to show how far they had
incorporated Terry's own attitudes towards learning and
the place of collaboration.   It will be remembered that
this group had been taught by Terry since the beginning of
their first year, within a timetable structure which gave
considerable weight to Humanities.   By the stage that we
asked these questions, at the beginning of their second
year, these children were therefore very familiar with his
style and methods - more so than for any other teacher at
the school.

As with the pupils in Islay's class, we gave the questions in two ways: first, as questions to be answered
individually by writing, and, two weeks later, as questions for informal tape-recorded discussion in small
friendship groups.   This allowed us to explore differences between subgroups within the class.   On the first

occasion, when the children wrote answers to the questions, 25 out of the 28 pupils in the class were present. For the second occasion, only 17 pupils were there.   The composition of the discussion groups was as follows:

GROUP 1
Esther, middle-class girl, a Music Scholar
Katie, middle-class girl, a Music Scholar
Victoria, middle-class girl
Sarah, middle-class girl, a Music Scholar
This group, consisting of four middle-class girls, three of whom are Music Scholars, represents a friendship group within the class.

GROUP 2
Ann, black working-class girl
Carol, black working-class girl
Sandra, black working-class girl
Valerie G., black working-class girl
This group, comprising the four black girls within the class, is a friendship grouping.

GROUP 3
Carl, a middle-class boy
Simon, a working-class boy
Stephen, a middle-class boy, Music Scholar
Timothy, a middle-class boy
Vincent, a middle-class boy, Music Scholar
This group, of mainly middle-class boys, is less homogeneous in terms of friendship than the two previous groups. Simon is not socially integrated among these middle-class boys; but the boys in the class have less fixed friendship patterns than the girls.

GROUP 4
Dave, a working-class boy
John R., a working-class boy
Tina, a working-class girl
Tracey, a working-class girl
This is the least satisfactory grouping as far as friendship patterns are concerned.   It is the only mixed sex group, and this mixture was imposed rather than chosen. The two girls would have been with two other working-class girls, who were absent.   The two boys would have normally been with other boys.   This particular grouping resulted from these four children being 'over' when the other groups had formed.

    The four groups treated the discussion task very differ-

ently.   In Group 1, the talk is 'managed' by Katie, who
sets a formal, analytical tone, and conducts the discussion in the manner of a BBC interviewer.   There is little
real debate, and even dissent, at first sometimes introduced by Esther, gradually peters out, as Katie comes increasingly to dominate the talk.   This means that most of
the content consists of Katie's quite full, rather adult,
overviews of the questions.   The other two girls, Sarah
and Victoria, who are close friends, speak less often and
less fully, but tend to reiterate or amplify each others'
points.

In Group 2, the discussion also tends to be dominated,
though to a lesser degree, in this case by Sandra, who
initiates the discussion of each question, sums things up,
and takes responsibility for moving on.   Ann and Carol
generally respond to Sarah's lead, and often provide evidence for what she has suggested.   Valerie volunteers
little, but gives her assent from time to time to what is
said.   Again, there is an absence of real debate;   consensus is reached very quickly.   However, all this
changes when the girls discuss their own issue;   at this
point, no one takes a special role in the talk, and all
four girls contribute, developing each others' ideas in a
genuinely conversational way.

Easily the most successful discussion is that conducted
by Group 3.   Apart from Simon - a rather shy and unconfident boy - the boys contribute equally to the talk.
Their standpoint seems to be that their discussion is
important to them;   they discuss questions at length and
considerable depth.   Unlike the talk of other groups,
this discussion seems genuinely conversational, with the
boys actually talking to each other rather than addressing
an audience.   There is often dissension, since these boys
are sufficiently confident of their views to venture and
defend minority opinions.   This dissension does not lead
to conflict, however, partly because Carl in particular
manages things with skill and tact.

Group 4's discussion is much the least successful, perhaps because the grouping was imposed and not chosen.
The negotiation of who is to ask the questions is the
occasion for a good deal of noise and banter, and throughout the discussion there are frequent lapses into giggling
and embarrassment.   Only Tina really contributes anything
to the discussion, with occasional supportive or cryptic
comments from the other three children.   Many of the
questions are not dealt with at all.

It seems appropriate to divide the six questions about
school work involved into three broad areas.   The first
two - about success at school, and streaming - are concerned with ability and attainment.   The last two - about
classes where different amounts of learning occur, and
classes where the teacher is liked but the subject disliked, or vice versa - are concerned with the differentiation of particular lessons.   The remaining two questions
- about homework, written work and exams, and pupil classroom talk - are concerned with traditional as against collaborative forms of school learning.

The children's responses, in writing and in discussion,
to questions concerned with ability and attainment, suggest that, as a group, they see both aspects as essentially open and accessible, rather than as fixed properties of
particular individuals.   In considering success at school,
only a minority relate this to innate qualities;   most
children explain success in terms of personal orientation
or relationships with others.   Their ideas about streaming also imply an assumption that educational attainment
is not pre-determined, but is the outcome of appropriate
learning opportunities.   The concern expressed by many
children, in responding to this question, that ability
segregation can prevent full social mixing, and that
school groupings can undermine the morale of some pupils,
also suggests an underlying opposition, on their part, to
hierarchical and competitive approaches to pupil differences.   From this point of view, the attitudes of this
group of children towards academic ability and atttainment
seem consonant with a collaborative approach to learning,
and with a mixed ability classroom context.

Attitudes towards the differences between school lessons seem on the whole similarly positive.   Almost unanimously, the children interpret successful or unsuccessful
lessons in terms of other people;   there is a sense that
lesson material however unpromising can be made personally
interesting and meaningful through the mediation of a good
teacher.   On both questions, a substantial number of
children emphasize the importance of a good relationship
with the teacher, implying that teachers are seen as genuine persons, not merely distant, inhuman authority figures.   For an approach to learning which entails teachers
as working partners rather than omniscient authorities,
this view seems a hopeful one.   Opinion about other
children as learning partners, however, is less clear.
Peers, according to these responses, are less salient than
teachers in explaining successful or unsuccessful lessons;

for children who do mention them, they are sometimes seen
as facilitating learning, and sometimes as disrupting it.
Perhaps most crucial of all are the children's attitudes
towards traditional forms of classroom learning, as
against collaborative ones.   Here, their responses suggest that most children do see the need to balance traditional forms with other forms of learning.   In writing
and talking about homework, written work and exams, the
group as a whole express reservations about these activities, implying the need to supplement them with other,
less formal, activities.   Towards pupils' classroom talk,
despite the fact that peers are sometimes seen as disrupting learning, there is a general willingness to see such
talk as at least potentially helpful.   Here again, therefore, the children seem to have a respect for non-traditional kinds of learning, as forming part of their classroom experience.

   Within these attitudes, generally favourable towards
collaborative learning modes, there are some subgroup differences.   In construing ability and attainment, middle
class children put much greater weight on personal agency
than do working-class children, who are more inclined to
explain them in terms of inborn attributes.   From their
small group discussions, it seems that middle-class girls
see good relationships with peers as particularly important for doing well in school, while middle-class boys are
more concerned with relationships with adults, not only
teachers but also parents.   The importance of relationships again features for both boys and girls, in considering streaming; for both, it is the effects on social
mixing which are stressed in discussing this question.
The perspective of working-class children is rather different.   Not only is doing well at school seen as the
product of largely predetermined differences, and streaming, concomitantly, viewed as generally sensible.   There
is also apparently some alienation from those who do succeed at school.

   Differences between pupil subgroups are less clear-cut
on the question of what makes lessons successful or unsuccessful.   Written responses seem broadly similar across
the various subgroups.   However, there are some differences of emphasis in the way small groups discuss these
questions.   Whereas all the groups stress the importance
of the teacher, there are differences in what aspects are
picked out as relevant.   What is put forward by both the
middle-class groups is the role of the teacher in creating
interest and enjoyment in the lesson;   the stance is one

of some equality with the teacher, with the girls discussing the teacher's personal approach, and the boys, from a teacherly viewpoint, considering the availability of resources.   In contrast, working-class children adopt a rather less equal position towards teachers.

Questions about social experience   The five questions about social experience were designed to throw light on several aspects of the way these children perceived their school and out-of-school lives.   Two of them relate to social relationships with other children: as friends, and across gender.   Collaborative learning depends on good relationships between children, and the absence of hostilities across gender.   Two other questions ask about the relationship between parents and the children themselves, first, in terms of parents' attitudes to their children's schooling, and second, in terms of the general level of understanding existing between them.   It seemed important to explore the children's perception of these areas.   If a disjunction was felt to exist between parents' expectations of school and the kinds of learning fostered by Terry, this would be likely to create some difficulty for the child concerned.   More broadly, a sense of mutual alienation from parents might carry implications of problems in relating to adults generally, and particularly in establishing the kind of equality and mutual trust towards the teacher that Terry's collaborative approach invites. The final question was designed to explore the children's sense of their distinctive identity as school pupils. Because collaborative learning demands a much more personal participation from the child than traditional learning methods, it must in the end depend on children's confidence that the context allows them to express their real personal identities.

Taking first the two questions about social relationships with other children, the responses of the group as a whole are highly positive.   Where friendships are concerned, shared experience and mutual support are very much more often emphasized than conflict and antipathy;   and friendships are clearly perceived as serving social solidarity rather than providing the ground for group hostilities.   The responses to the question about mixed schooling, far from expressing themes of warfare between the sexes, show a high level of approval of boy-girl mixing, both as currently valuable and as important for future adult life.   From this point of view, therefore, these children seem to experience relations with other children in the positive ways that genuine collaboration demands.

In considering questions about parents, the children's responses are less homogeneous. Parents are perceived as endorsing the usual priorities within the curriculum; the fact that English and literacy skills are given so high a place perhaps indicates that the content of Terry's Humanities class is thought to be particularly valued by parents. Some children portray parents as wanting school to support more personal kinds of satisfaction; for this minority, the essentially personal mode of collaborative learning might make particular sense. When it comes to the question of parental understanding, the responses are on the whole less encouraging, though again, there are variations. Most children evidently see a gulf between parents and their own generation, because of different experiential heritages. For some it is a gulf that can be bridged, for others, not. To the extent that real mutual incomprehension exists, this seems likely to undermine the possibility of a close personal relationship with a teacher in a collaborative classroom.

The last question is concerned with differences of identity in and out of school. Most children endorse the idea that such differences do exist, and relate these to the different social contexts and social relationships involved. Implicitly, behaviour is attributed to interpersonal process rather than to pre-determined factors - a view which supports the emphasis, in collaborative modes, on classroom relationships. On the other hand, for many of these children, school essentially means constraints, and to this extent, the freedom and opportunities of a collaborative classroom may radically conflict with their expectations.

Again, some differences exist among the pupil subgroups of this class. In the first sphere - that of peer relationships - no clear divergences are apparent in the discussion of boy-girl relations, but different themes emerge when friendship is the topic. What is striking is the different perspective taken by the two groups of girls. Whereas the four black girls clearly locate friendships in an out-of-school context, the four middle-class girls place them firmly within a classroom context, emphasizing school interests and academic ability as the basis of friendly relationships. Though no clear differences appear to separate the boys, these responses suggest that, for these two groups of girls, friendship may serve a very different function. It seems that for this subgroup of black girls, their friendships have very little to do with school, while for the subgroup of white middle-class girls,

there is complete continuity between school and friendship, with their friends actually serving to support their
academic interests and achievement.

In general, the responses of the various subgroups to
the questions about parents, while not strikingly different, suggest a greater integration between home and school
for middle-class than working-class children.   It is the
middle-class boys who, in talking about parents' aspira-
tions for their children's schooling, compare home and
school as contexts for learning, and portray parents as,
in a sense, teachers.   When it comes to the question of
parental understanding, in contrast to working-class black
girls, who see parents as irrevocably committed to the
excessively strict upbringing they had themselves, there
is agreement among at least some of the middle-class boys
and girls that possibilities of mutual understanding exist.

There are also some distinctive perspectives, among the
subgroups of children, as to the effect on personal identity of the school context.   The middle-class girls stand
in marked contrast to the black girls;   again, it is the
middle-class girls who convey a sense of continuity
between home and school, insisting that no difference
exists, unlike the black girls, who say people are quite
different in the two contexts.   The other two groups also
see school identity as unlike out-of-school identity, but
stress slightly different factors.   Whereas the working-
class boys and girls suggest that school imposes a 'goody-
goody' role, the middle-class boys see its restrictions,
together with the presence of friends, as conducive to
generally mucking about.

Additional material introduced by Groups 2 and 3   At the
end of our list of questions, we asked the children if
there were any questions we ought to have asked, but had
left out.   Neither Group 1 nor Group 4 took the opportunity to introduce any new theme, but both Group 2 and
Group 3 did so.

In terms both of length, and of general urgency of
tone, Group 3's contribution is the less substantial.
The boys raise the question of school rules, from the
viewpoint that the school council is ineffective and disappointing.   They then move on to the question of school
uniform, but disagree about whether it is a good idea, and
whether it is actually enforced.

The four black girls in Group 2 take the opportunity to
discuss prejudice in the school; their talk about this is
nearly as long as their discussion of all the other questions together, and represents a genuine debate, in contrast to their earlier somewhat stilted discussion of set
questions.   They begin with a claim by Ann that 'some
teachers, I'm not saying all, but some teachers are prejudiced in this school'; Ann documents this with an anec-
dote about a black child who retaliated.   The girls then
agree that, as Ann says, 'You don't really see the teacher
doing it to children his own colour'.   Carol suggests
that prejudiced teachers are out of place in a racially
mixed school, and this is endorsed by the others.   The
girls go on to discuss segregation.   There is consensus
that mixing is better.   However, this leads on to a consideration of what mixing actually means in their own
case, where, as only four blacks in the whole class, they
feel greatly outnumbered.   As Sandra puts it, 'You mean
to say that a class that's mostly got more whites than it
does coloureds isn't quite equal.'   All four girls echo
this feeling.   They then revert to the issue of how
teachers treat black children.   Carol describes an incident she saw on television where a Jamaican child with
difficulties in speaking English was picked on and shown
up by the teacher.   This leads Ann to describe her own
experience of being discriminated against for using
'Jamaican tone' soon after she came back from Jamaica.
All four girls agree, with considerable feeling, that
their own language is treated in school as inadmissable;
Sandra sums this up by saying 'teachers prevent you from
speaking your own language or something'.

The pupil subgroups   Bearing in mind that the four discussion groups gave very different levels of commitment to
the task of talking about the questions, and that Group
4's discussion was particularly thin, can anything be said
about the implications of their responses for their
general stance towards Terry's collaborative learning
modes?   Perhaps some cautious inferences can be made
about what appear to be certain differences in their
general orientations.

Though Group 1's discussion was somewhat stilted and
artificial, some themes do recur in their talk about the
various questions we asked them to consider.   It seems
that as a group, these girls probably experience a high
degree of continuity between their school and out-of-
school worlds, and, in particular, find their friends

supportive of their academic interests and achievements. Their attitudes to school seem very positive, and their orientation towards teachers seems to define them as persons rather than remote authority figures.   Finally, they have a sophisticated and non-traditional conception of learning, in which the idea of intellectual exchange has a place.

There are also, certainly, limits as to what can be confidently concluded from the discussion of Group 2. The 'official' part of the discussion was generally impersonal, and sometimes quite perfunctory; it was quite unlike the highly engaged and personal spontaneous discussion which came later.   However, again, there are some suggestive themes.   On the whole, these girls' comments seem to imply much less personal involvement in schooling than for Group 1.   They clearly separate their school lives from their lives outside it, and see friendships as having their existence outside school.   Learning, for them, appears to be generally less open to personal agency than for the middle-class white girls; and success in school is less positively evaluated, even though a good education is clearly valued.   Classroom learning seems dependent on teacher control, and perhaps is not expected to be very personally engaging; traditional methods seem to be generally more favoured.   If this group of girls does find some degree of alienation from school, their highly personal discussion of their own situation seems to go a long way to explaining it.   As a small ethnic minority within their class group, they feel greatly outnumbered by white children, and, even though they are careful to acknowledge that not all teachers are prejudiced, they are all very familiar with discrimination, particularly in the area of language.

Group 3, clearly more at home with the whole mode of discussing set questions in a small group, produced a much fuller and more personal debate than any of the other groups.   What seems characteristic of their stance as a group (in which Simon, the only working-class boy, did not say much) is a generally highly positive experience of learning, which is by no means restricted to the school context.   Like the middle-class girls, these boys convey generally good feelings about classroom learning, which include an expectation of finding work interesting, and a position of relative equality towards teachers.   They have an even more sophisticated view of schooling than the girls; and are clearly convinced of the educational value of classroom talk.   What is perhaps most striking in what

these boys say is their continual reference to the encouraging and supporting role which parents take towards
school learning, and to the fact that home itself represents a particularly rich learning context in its own
right.

It seems unwise to draw any firm conclusions about the
attitudes of children in Group 4.   Very little was said.
The few comments which were made expressed anti-talk, and
also anti-hard work (being a goody-goody) feelings, the
sense that people are different out of school, that the
presence of friends leads to mucking about, and an apparently instrumental view of school.   However, since many
of the questions were not dealt with at all, while others
received only a single comment, it is impossible to know
how far these views really reflect the attitudes of the
four children involved.

(iv)   The views of six working-class children and one
middle-class boy

In this part of the study, we were concerned to explore
attitudes among a group of pupils with whom Terry was particularly concerned: those who, as members of a working-
class culture, had the potential for dropping out of
school.   Could the kinds of personal engagements available in a collaborative classroom counteract feelings of
alienation from school?   Perhaps this depended on how
children saw teachers, the curriculum, and school generally.

Our interviews aimed at these three areas of perception.   First, how did these particular children see
teachers, and what differentiations did they make between
them?   Was teaching seen in terms of techniques, style,
lesson content, kinds of task set?   What difference could
a good teacher make, where the subject was not interesting?   How did the children interpret the informality of
collaborative teaching methods?

It seemed to Terry, and to us, just as vital to know
how these children saw the curriculum.   What did they
really want to know about?   How traditional were they in
their expectations of lesson content, and how ready to
accept the integration of school with out-of-school knowledge?

Collaborative learning depends on the sense that school

life can be consonant with one's own personal concerns and
identity.   For these children, how far did school mesh in
with personal and home values?   What, essentially, did
they expect from school?   How did they feel they personally stood within the whole school institution?

   Mid-year, we interviewed individually two working-class
boys: John R. and Kenny, and four working-class girls,
Sandra, Tina, Tracey and Valerie G.   For contrast, we
talked to Stephen, a middle-class boy who was also a Music
Scholar.

   In presenting the material, let us consider each of the
three attitudinal areas in turn.

   For children who are becoming alienated from school,
teachers are likely to be seen as non-persons, with whom a
genuine human relationship would be impossible.   This
certainly does not seem to be the case for the children in
this group.   A clear theme running through the interviews
is that the personal qualities of the teacher matter fundamentally, and that mutual friendliness and liking,
between teachers and pupils, are essential.   John, who
expresses strong disapproval of strictness and coercion in
teachers (giving hard work, using detention and the cane),
emphasizes the importance of kindness (kind teachers 'just
make it sound interesting').   Both Sandra and Valerie
stress easiness between pupils and teachers, and Sandra
contrasts this with the repressive, tension-inducing
approach of some teachers ('It would be tense, tense all
the time').   Tracey, who talks about a basically disciplined, formal relationship, nevertheless argues for the
need for teachers to respect the children in their classrooms, expressing resentment towards a teacher who had
been 'funny' with her.   Several children hint at a genuinely reciprocal relationship.   Sandra refers to
teachers with whom children would be likely to prolong
chat indefinitely ('They take the excuse to keep talking
to the teacher').   Tina and Valerie talk about having a
laugh with the teacher.   Tina, who has most to say about
the personal differences between teachers, talks about
mutual liking between pupils and teachers, and goes on to
discuss teacher differences from an essentially equal
standpoint;   she considers, for instance, how far they
show integrity in their personal style 'Like Miss M., she
just dresses how she feels comfortable, and I don't know
why, but it just suits the way her lesson goes.'   Of all
six children, only Kenny suggests a sense that the teacher
behaving in a personal and human way might not always be

entirely welcome: 'She'd rather just look at you.'   What
he says conveys some feeling of embarrassment and discomfort towards the intimacy and personal directness of
'soft' teachers.

In the centrality which they give to pupil-teacher relationships, these working-class children are, if anything, rather more emphatic than middle-class Stephen.
The significance which, as a group, they attribute to
these relationships is, however, not quite the same.   For
his part, Stephen is unambivalent; he sees relaxed, informal relations between children and teachers as entirely
conducive to effecting learning: 'It's all sort of, very
relaxed, and I don't think anyone would want to walk out.'
Most of the working-class children are not so sure about
this.   Kenny, Tracey and Valerie all believe that informal teaching approaches result in mucking about and not
learning much.   Sandra also thinks people learn more in
the tension-ridden atmosphere of an authoritarian class.
However, several children describe informal, friendly
teacher-pupil relationships as particularly important for
people like themselves.   In describing as 'a bit upper-
class' pupils who get on well with strict teachers, John
is clearly differentiating himself from them.   Similarly,
Sandra refers to 'posh' people, and those who are good at
school work, as doing well in authoritarian classes; her
own empathy is obviously with people who have difficulties, and need to ask about their work.   The same psychological distance is evident on Tina's part, when she
refers to the 'snobs' who become pets of strict teachers,
as against those, with whom she evidently identifies, who
are scared of teachers like that, and so cannot express
their problems about work.   Kenny, to whom friends in
school are clearly important, says that though people who
like to work alone get on well with strict teachers,
others, who like working with friends, would be less
happy.   From the standpoint of pupils who might sometimes
find school work difficult, several children suggest how a
good relationship with the teacher can mediate learning.
John, who describes lessons as often boring, refers to
kind teachers as making the work interesting.   Sandra
thinks teachers whose relationships with pupils are open
can help them overcome their dislike of a subject; and
Tina gives a personal example of this, in her own change
of feelings about Humanities, after getting to know Terry.
'I used to hate Humanities, I used to, you know, bunk off
and everything.   Then I got to know [Terry] and now, you
know, we get on very well because he's a very nice
teacher.'   Valerie believes people listen in a lesson if

they like the teacher, and 'you learn even if the subject
is boring'.

It is worth noting that four out of these six children
spontaneously refer to Terry himself with considerable
warmth of feeling.   Tina's comment about her changed
attitude to Humanities has already been mentioned; she
also takes Terry as an instance of the ideal teacher, who
can take a joke, but stops things before they go too far.
John uses Terry as an example of a kind teacher, whose
lessons pupils enjoy.   Like Tina, Kenny makes an approving comment about Terry's capacity to keep things in
order.   For Tracey, it is Terry's respect and helpfulness
towards his pupils which are salient.   'I like [Terry].
He helps us, and then we have to figure it out ourselves,
but if we're really stuck he tells us.'   These comments,
quite unprompted, suggest that Terry himself is highly regarded by this group of pupils; and that his concern for
human relationships, and for enjoyment in class room work
- basic to his collaborative approach - are particularly
appreciated by them.

Disaffection from school means a lack of involvement in
the school curriculum.   How do these children see their
school work?   For those who talk about particular curriculum areas, there is some differentiation.   John, though
he says little about these, mentions liking Cookery.
Kenny expresses positive feelings towards a number of subjects, as relevant to his possible job future, and also
towards Media Studies, as interesting in its own right.
Conversely, he sees French as irrelevant.   Sandra describes Geography and Science as involving different kinds
of learning; she also thinks Humanities is important, and
generally interesting.   Tina also expresses positive
feelings about Humanities, on the unusual grounds that it
disguises the three subjects you are learning: 'You don't
realize you're doing Geography and History.'   However,
Maths, which offers a great deal to learn, is her favourite subject.   Tina argues against RE in school, as conflicting with some children's beliefs.

On this evidence, the school curriculum is neither un-
differentiated nor without the possibility of positive involvement for this group of working-class children.   It
does not seem to be the case that school work has a purely
instrumental value.   Although Kenny explains his likely
choice of options in terms of job relevance, he also
refers, with some enthusiasm, to the intrinsic interest of
Media Studies.   Sandra thinks Humanities broadens and

generally enriches your mind.   Tina, in her comment about
Humanities disguising the subjects it includes, seems to
be saying that the curriculum can be personally interesting if it is not too academic.   She enjoys learning for
its own sake, as her comment on Maths shows; but she is
concerned that school work should be consonant with personal beliefs.

   For this small group of working-class children, therefore, the school curriculum is clearly not without interest, and the potential for personal engagement.
Although their experience of its range and depth is
less extensive than Stephen's, in terms of positive attitudes towards school work there is no very obvious difference.   Where they do seem to differ is in the degree to
which they feel confident of their ability to engage with
the school curriculum without the mediation of teachers.
In Stephen's talk about his school experience, a recurring
theme is the possibility of learning independently.   He
describes the casualness of his Latin lessons, in which
people work throughout the lesson on their own, following
the teacher's setting out of the task.   He refers to the
resources of his out-of-school life - parents who take a
close interest and offer guidance and help, music groups,
orchestras and courses, instruction in the Scouts, and so
on.   Perhaps most significantly of all, he defines large
sections of the school curriculum as being a matter of
personal interpretation, rather than having right or wrong
answers.   Such a viewpoint does away with the heavy
authority of teachers, and makes the curriculum directly
accessible to the learner.

   By contrast, most of the working-class children do not
seem to assume that things could be learned without the
help of teachers.   We have already seen that, for several
children, work in school is seen as requiring some degree
of teacher coercion.   There also seems to be a general
consensus that teachers are constantly needed.   John, in
particular, feels that people learn nothing if they have
to work on their own, and that books, which one might fail
to understand, are no substitute for teachers, who can explain things.   The theme of failure to understand also
runs through the comments of other children.   Kenny
refers to many teachers going too fast, and not explaining
the work.   Sandra complains at some length about the difficulty of not knowing exactly what is required in homework, and says that this situation often arises.   Valerie
mentions having been unable to understand the work in
Maths lessons.   Several children talk about the blocks

and difficulties in school learning, which need the help
of teachers if they are to be worked through.

   It may be that children with some doubts about their
capacity to engage independently with the academic side of
the curriculum feel more confident about their understanding of its more personal aspects.   Judging from the comments of three children about the tutorial sessions concerned with smoking, this seems to be true.   All three
speak with evident familiarity with both the propaganda
and the practice of smoking;   they have not apparently
learned anything new from these tutorial sessions.   However, this sphere of the curriculum is obviously not serving as a bridge between school knowledge and out-of-school
knowledge.   On the contrary, it is unanimously rejected
as not a proper part of school work.   Kenny thinks the
tutorial sessions have no effect: 'people learn outside,
from their older mates.'   Sandra believes people are un-
affected by official instruction, but would be influenced
by encounters with real life tragedies, like someone in
the family dying of lung cancer.   She criticizes the in-
clusion of these sessions in the school timetable, on the
grounds that they are not what people come to school for:
'you don't include it as school work'.   Tina echoes the
idea that these tutorials are ineffective in influencing
behaviour;   she thinks giving up smoking has nothing to do
with discussions, but is a matter of will-power: 'if you
smoke, stop it, or don't start at all.'   It seems, therefore, that this particular way of bringing children's personal experience into the arena of school is not acceptable to these working-class children.

   If school is seen as having no real right of access to
personal matters such as smoking, does that mean that
these children draw a boundary line between their school
and out-of-school lives?   One way of answering the question is to look at what they say about friends, and the
part they play in school experience.   Here, although some
children stress the opposing pressures of other children
and school work, there are also several references to
friends supporting learning.   Sandra, Tracey and Valerie
all mention the distracting qualities of other children
within the classroom.   However, none of them is talking
about friends as such.   All those who do talk about
friends indicate the possibility that they might play a
positive role in classroom learning.   John refers to his
three mates copying from him.   Kenny, despite believing
that in general friendships disrupt school learning, and
would need to be neglected in the later years of schooling,

does describe his own regular collaboration in lessons
with his friend Jose: 'I help him with some stuff, he
doesn't get it, you know, and I tell him what to do.'
Finally, Tina, who differentiates sharply between friendly
and antipathetic relations with peers, clearly feels that
friends can help each other in class, and instances her
own regular collaborative foursome: 'Like, there's four
of us, we sit next to each other, and we always learn each
other things.' In this area of their experience, these
children do not seem to be very different from Stephen,
who, while referring to his work with other children, and
particularly with his friend Carl, also mentions other
boys as potentially disrupting classroom learning, through
their involvement in 'gang warfare'.

   A far greater difference is evident between this group
of children and their Music Scholar counterpart, in
another aspect of the relation between school and out-of-
school life. When it comes to the question of the part
that parents play in his school learning, Stephen portrays
a role of constant, informed involvement, encouragement
and stimulation. He describes his father as giving careful attention and guidance in homework, commenting that he
always makes sure he understands what the work entails;
his mother, similarly, is able to help in the relatively
abstruse area of Latin declensions. The future occupa-
tion which his mother has suggested - a violin teacher -
is itself one which endorses and extends his current
school learning, and which contains an implicit positive
valuation of teaching.

   The picture which emerges from the way the working-
class children talk is very different, and stands in contrast to Stephen's experience of close integration and
mutual support between school and home. For Sandra and
Tracey - the two black girls - parents are often not
available for help with homework; as Tracey says, her
mother is frequently too busy to help, while Sandra adds
that even if parents are not too busy, they are likely to
be out in the evenings. Still more common is the perception that parents cannot help with school work because
they simply do not understand it well enough. John says,
'Sometimes my parents don't know the answer.' Kenny, in
a poignant comment, remarks that 'If the parents, you
know, didn't learn much at school, then the children might
be dumb. My parents don't know that much, so I don't
learn that much.' Sandra thinks most parents are out of
sympathy with what happens in school, and, in particular,
do not see the point of much of the curriculum. Tina

also believes parents are out of touch with schools. It
is clear that these working-class children lack the well-
informed concern and support from parents, in their school
learning, which Stephen, the middle-class Music Scholar,
describes.

Given that this group of children lack rich resources
in their out-of-school lives to support their school
learning, do they generally see school as irrelevant, or
themselves as school failures? Certainly none speaks of
such a wide range of good learning experiences as Stephen
describes. Yet in no case do these children imply personal alienation from school, or a sense of hopelessness
about their own position. Tracey, who is perhaps the
most critical of school and teachers, nevertheless volunteers a comment about her positive feelings towards Terry,
and remarks that most pupils are happy with their teachers.
Valerie and John, both of whom refer to the boringness of
some lessons, each say that school work can be interesting
and enjoyable. Sandra and Kenny speak with some enthusiasm about particular areas of the curriculum. Tina, of
all six children the most pro-learning, describes Maths as
her favourite subject because it is difficult, and there
is a lot to learn.

Though these children have evidently not become
switched off from their classroom learning, the position
from which they speak about it is clearly not that of
Stephen, with his special status in the world of school.
Throughout their talk runs the theme that, as pupils, they
have differentiated themselves from those who are successful in school. The many references to difficulties in
understanding school work have already been mentioned.
These children talk of difficulties, of not keeping up, of
being confused, and of not being able to remember. Unanimously, they express a sense of distance from those of
high ability. Valerie describes herself as an erratic
learner. John thinks upper-class people would do well in
lessons where the teacher gives no special help, unlike
people like himself who need teachers to be kind. Sandra
similarly contrasts herself with the posh pupils, who are
naturally good at lessons, and do not need to ask the
teacher. Tracey also refers to the snobs and posh people
in school. Even Tina, the most confident member of the
group, thinks that it is snobs who do well, despite uncon-
genial teachers, whereas she depends on having teachers
whom she likes. Kenny, in the remark quoted, describes
himself as not knowing much because his parents had also
failed to learn much in school.

Summarizing the evidence from these interviews, it
seems that, in the main, this small group of working-class
children have remained pro- rather than anti-school.   In
terms of their attitudes to teachers, they clearly value
personal qualities, and see a genuine relationship as
desirable;   the references to Terry himself suggest that
this has been their experience of his class.   As far as
collaborative teaching methods are concerned, again, the
positive references to pupil-teacher relationships, and to
Terry himself, suggest generally favourable attitudes.
However, several children express some suspiciousness of
informality and a sense of learning as dependent on
teachers, and, to this extent, they may not be willing to
see themselves and other pupils as prime resources in
school learning.   The curriculum itself clearly contains
potential interest and engagement for these children,
though, again, this seems to be dependent on the mediation
of teachers.   However, as a group, it seems that they set
limits to what is appropriate for the school curriculum,
and see purely personal areas as outside its business.
Finally, this group, though they lack a close integration
between home and school, do not see their friendships as
opposed to their school learning, and do not express personal alienation from school, though they evidently
approach school life from the standpoint of less able
pupils.

(c)   THE DYNAMICS OF INTERACTION

In thinking about this class of children and how far they
lived out Terry's philosophy during the year we saw them,
it seems right to start with Terry's own relationship with
those involved.   Terry believed that good feeling among
pupils was itself a function of the teacher's stance.   He
saw his own relationship with children as crucial.   From
what we witnessed, Terry was very active in developing
sociality between himself and those he taught.   He seemed
equally attentive to both sides of a mutual understanding.
On the one hand, he constantly acknowledged individual
children, encouraging, teasing, responding, and generally
affirming them as distinctive, and valued, people.   In
classroom work he habitually welcomed his pupils' initiatives and suggestions, and often took up their ideas as
worth developing further.

But Terry was equally concerned to make himself accessible and understandable to the children in his class.
This meant a good deal more than meeting their ideas, and

joining in with their fun.   It also entailed explaining himself and his expectations.   Terry took care, through-out the time we saw him, to provide a clear and explicit framework for the tasks he set.   In concrete terms, this involved, for instance, writing up on the board exactly what he was asking the children to do.   More subtly, it meant making visible the hidden curriculum concerning col-laboration.   In asking children to work together, Terry regularly spelt out how they should set about it, what kinds of work he expected them to produce, and what they were likely to gain from working in this way.   He also set up tasks which would enable collaboration between pupils to be both feasible and productive.   For example, the children were asked to devise interviews, produce arguments, or plan newspaper features.   Resource books were provided, but children were also invited to draw on what they already knew.   The time scale - about a month for each project - allowed adequate space for talking, planning and making rough notes before the work was final-ly produced.   In this way, the explicit demands and limits provided by Terry offered a definite framework within which children could engage in a joint enterprise, express their own individuality, and draw on their differ-ent areas of expertise.   He also clearly expressed his own expectations of classroom work through the position he took towards what was happening, moment by moment.   Though tolerant of a good deal of noise, Terry regularly intervened if talk had veered away from work, and brought the children back to the task, occasionally delivering a lecture on time-wasting.

From all that we saw, Terry's high level of commitment to building teacher-pupil sociality had paid large divi-dends in his classroom group.   We had a clear sense that the children felt comfortable and at ease;   when we first met the class, they were already familiar with Terry's approach.   What they said about his lessons strongly bore out this positive orientation.   As a group, they unani-mously expressed appreciation, often enthusiastic, of Terry himself.   Towards his curriculum, feeling was more variable, just as, in what we observed, some children obviously invested themselves more than others in the work they did in class.   On the whole, however, the general level of commitment to class work was high rather than low;   and on the whole, the experience of Terry's lessons seemed definitely positive.

Subgroups of pupils

Important though Terry's own relationship with the class
must have been, the children's relationships with each
other were clearly also crucial in governing the ethos of
the group.   To a large extent, this is a matter of the
separate, and rather different, social cliques within the
classroom.   From this point of view, the five broad
social groupings of children stood for particular positions towards Terry's learning modes, some of them endorsing these more positively than others.

     In these terms, it was obviously the two middle-class
groups, further differentiated by their special, Music
Scholar, status - whose position towards school learning
and collaborative methods was closest to Terry's philosophy and who, concomitantly, embraced his approach most
enthusiastically.   If we look first at the six middle-
class girls, the homogeneity of their attitudes is very
striking.   For these girls, school experience was highly
positive, and essentially integrated with life out of
school.   One aspect of this was that they not only saw no
disjunction between school life and their personal friendships, they even expected to find these friendships at
least partly centred on school interests.   From this
point of view, it is not surprising that these girls generally found collaboration among themselves so natural, and
typically made such good use of it.   Their high level of
commitment, and enjoyment, in Terry's lessons also accords
with how they perceived his curriculum.   Within the context of a knowledgeable attitude towards the whole school
curriculum, these girls unanimously put Terry's subject
first.

     Though not so encapsulated a group, in their lesson
interactions, the four middle-class boys expressed equally
homogeneous attitudes and were quite alike in how they
stood towards Terry's methods and curriculum.   In their
class work, these boys were, from what we saw of them,
even more committed and absorbed than were the girls.
They seemed particularly confident in situations requiring
an active role in developing knowledge, and the ability to
draw on their own resources.   When they talked and worked
together, their high level of mutuality was notable, as
was their ease in handling any differences of opinion -
something other children often found problematic.   Like
the middle-class girls, these boys seemed, from what they
said, to find no disjunction between their school and out-
of-school worlds - indeed, to experience their family

contexts as highly supportive of school learning and themselves as particularly rich in learning resources.   For
them, as for the middle-class girls, classrooms appeared
to offer generally positive experiences, and among these,
Terry's classroom was clearly specially highly valued.

For another, very close-knit group of children, the
situation was rather different.   The four black girls in
Terry's class represented a subgroup whose function seemed
essentially social rather than educational.   Fundamentally, this probably met the crucial need for mutual support
in a situation where these girls felt, at best, exposed
and, at worst, subject to discrimination.   The strong
comments which all four girls made speak of a familiarity,
in their school lives, with racist attitudes on the part
of teachers - though, as Ann was careful to point out,
'not all teachers'.   Even in Terry's class it was clear
that these girls had a sense of their minority group
status: Sandra's comment, echoed by the others, was 'A
class that's mostly got more whites that it does coloureds isn't quite equal.'   It does not seem surprising,
given these feelings, that these four girls looked to each
other as a source of solidarity, and used the opportunities of interaction for mutual personal acknowledgment and
support.

When we saw these four girls talking together, their
talk was generally about matters unrelated to work.
Once, exceptionally, we did observe Sandra and Ann devot-
ing their shared attention to the task set by Terry - com-
posing a newspaper feature - and managing this very com-
petently.   Much more often, though, the talk of all four
girls dwelt on topics quite unrelated to classroom work.
Personal relationships among themselves, a dance they were
putting on, experiences in the out-of-school world - these
formed the focuses of their conversations together that we
witnessed during the year.   In this context, their dealings with each other were both supportive and delicate.
Both generally, and to the extent that their talk touched
on the work they were doing, the girls were noticeably
sensitive and tactful towards each other.   This was particularly striking in relation to Valerie who had, in
fact, been judged ESN.   The other three girls consistently avoided highlighting the obvious difficulties which
Valerie was having in class work, while regularly including her in their social group.   This personal affirmation
must have acted to maintain Valerie emotionally in a situation in which she was, potentially, doubly vulnerable.

If the impressive sociality between these four black
girls involved personal rather than strictly educational
concerns, this does not mean that they did not work in
Terry's classroom.   Apart from Valerie, whose great difficulties with class work often led to her visibly giving
up, this group of pupils was, from what we saw, both generally hard-working and anxious to do well.   They did,
however, characteristically work on their own rather than
together.   Concomitantly, more structured tasks, involving individual written work, seemed to call forth greater
commitment from them than did open-ended tasks demanding
small or large group discussion.   We noticed that they
seldom contributed to class discussions, despite the fact
that these were generally lively;   all four girls seemed
unenthusiastic about this side of Terry's lessons and on
one occasion we remarked that Carol appeared totally
switched off.

How does this stance towards Terry's classroom fit with
the general attitudes these girls expressed?   Again, from
what evidence we have, there was a high degree of agreement among this group.   Both Ann and Sandra, in construing children generally, were much more concerned with out-
of-school life than life inside it, although what they did
say about school suggested a generally positive rather
than a negative orientation.   Talking about school in relation to their lives generally, all four girls conveyed a
sense of disjunction between formal education and everyday
experience.   They saw friends as sharing out-of-school
concerns, felt that parents did not generally understand
the school context, and agreed that personal identity was
different in and out of school - as Ann put it, 'children
act different and probably speak different'.

This general separation of personal and social concerns
from the world of school seems entirely in accord with the
way these four girls used the opportunities for talk, in
Terry's class, for social rather than for educational purposes.   How they reacted to Terry's curriculum and his
methods also seems to make sense in the light of what they
said.   Throughout these girls' comments ran the thread
that school achievement, opportunities for learning, were
valued.   However, it was for Maths - a crucial qualifica-
tion for employment - that all four girls expressed the
greatest enthusiasm when they rated a variety of curriculum areas.   Towards Humanities, they were much less enthusiastic, although, again, characteristically, Sandra
expressed some appreciation of its instrumental value as
enabling people to write good English.

Just as their greatest concern, in the school curriculum, was with aspects traditionally associated with individualized work, so these four girls, in what they said,
conveyed a reliance on teachers rather than pupils as resources in learning.   Talking about classroom work, they
emphasized the importance of strictness on the part of the
teacher to ensure that pupils learn, while expressing some
mistrust of classroom talk.   Again, given these attitudes
to different classroom modes, it is not surprising that
Sandra, Ann, Carol and Valerie took individual written
work more seriously than the large group discussions, or
the more intimate interchanges in which Terry constantly
invited them to engage.

Turning from black to white working-class girls means
considering a rather different subgroup within Terry's
class.   In the first place, this is largely a story of
only two girls, Tina and Tracey, since both Sally and
Valerie O. were regular absentees.   Tina and Tracey, despite their constant close involvement in Terry's lessons,
expressed attitudes which in some ways were quite dissimi-
lar.   Both girls conveyed the sense, in what they said,
that their out-of-school experience was more vital, more
involving, than what happened within school itself.   But
towards the school context, and the formal learning situations it offered, Tina and Tracey adopted rather different
positions.

Tina's orientation towards school learning was strikingly confident.   She was able to discuss school lessons
almost as though she was a teacher herself;   she debated
the relevance of the curriculum for particular pupil
groups, she considered different teaching styles, she
examined the choice of school texts and suggested alterna-
tives.   For Tina, teachers were highly differentiated,
and she discussed their personalities and approaches in a
very thoughtful and subtle way.   Where she valued
teachers, it was for their human qualities and their capacity to engage with pupils in a genuinely mutual relationship.   While appreciating teachers as persons, Tina
clearly did not feel dependent on them to mediate learning;   in fact, she expressed resentment of those who constantly taught pupils, instead of letting them get on with
the work by themselves.   This sense of confident independence also seemed to inform Tina's approach to complex and
difficult learning situations;   she was enjoying the challenge of Maths precisely because the subject had got
harder.

Her friend Tracey spoke from a very different perspective.   She clearly saw her own position, towards school
learning, as that of the less able pupil and frequently
made reference to the experience of difficulty with the
curriculum, and the sense of being at sea in lessons.
Her attitude to teachers was in marked contrast to Tina's.
For Tracey, school learning seemed to be highly dependent
on teachers, to whom she looked for a strict management of
the class, together with an insistence on traditional,
individualized work.   So far from endorsing Tina's expectation of relative equality in teacher-pupil relationships,
Tracey mistrusted free-and-easy classrooms, and saw
teachers as distant authority figures rather than accessible human beings.

As part of these different perspectives on school
learning, the two girls expressed contrasting views about
classroom collaboration.   Whereas Tracey saw the potentially disruptive effect of friends, and conveyed general
mistrust of talk and informality in lessons, Tina commented positively on the learning possibilities of pupil-pupil
interaction, though she saw these as dependent on the relationships between those involved.   In talking about pupils
working together, Tina did in fact refer to her own group -
herself, Tracey, Valerie O. and Sally.   As she said,
'There's four of us, we sit next to each other and we
always learn each other things.'   It seemed to be Tina's
ease with the teacher, her confidence towards the material
of lessons and her belief that friends could easily and
naturally learn from each other which, in practice, governed the nature of her interactions with Tracey in Terry's
classroom context.   In what we saw of these two girls
during the year, Tina's characteristic, often enthusiastic,
commitment carried her less able friend along, often producing real involvement, and her own initiatives, for
Tracey, in work they were doing together.   Tina's high
morale and her readiness to help her friend, did not
always overcome Tracey's difficulties;   on one occasion,
after a long period in which Tina made various practical
suggestions and showed Tracey her own work, we saw Tracey
abandon the task in despair, crumpling up the work she had
done.   More often, however, the two girls were to be seen
involved, often absorbed, in the work they were doing
together, proceeding without reference to the teacher.

The firm friendship of these two girls was clearly
based on out-of-school concerns.   The fact that they were
able to turn it to such account in Terry's classroom -
despite Tracey's generally negative experience of lessons -

is probably due to the mutual sensitivity of the two
friends.   Tina herself was thoughtful and perceptive
towards others; she set a high value on personal relationships, in which she looked for mutuality and trust.
Certainly, in what we saw of her interchanges with Tracey,
she demonstrated these values.   It was clear that she
appreciated Tracey as a friend, and that, towards their
clearly unequal academic abilities, she took an un-super-
ior position, tactfully helping Tracey where this was welcome, but not insisting, or dominating her friend.   For
Tracey, a sense of being respected was crucial; she expressed some bitterness towards a teacher who had been
dismissive.   It seems likely that her friend's appreciative attitude and delicate handling of her academic difficulties were the critical factor in enabling her to invest
herself, to the extent that she did, in the work of
Terry's class.

Terry's encouragement of this relationship, important
to both girls, led in turn to a highly positive valuation
on their part of his lessons.   Tina and Tracey both gave
Humanities the highest positive ratings, Tracey adding
that it was 'very easy and nice to do', while Tina said
Terry was 'a great teacher'.   This positive feeling
towards the class might not have come about.   For both
girls, life outside school was clearly more important.
Tracey, who found school work so difficult and frustrating, described hard-working pupils as 'goody-goodies', and
clearly felt herself to be incompetent, could easily have
experienced an alienation in Terry's class.   On her side,
Tina strongly rejected much of the school curriculum,
usually because of personality clashes with the teacher.
Since she set supreme importance on her social relationships, her feelings about Terry, together with his willingness to make room for her friendship with Tracey in
lesson work, were obviously critical.   In the case of
both girls, therefore, the mutual benefits of their personal friendship and Terry's Humanities lessons were particularly marked.

Of the five subgroups in Terry's class, we have looked
briefly at middle-class girls and middle-class boys,
neither of which groups, apparently, had any difficulty in
working productively and with enjoyment in the framework
he provided.   Then we considered the black working-class
girls, who clearly appreciated - in fact probably needed -
the mutual social support available in Terry's lessons,
but did not, to nearly such an extent, integrate this with
their academic work.   Finally, we examined the inter-

action of two white working-class girls, and found that,
on the whole, they made Terry's classroom work quite central to their mutual involvement in his lessons.   This
leaves the nine or so white working-class boys - the group
with which Terry himself was most particularly concerned.

Across the year, though there was some variability,
these boys generally showed a relative lack of involvement
in the work of Terry's lessons.   Certainly they stood, as
a group, in marked contrast with the committed, active,
enthusiastic middle-class boys.   From what we saw, this
group of children typically gave little real personal commitment to the open-ended projects set up by Terry,
although they usually did enough work to get by in
lessons.   Their general indifference was most marked when
Terry invited the whole class group to discuss personal-
social questions.   For instance, in a public expression
of views on matters such as how to bring up children, and
the impact of unemployment - matters which were certainly
of consequence to everyone in the class - these usually
talkative and articulate boys offered virtually nothing.

There were some notable exceptions to this general lack
of participation.   This was to some extent a question of
the individual boys concerned.   Several times we noticed
that John R., a dynamic, buoyant and confident boy, was
acting both to energize and sustain his companions -
usually Dave and John T. - in class work.   However, where
this happened, the work involved was typically quite
structured.   John T., for instance, regularly worked conscientiously with his friend, Kevin, on such tasks as comprehension questions.   Where more personal, creative
efforts were required, we did not see any evidence that
boys within this subgroup were willing to invest themselves in a common endeavour.   What we did see, where
Terry's work was of that sort, was that some individual
boys were temporarily drawn in and swept along by the
interest and enthusiasm of members of the class who were
outside their own subgroup.   When Kenny, in this subgroup, worked with Jose, outside it, the two boys maintained an impressive and sustained commitment to an essentially creative project, involving the preparation of
newspaper copy.   This was also the case when Simon,
usually passive, even apathetic, in Terry's lessons,
worked with middle-class Stephen.   Again, though, it was
Stephen who clearly took the lead in planning illustrated
folders about the North American Indians;   Simon maintained, throughout the work, the role of willing audience
and follower, occasionally volunteering initiatives of his

own.   From what we saw, however, the commitment of these
boys to such personally involving class work was essentially dependent on moment-to-moment contact with someone
else's confidence and enthusiasm.   We noticed, too, in
the interchanges we saw between Stephen and James, that
the prior commitment of another pupil did not necessarily
succeed in drawing in a working-class boy whose current
level of involvement was minimal.

   If we consider the attitudes which this group of boys
expressed, certain themes emerge which seem to fit with
this general unwillingness to make a genuinely personal
commitment to the work of Terry's class.   Although we
did not have a complete sampling of the boys involved,
we had at least some access to seven of them - only James
being absent from all the assessments we made.   In what
these seven boys said, there is quite a lot of common
ground.   These boys expressed the sense that personal
identity in and out of school was very different, peer
group relationships were experienced as located outside
school, and there were expectations that friends would
disrupt school learning.   Given that they also emphasized
the supreme importance, for them, of peer group solidarity
- both as the main source of fun, and as critical to sur-
vival in a world of conflict and violence - this adds up
to a stance in which the formal concerns of school were
essentially marginal to the vital concerns of personal
life.   It is perhaps not surprising that these boys went
on to express some discomfort and potential alienation in
formal learning situations.   This was conveyed by the
characterization of school work as generally boring and of
pupils as needing coercion to apply themselves to it.
These boys also portrayed themselves as academically less
able, with a definite personal distance from 'snobs' and
'brain-boxes'.

   For pupils who saw school learning in this light, how
were Terry's particular modes and expectations likely to
be experienced?   What is most striking is that, for all
six in this subgroup who expressed their feelings towards
different school subjects, Humanities, along with the other
four academic subjects, was unanimously given a low rating.
Characteristically, these boys barely differentiated the
formal educational curriculum - Terry's subject, along
with others, was judged to be generally boring and use-
less, while only Games, itself outside the academic business of school, received an enthusiastic rating.   As
John R. said of Humanities, 'it can become a drag'.   It
seems likely that Terry's attempt to integrate school

learning with real and lively personal experience met, in
these boys, a sense of resistance, in so far as they expected the curriculum to be separated from out-of-school
life, and were critical, for instance, of tutorial sessions which ventured into areas of personal behaviour.
Finally, in that Terry's approach demanded that pupils see
themselves and other pupils as valid resources in school
learning, these boys' view that teachers represented the
repositories of knowledge and the disciplinarians of
learning provided still another obstacle to their ready
engagement with his methods.

Yet there is no doubt that, as a group, these working-
class boys benefited personally from the classroom set-up
established by Terry.   The space which Terry made for
their sense of peer group solidarity provided opportunities for laughter and fun which, although generally at a
tangent from class work, did not actually undermine it.
The fact that such episodes were allowed, and often
actually shared, by Terry, meant that these boys, whose
interactions were typically boisterous and exuberant, were
nevertheless validated as members of the class, rather
than being seen as disruptive pupils.   It was probably
because of this confirmation, both of themselves as individuals and of their personally important group solidarity, that these boys were prepared - if not to invest
themselves personally and wholeheartedly in Terry's curriculum - at least to meet the minimal requirements he
made.

Form 27 was notable for its five relatively distinct
subgroups of children.   As we have seen, each of these
subgroups had, to some degree, its own particular outlook,
and, to a large extent, the subgroups kept to themselves
within Terry's classroom.   Terry himself thought that
existing friendly relationships provided the only viable
basis for working together in lessons;   he did not believe
in interfering with the natural groupings of the children
in his class.   When, occasionally, he did so, the results
were not always successful, and seemed, to some extent, to
confirm his own doubts.   For instance, although the partnership he set up between Stephen and Simon took off, the
pairing of Stephen with James definitely did not, James
remaining as bored and apathetic as usual.   In so far as
Terry's approach endorsed existing friendship patterns,
his lessons acted essentially to confirm and even crystal-
lize the subdivisions within this class group.

Among the girls in Terry's class, the three cliques

were clearly divided on lines of race and class.   The
middle-class girls, all of whom were white, formed a distinct group, linked not only by their social background,
but additionally by their special school status and the
shared out-of-school activities which this entailed.   The
working-class black girls, because of their own sense of
apartness in a predominantly white class, formed an
equally separate, close social clique, similarly, on their
own.   One of the inevitable by-products of this segregation, among the girls, was a division on lines of academic
ability - the middle-class girls being, as a group, more
academically successful than the other two groups.

In the way they worked within Terry's classroom, these
three groups of girls characteristically kept apart.   We
never saw any instances of collaboration across cliques.
Yet we also saw no signs of inter-group hostility or competitiveness between the three groups.   On the contrary,
feeling across cliques seemed generally friendly, and
there was regular, if brief, social interaction between
members of all three groupings with each other.   That
this was so was probably due partly to Terry's position
towards the children in his classroom group.   In the
first place, as we have seen, he continually made clear
his own personal appreciation of individual children,
being particularly sensitive to those he saw as potentially alienated.   Terry also constantly de-emphasized compe-
tition.   While not ignoring the very wide range of academic ability within the class, he was concerned to encourage the less able children to reach something of the
high standards of the very able - rather than defining
certain pupils as inherently lacking competence.   Through
the obvious liking and respect for Terry himself among all
these groups of girls, it is likely that they assimilated
something of these attitudes towards each other.

Six particular children

The mutual social stance which the three girls' cliques
adopted must also have been a function of the individuals
within them, and particularly, those individuals who were
specially influential.   In the middle-class group, Katie
seemed a highly salient member, just as Sandra apparently
was among the black girls, and Tina, among the white working-class girls.   As far as Katie was concerned, her
social orientation in class was certainly integrative
rather than divisive.   We saw her role towards the other
girls, both within and outside her own clique, as charac-

teristically friendly and constructive.   Katie was clearly well liked by the other girls generally.   In her own
group, Esther, who often preferred to sit alone, seemed
happy to sit with her.   We also noticed Katie sitting
quite often with Ann, one of the black girls, though the
two never joined forces in work.   Katie, in the attitudes
she expressed, showed a broad social sympathy and concern.

Despite her own elevated school status and her general
enjoyment of formal learning, Katie was able to feel empathy with less able pupils, commenting that in school
they were apt to 'be made to feel odd, and become
depressed'.   She not only apparently set a high premium
on human communication, she also clearly valued the sharing of experience across a wide social range.   As she
said, 'One of the reasons we come to school is to learn to
mix with other people, and share our views.'

If Katie, in the role she took in Terry's lessons,
acted to mitigate the potential divisiveness of its social
cliques, it was Sandra who most clearly ensured that her
own small clique did not withdraw into an isolated, alienated island in the class.   From what we saw, Sandra
seemed to be the pivot of the subgroup - the person who in
some sense defined their orientation towards Terry's classroom.   Like the other three girls, Sandra, in what she
said, conveyed the centrality of her minotiry group status
for the way in which she perceived herself.   But because
of her sensitive understanding of the other black girls
and her generally positive feelings about Terry's curriculum, she represented both a source of support for her
friends in his lessons and a bridge between them and his
classroom ethos.   Sandra's acceptance of Valerie's academic difficulties, together with her delicate proferring
of help, must have done much to forestall total frustration for Valerie, just as the mutually supportive relationship Sandra shared with the three other girls must have
helped to sustain their morale in Terry's classroom.

It seems significant, too, that, despite the reservations which Sandra, like Valerie, Ann and Carol, had regarding the personal significance of school, she nevertheless saw at least the possibility of real involvement in
the formal curriculum.   More particularly, Sandra greatly
appreciated Terry himself, and valued the open and human
relationships he offered children.   Her sense that, in
classrooms such as Terry's, she could feel at ease, and
talk to the teacher about any problems that arose, must -
given the high level of rapport within this group - have

influenced the interpretations that the other three girls made of Terry's lessons.

Among the white working-class girls in this class group, Tina, without doubt, was the most dominant. As we have already seen, Tina adopted a highly positive stance towards Terry's lessons.   Central to this was her enthusiastic appreciation of Terry himself; we saw her express this publicly in the obviously enjoyable interchanges she had with him in class.   Tina was also exceptional among the working-class children in her sympathetic understanding of Terry's collaborative learning modes.   She believed in informality, in independent learning, in the possibilities of collaboration between friends.   We have seen that, in fact, she put her collaborative opportunities to good use in working with Tracey and that this collaboration maintained her potentially alienated friend. Tina's influence, though, spread much more widely than this.

In some sense, Tina seemed to be the lynchpin of the class.   Although, in our observation, she had little to do with the middle-class girls, she mixed often and easily with the black girls in the class, and, in contrast with many of the other girls, had an open, free-and-easy relationship with the boys in the class.   Tina therefore seemed to hold a dominant social position within the class group; for other children she must have carried a highly positive orientation to Terry's lessons.   Had she adopted an antagonistic stance, as she obviously did towards other, rather different, classroom practices, Tina might well have drawn many other children with her into anti-teacher, anti-work feelings.

The situation among the boys in Terry's class was, as we have seen, rather different from that of the girls. Where the girls subdivided themselves into three clearly separate groups, this did not happen with the boys, whose social relationships were much more open and fluid. Their altogether freer interactions allowed collaborative working among a number of different pairs of small groups, occasionally crossing boundaries of social class.   Nevertheless, one boy, Rana, appeared frequently isolated and excluded.

To a large extent, this situation seems to have been an outcome of the attitudes of the highly able middle-class boys, none of whom were apparently elitist or competitive in their orientation to school learning.   We saw all four

boys - Carl, Chinekwu, Stephen and Vincent - helping less
able children.   When, as sometimes happened, other children admired the work these boys had produced, they typically adopted a modest stance.   All four seemed very
ready to work with others, in pairs or small groups, and
appeared to gain real pleasure from the opportunity to
share ideas and develop them jointly.

Stephen's contribution to this general openness among
the boys was probably considerable.   It was Stephen whom
we saw in a sustained, successful joint enterprise with
Kevin, a working-class member of the class.   His joint
endeavour with James, a little later, was much less successful; but it is significant that Terry selected him
for the extremely difficult task of engaging a very bored
and unmotivated boy.   For Terry, Stephen probably represented a catalyst through whose ebullient energy and enthusiasm other children might be drawn into participation
in classroom work.

There is no doubt that Stephen, in his position towards
the work of the Humanities class, carried a philosophy
that was very close to Terry's own.   His strong belief in
informality and the value of talk for 'discussing things
and exchanging opinions', his confidence towards difficult
areas of the curriculum and enjoyment of challenge, above
all, his sense that, in spheres such as this, knowledge
was constructed, not received - all these things marked
Stephen's very strong commitment to independent, participant learning.   He was, besides, an outstanding examplar
of the use of classroom collaboration in productive and
personally enjoyable ways.   With his rich experience,
both in and out of school, of shared learning, Stephen
took Terry's opportunities for joint work easily and
naturally, and often put them to outstandingly good use.

All this might, nevertheless, merely have served to
accentuate Stephen's elite status, and separate him from
other, less academically oriented boys.   The fact that it
did not do so must be due to Stephen's own attitudes to
his peer group.   Within Terry's classroom, as we have
seen, Stephen did not claim a special status.   Not only
did he mix freely, and with evident enjoyment, among the
group of working-class boys, including individuals among
them, if this was called for, in his classroom work;   he
also expressed feelings towards his situation that were
strongly anti-elitist.   Acknowledging that, on his arrival at secondary school, he had been thought 'a bit of a
snob', Stephen believed this had changed, and, on his

side, quite vehemently denied ever having had a sense of
social or educational superiority.   He was equally emphatic in rejecting the separation of children in school on
grounds of academic ability, commenting that it would be
'like the Conservatives, the rich get richer, and the
poor, poorer'.   More subtly - but probably just as important - Stephen shared the perceptions of the boys' working-class subgroup, that relations among boys contained a
strong element of conflict and violence.   In this area of
commonality, Stephen lived in the same experiential world
as the working-class boys with whom he shared Terry's
classroom.

As far as the working-class boys were concerned, John
R. seemed particularly influential in establishing the
generally friendly stance of this subgroup towards others
in the class.   As with Stephen, Terry sometimes deliberately used John to draw in relatively isolated or unengaged boys;   we saw this happen in the case of John T. and
of Dave.   In these situations, John did, from what we
observed, largely succeed, not only in involving the other
boys socially, but also in initiating, and then sustaining, their engagement in classroom work.   He did this by
keeping up a running commentary on his own work, checking
what they were doing and generally reminding them, and
himself, of what they were supposed to be doing, and how
they were getting on with it.   Because of his own exuber-
ance and sense of humour, John usually found some occasion
for jokes and fun in the situation he was in, and it was
obvious that other boys enjoyed his lively presence.

Given his general sense of school as marginal and
school work as boring, John might well have adopted an
oppositional stance towards Terry and his lessons - a
stance which would probably have affected the other working-class boys, among whom he had considerable influence.
It does not seem that Terry's Humanities had much personal
significance for John;   like the other working-class boys,
he made little differentiation of the academic curriculum,
and commented that Humanities could be a drag.   The vital
factor in his positive orientation was probably the large
opportunities Terry's Humanities lessons offered for
social interactions.   For John, to whom relationships
with other boys were apparently the major source of enjoyment, classrooms which suppressed all verbal and physical
interchanges must have been barely tolerable.   In Terry's
classroom, he found a setting in which the teacher not
only encouraged social interaction, but affirmed the value
of John's own capacity for sociality with other children.

Apart from the persistent absentees, virtually all the children in Terry's class were included in social interactions among them, if not necessarily - as we have seen - in collaborative working.   There was, however, one exception - Rana.   Throughout the year, we noticed that Rana was either sitting alone in lessons, or alongside, but not within, an ongoing group.   Although, occasionally, he joined in the jokes and laughter of John R. and his friends, much more often, we saw him looking wistfully on, unnoticed by the other boys.   Typically, he was reduced to working alone, writing in an apparently desultory way, or, when he got stuck on the task, resorting to doodling on the paper.

It is not altogether clear why Rana, alone among these children, should have been so excluded.   If we examine what he said about his experience in and out of school, it is clear that he shared quite a lot of common ground with the working-class boys in Terry's class.   Like them, he took an instrumental view of learning, and respected traditional rather than informal classroom modes.   As they did, he felt that school imposed its own, constrained identity on children, and that, in boys' more natural interactions, conflict and tension were endemic.   But Rana spoke of such interactions from an apparently rather different perspective from that of most working-class boys.   Race was obviously a highly salient dimension in his perceptions.   Unlike the white boys, Rana saw race as a major factor in differentiating children, and thought that membership of a minority racial group was likely to be the basis of friendship among boys.   He applied this to himself, saying that he would have as a friend someone who was the same colour as himself.   There are hints, in what Rana said, that minority group membership carried connotations of potential victimization: he referred to people calling him names.   It may be, therefore, that despite Rana's evident wish to take part in the lively encounters of the white working-class boys, his own invisibility to them bore out his sense of racial barriers.

Concluding comments

This class group was characterized by differences among the children in gender, race, social class, and an exceptionally wide academic range.   As we have seen, Terry's approach to collaboration did not much challenge the existing subdivisions in the group - subdivisions which were probably being explicitly endorsed outside his classroom.

Yet this did not, from what we saw, lead to a breakdown in commonality and sociality within the group.   The perceived differences among the children had not degenerated into rifts between them;   there were no signs that the different subgroups viewed each other with mistrust, contempt or incomprehension.

That this was so seems to have been due to two factors.   On the one hand, Terry himself actively worked to develop sociality between himself and all the children in his group.   This seemed to result in the growth of considerable commonality between them;   all five subgroups showed a personal appreciation of their teacher, and a sense that his lessons could be enjoyable.   The second crucial factor, apparently, was the presence in the class group of particular individuals.   These individual children acted to develop commonality more widely within the group, and to extend sociality beyond their own particular subgroup, so as to include others in their sphere of social concern.

Chapter 6

Rachel's second and third year Humanities (Drama) and English class

RACHEL'S FRAME OF REFERENCE

Rachel's post at Newlands partly involved her in teaching lower-school Humanities under Terry, and partly gave her responsibility for Drama in the creative arts department. A highly enthusiastic and energetic teacher, she took on responsibility for running after-school drama groups with several forms, and organizing productions for the school both of material improvised by pupils and existing written plays. Several times she was heard to say that every subject in the curriculum ought to be infused with drama and that children should be given the opportunity to learn through drama wherever possible.

In the first term (the children's second year of secondary schooling), the class was taught by Rachel for two periods per week for a Humanities course which combined History and English. History was mainly done through project work in folders, but there was a great deal of overlap between the two areas as a matter of departmental policy. For example, children might be asked to write semi-fictionally about an historical episode or their History work might provide material for consideration of English grammar and expression.

Topics covered during the year were quite varied. A number of works of fiction were read in class during the year and story writing or comprehensions based on them. The class also worked from time to time on conventional grammar exercises from a text book. Because of time-tabling we monitored Drama or English lessons rather than classes given over to History.

During the second year (the children's third year)

History and English were taught as distinct subjects by
different teachers from the children's third year in
school.   We monitored the English curriculum taught by
Rachel and had no contact with their History teacher.

There was a great deal of latitude in the third year
for English teachers who interpreted the curriculum in
quite individual ways.   Rachel used fiction available in
the school stocks, and also worked through a project on
Autobiography which was available in the school, but
devised her own curriculum as she went along.   She did a
great deal of drama, group discussion leading to writing,
and tended to teach grammar and expression by using the
children's own work as examples of good or bad practice.

Relationships between pupils and the teacher

In the frame of reference which we will describe for
Rachel, her commitment to the generation of shared experience and mutual understanding in classroom settings will
become apparent.   Where many teachers see their role as
the imparting of information, or facilitating understanding of a 'subject', Rachel felt that the concepts of teaching and learning had no validity without prior attention
to the nature of the relationships between teacher and
learner, and between the learners themselves.   Many
children were indifferent or disinterested in what school
had to offer and it was up to teachers to stimulate them,
not to blame the children for failing to share their enthusiasm for their subject.   If teaching was to 'take',
children had to be receptive and responsive and teachers
had to prepare the ground via their relationships with the
pupils: 'You can't expect people to do things unless
you've engaged a relationship with them ... [fostering]
real learning means having responsibility for the engaging
of their interest....'   In Rachel's view, in a constantly
changing dynamic classroom, successful relationships had
to be based on honesty: honesty underpinned the whole
ethos of her teaching, and was the bedrock, hidden curriculum which validated or negated her work in the class.
Honesty was a superordinate construct with a wide range of
convenience.   For example she talked about teachers who
were unable or unwilling to be honest about their own life
situation and feelings, and encouraged in children a false
sense of teachers' separation from the ordinary world of
humanity, which they knew and understood out of school.
She explained that being honest with her class meant she
was prepared to reveal her own vulnerability and share her

problems as a teacher, expecting in return that the children would take her seriously:

'I started a creative arts lesson the other day, but
couldn't get their attention so I said, I've got a
really bad problem and I sort of told them honestly
that I had such stomach problems, you know because I
had to lose my temper at the beginning of every lesson,
or pretend to, I explained this exactly to the kids,
that it was really affecting my health, and was there
any way that I could get them to stop talking without
actually having to shout at them, and they knew that I
was being honest because they know that I've been away
... so that's a perfect example of just me being
straight about me and my limitations.'

Having shared her problem honestly with them, she asked
the pupils to meet her as equals in finding a solution,
which she would then act upon:

'I asked how am I going to avoid getting so ill that
I've got to give up teaching, what can I do to get you
to be quiet.   I said I'll give a prize to somebody who
can think of good ideas ... one kid said take off your
jacket.   So the next week I remembered to put on the
jacket, and then took it off, and it was a joke, but
they all sat down, it was a joke enough for them to
sit, to see if it could work....'

Another facet of honesty dealt with was who one was and
what one believed in:

'You're saying to these other human beings, this is
what really caught my interest today, or I felt dis-
tressed when I saw something on television, or if a kid
does actually say to you, do you believe in marriage or
whatever, you do, apart from the way you discipline
them or cope with the classroom and them in the classroom, be an honest human being.'

Adolescents have a capacity, Rachel thought, to see
through the smokescreens erected by teachers and responded
to the 'real reasons' when a teacher reproved them or was
dissatisfied with their work, recognizing the difference
between discipline based on authoritarianism, and genuine
concern for their problems with work, and their improvement.

In a reciprocal relationship authoritarianism was not

appropriate, and discipline more a matter of explaining to
children that their own progress depended on their co-
operation.   However, reciprocity between teachers and
pupils did not preclude normal human reactions:

> 'I think that disciplining in an honest way ... is not
> to say shut up, be quiet etc., for _me_, but that we can
> get more accomplished, you know, if you can hold back,
> now, ... and then it's equally, that if you are finding
> things frustrating, I think sometimes even an explosive
> reaction is very good for the kids.'

The methods she had evolved in her classroom were not
always trouble-free or entirely successful.   But if the
process and not just the product were the point of a
lesson, she reckoned on dealing with conflict as part of
the process of learning.

Just as she regularly reminded the class of their relationship with her, of their mutual dependence if work was
to get done, and that they had to allow for her limitations, whether physical or in time, she let the children
know that she understood their point of view, and was explicit about her perception of relationships between them:

> 'You say, look this good group isn't working because
> you're refusing to let so and so join in, or you've got
> a bad feeling in the group.... That rears its head
> quickly in drama, but not so much in ordinary formal
> learning.'

If a teacher was going to put pupils in positions of power
in the classroom, she had to recognize the risks they had
to take, and take seriously the relationships with each
other that they were putting on the line.   If they
started taking over lessons, they might find themselves
failing, or being disciplined by other pupils.   For her
part, she contributed to the openness of the situation by
being prepared to apologize to them if she had hurt them,
even in jest, and in return knew they wouldn't go too far,
either with each other or with her.   This was because
they knew she had control but also because:

> 'subconsciously, they just don't want to hurt me.... I
> feel that they are friends, and I feel that they are
> trying to be friends of mine, and therefore, the atmos-
> phere, thank God, is very supportive of me.'

As well as the teacher acknowledging her own fallibility

in the classroom, Rachel believed in extending feelings
and articulating to the children explicitly her awareness
of their situation and susceptibility to outside influences: 'it all seems to me to do with just explaining
things which teachers often leave unexplained....'   Sometimes this had to do with the teacher explaining herself
to the children:

> 'maybe walking in and saying, you know I'm sorry that I
> haven't marked these things for a long time, because it
> must be really annoying for you, or simply just say,
> look I've been away for two or three lessons last week,
> so we'll really have to listen to each other this
> lesson, because I've got to organize a lot of work.'

Rather than just reprove them she might comment on their
behaviour in ways which gave them psychological space:

> 'little remarks like, just saying, oh you've all come
> from lunch and you all look hectic, and I know you're
> all over the place or whatever, so let's do something
> to calm us all down, but just a sympathy thing all the
> time, sympathy, understanding what it's like for them
> to be in this place.'

A straightforward response to children's moods sometimes facilitated the adjustment of an individual to the
group, and dealt with the child's true problem, rather
than the teacher's desire for conformity, or to assert
authority.   If a pupil seemed to be in a bad mood, or was
behaving in anti-social ways, she felt it was more productive to ask why, which was one's true concern as a
teacher, rather than dwell on failure to meet classroom
norms: 'cut through all the business of "I'm the teacher,
you're not behaving" ... but ask what's happening to him
and his work.'   Sensitivity to children's psychological
state was also a way of integrating a difficult pupil and
helping him to get something from a lesson:

> 'Like Andrew came in after having been away a long time
> and said, why don't you just send me out now, I want to
> go, and I said to him ... it's quite a threatening
> remark, really, and I said, you might just enjoy the
> lesson Andrew, ... but didn't get cross with him, said
> you might just enjoy the lesson, sit down and shut up;
> and we were reading and I got him to read instantly and
> said in front of the class, Andrew's really good at
> reading, can you read?, and his stupid little ego is
> immediately ... you know he was "in" on the lesson and

then at the end of the lesson we played a game where
you have to be a person in the school who we all know,
and we all have to ask opinion questions and find out
who the person was in the school, and he wanted to do
it the whole time and of course that was a very active
thing that he's very good at.'

From the children's point of view, it was not enough
for the teacher to present herself as a sincere, genuine
human being.   Reciprocity implied that she recognize the
validity of children's experience.   The corollary was for
the children to perceive that they could legitimately
bring into the class, issues which might have seemed inappropriate in another school context.   The children had
to learn new and radical definitions of the classroom and
for this understanding to really take root, and the class
to accept their own positive role in the development of
their learning, involved a basic trust between each other
and the teacher, and honesty about themselves.

A collaborative setting focused on children's relationships with each other, helped them to get to know and
trust one another and above all ensured that they made an
honest response because they really cared about the content of the work, which was their own lives.   She gave as
an example Jonathan and Duncan who had not only been marginal in the peer group but unwilling to take risks in
their relationship with her:

'I mean people like Jonathan and Duncan are really
speaking out with me and taking the mick out of me and
there's just a very relaxed jovial business you know
and also interesting that Jonathan and Duncan are both
mentioning things to do with sex in what they're writing ... and I mean ... not because of me but I feel
that they do feel a freedom of expression.'

Relationships between pupils

A collaborative, non-competitive ethos was essential for
children to develop an open but self-critical view of
themselves and their work, self-evaluation had to occur
with reference to other people's efforts, perspectives and
responses.   This might entail potentially 'cruel' pub-
licity and exposure (to use Rachel's word) unless the
atmosphere was not just non-critical, but positively supportive.   She set out to create non-defensive good feeling between all the pupils, not just the kind of mutuality

that one might expect between friends.   She felt that
there was a difference between the kind of familiarity
that sharing a class base engendered, and genuine trust
and openness towards someone, who was not necessarily a
chosen friend or member of one's clique, gained through
working on common tasks.   In many classes a competitive
spirit developed, which resulted in global judgments such
as 'Oh this is so good', or 'this is a load of rubbish' if
work was read out, or books passed to others to see.
Such generalizations foreclosed on genuine appreciation or
prospects of learning from each other's efforts.   What
she hoped for was mutual respect and tolerance, extending
beyond the bounds of friendship, so that children who were
asked to look at each other's work, or work together on a
project, were able to gain something from it.   Sharing
one's own work and seeing how it compared with another
person's, and reference to someone else's insights and
perceptions could lead to critical self-evaluation: 'not
just reflecting on your own work, but seeing what can be
done by other people without your psychological limitations ... you know ... the inspiration of others.'   In
practice, creating an atmosphere of mutual trust required
that children who normally hardly mixed had the opportunity to find out more about one another, and develop a
respect for each other's potential, qualities or problems.

As an example of the tolerant non-judgmental approach
she hoped for, she mentioned the class response to the
work of Kurdo who at that time had little fluency in
English:

'He has written his life recently for me, which he's
typing up here in English lessons ... and I'm going to
photostat it and we're going to read it together ...
and yet you know there have been times when kids have
just looked at his folder and just kind of chucked it
around, because it's all a mess, and then another one
has quickly said ... "Yes but Miss M. says this is
like, you know his fourth language" ... and they're
just stopping to think about his problems....'

It was foolish to suppose that children would be prepared to put themselves in exposed positions in front of
other children or the teacher, without testing the water
to see whether their vulnerability would be exploited.
The teacher set the tone and the ground rules by pointing
out to the pupils that there was no threat or hidden sanc-
tion, by saying 'well it's just you, and you're carrying
on learning, or whatever':

'I don't think that children can even begin to become
honest in the classroom unless the classroom provides
situations or whatever, where they just carry on being
themselves, bringing their knowledge to the classroom.
It's not like a "different stage" which is nothing to
do with their lives ... a sort of theatre of the classroom where all sorts of very odd bits of behaviour
start happening....'

Adolescents were particularly susceptible to the 'generalized view', distortions or simplifications of the media,
or gang norms. One of the most crucial areas of secondary education ought to be to counteract stereotypes and
give children the insight which saw beyond generalizations:

'The lack of the particular insight is very damaging
... one of the things I think about almost every day,
is of them thinking honestly about the actual world
they're moving around in ... that's the difference
between lying to yourself about life through blindness,
and actually seeing in the particular.... To try and
help children to reflect honestly on their own conscious existence is one of the most important roles of
an English teacher.'

At the same time, it was up to teachers to encourage
children to stand back and compare their own society with
other cultures. She felt this particular aspect of education had been neglected in her own schooling, and did
not always get sufficient attention now. Children could
become increasingly perceptive about themselves and their
position in society through an exploration of reality and
fantasy. This was a theme to which adolescents were particularly sensitive and was a rich resource for new insights into themselves and their own problems. It was
also helpful for them in achieving an honest perspective
on themselves to deal with the confusions, frustrations
and misunderstandings that arose in their dealings with
adults. Some of the introspection and reflection that
such work necessitated would be very private but much of
it would involve sharing of experience:

'I think that when trying to deal with the world a
little bit from their point of view, like I've been
doing a lot about fantasy, fantasising, and the problem
about muddling your fantasy and your reality, and
they've been doing a lot of writing about the problems
of mixing fantasy and reality and that has given them

an avenue to explore their problems ... the real complex convolutions of being an adolescent.'

The joint creation of the curriculum

The preceding paragraphs have already suggested that there
was a close mesh in Rachel's concept of the content of the
curriculum, her aim to break down defensive barriers both
between children and between herself and the pupils, dis-
courage competitive, hierarchical relationships based on
ability, and encourage an honest exploration of one's own
values and experience.

She viewed the curriculum of English as something to be
jointly created between her and the particular class she
was working with:

'I don't know how I could begin to teach a set syllabus
... the syllabus, the lessons and learning will never
ever be the same with any other group, so their syllabus is going to be their syllabus ... it's a progres-
sion of particular relationships.'

She had considerable freedom, particularly in the third
year and worked very little from set texts.   Much of what
happened in the classroom was jointly developed by pupils
and teachers, often using children's work or ideas, in
dramatic work and discussion:

'The particular subject which I teach would be best
described as a happy mixing of an idea that I might
give them with their return on the subject and then
that would maybe become a particular subject for the
next lesson.'

When children really became involved they achieved a fluency and sincerity which set their work apart.   But they
needed feedback - recognition of their sincerity or failure to write with honesty:

'Particularly in your response to their writing, giving
back work and things, saying I don't think this is you
talking on paper or Warren wrote something wonderful
about a friend of his and I said this is fantastic
writing, because I know that you're really interested
in what you're saying, and that this is just effortless
for you, and I don't feel it was something that cost
you a lot of self-discipline to write, and he said no,
it was very easy to write.'

As well as involving the class in the creation of their
own curriculum, she felt it was important to give children
a sense of purpose and perspective on their lessons:

'There ought to be so much more discussion back over
things and then that'll make them see ... I think
teachers are always pushing on and on but not getting
the kids to see what is happening and what's helpful
... there's got to be collaboration between the teacher
and the kid about his achievements.'

The joint creation of the curriculum by pupils and teacher
implied an equality of relationship which was usually
denied by teachers: 'Letting them bring in their jokes
and their world and letting them take over lessons, and
try and fail ...' but also, drawing on their 'underworld
of interest': not just their isolated interests but the
dynamic social world that they lived in, things going on
between them in class and out of it.

Her starting point in this pupil-centred curriculum was
their experience of childhood, and getting the class to
explore and articulate what she saw as their area of expertise: 'Teaching from a position of strength, so that
they feel as if they're the specialists, they <u>know</u>, and
then to be extended again by the teacher.' She liked to
draw on: 'their particular knowledge and their particular
insights, that you don't have any more [as an adult] and
valuing and making sacrosanct the area of childhood, and
saying "I've forgotten, but you know".' As an example
she quoted two recent writing tasks she had set, and how
she had developed children's own themes:

'One of their homeworks last week was to write about an
argument they'd had with an adult but to write about it
as a diary entry from an adult point of view, so they
had to adopt a different writing style, which some of
them managed to do very well and very interesting for
me, writing from their mother's point of view, about a
recent argument they'd had with themselves.... They've
just done a homework where a child gets into trouble
because he mixes his make-up world with his real world
and then one hopes that things which they're finding a
problem will come out, and then he looked back on, and
read out, and shared.'

In the context of a jointly developed curriculum Rachel
saw her particular role as harnessing the children's perceptions and knowledge, pushing the limits outwards,

largely through collaboration with others and then developing their written work from the active shared experience
and articulation of ideas:

'So I might bring in or give them some written work to
do which will ... which hopefully will extend them to
a greater leap of the imagination beyond that, which
will extend them from a subject they're interested in,
in a way that they wouldn't do naturally themselves,
which is a thing that I think teachers and teaching
really lacks ... the confidence to push kids, to give
them new perceptions.'

Rachel referred to 'deep participation' as the primary
kicking off point for writing. This evolved through personal involvement and active creation of one's knowledge,
as opposed to passive ingestion of other people's ideas.
Deep participation was also crucial in their response to
and understanding of the written word. She wanted children to respond to literature or to write because they felt
personally moved to express themselves, not just to comply
with school rules: 'Having discussed their view of the
world getting them to write honestly ... giving them a
good feeling about writing ... getting them to write a
lot.'

A flexible curriculum which drew on children's knowledge and interests rather than imposing content on them,
was also valuable in integrating failing children and enhancing their self-esteem. One could use all the children's knowledge and social insights in productive ways,
even those who were academically weak. Rather than
patronizing failing pupils with false praise, one could
highlight strengths which would have validity within the
terms she had set. A supportive, tolerant atmosphere was
encouraging for any children who were struggling or demoralized; other children responded less critically to
their peers if the teacher set the tone. They always
knew who was having difficulty academically, and preferred
to see praise rather than blame being dealt out. More-
over, they generally enjoyed being part of a benign atmosphere:

'Children who really do find things hard, and all the
other children know ... they love that feeling of
benign slapping on the back ... if you make a fuss of
someone, they'll say "oh wotcher, well done" and the
good feelings that they can bring out, and do, to support the other kids, if you just open the door and get
a demoralized kid or group praise from the other kids.'

Furthermore, in a context where pupils had been working
together, and understood personally how much effort had
gone into a partner's work: 'the praise was actually
valid, as opposed to just dramatic.'

Rachel saw one of the main functions of schooling as
the enhancement of children's self-esteem:

'The amount of confidence and by that I mean real confidence that you've acquired, and the self-image you've
been given at school, or how much school has actually
set you back emotionally ... your confidence to deal
with anything ...'

these were really the criteria on which school should be
evaluated, not just on whether children had assimilated a
body of facts, or acquired some skills.

Confidence and feelings of self-worth were intimately
tied in with what Rachel referred to as a 'sense of agency'
in their lives. She felt that to give the class itself
an active role in the creation of its curriculum involved
two different but related themes. She believed that
children developed a sense of agency in their learning
when they participated in this way and that this was valuable experience in itself, with implications for their
role in society. For the children to be active agents of
change implied not just that she would take up their suggestions, but that they regularly and actively participate
in the dramatic work which would form the basis for their
lessons and their subsequent writing. What they did, and
how they chose to interpret the situations and tasks, as
well as the actual situations they chose, would form the
real work of their curriculum.

The passivity and obedience to authority which school
demanded and the lack of real power to change anything,
flooded over into many children's perceptions of their
role in the outside community: they tended to regard
society as monolithic, inflexible and impermeable to them.
She was disturbed by their ignorance of outside events and
felt they were 'totally unequipped for the adult world'.
One of her regrets was that she had not got them to look
at society more critically.

She realized that the often conventional interpretations
that pupils brought to the classroom mediated between what
the teacher hoped for and was actually able to achieve.
If they failed to perceive drama and active participation

as 'real work' it might be necessary, initially, to rely on 'tricks or ridiculous games' which worked simply because the children were enjoying themselves. At this stage, the pupils would probably not regard drama as 'real work' and would only do so when they perceived how oral and group work generated the material for written work, and made it more meaningful:

'I was just thinking about how their attitude to doing things like dialogue, interviewing each other, or role playing or drama - like we did this game of blocking and accepting, when two people stand behind two other people and you give them a controversial discussion and then the person behind says "block", and then they'll say "accept", and you have to keep changing, you block the argument if you're told to block it and accept if you're told to accept, and they will do that kind of thing now without saying it's not work because they've had the satisfaction of knowing that that gets them to some sort of truth and understanding of something, which then opens the floodgates and they can write because they now know what they're meant to be thinking about, or they know what they think about.'

(b)   THE PUPIL'S FRAMES OF REFERENCE

Rachel's class group (Form 20)

Only 17 children were on the roll for the full two years of our study of Rachel's class.   Of those who made up the class for all or part of this two-year period, there were 14 girls and 18 boys.   A number of pupils left or joined the class during these two years.   Additionally certain children were regularly withdrawn from the class group for additional tuition.   Three pupils - Alfonse, Dave and Steve Y. - were withdrawn for basic skills classes.   Two - Jenny and Kurdo - were withdrawn for ESL tuition. Three boys - Duncan, Jonathan and Sandro - were withdrawn for Latin classes.   Finally, two children were persistent truants: Robert and Yolanda.

(i)   Perceptions of Humanities

One aspect of our interest in Rachel's classroom group was how the children perceived her curriculum.   We wanted to know how generally popular Humanities was with them, and how they saw it in relation to other school subjects.   Of

course it was also important to discover whether the children's perception of Humanities changed as a result of
their experience of Rachel's collaborative teaching
methods.

   We used the format already described.   As with our
other semi-formal assessments, we gave the questions to
the class group during the first part of one of Rachel's
lessons.   On the first occasion, half the children (11
out of 22) used the opportunity to add their own comments
about Humanities.   On the second occasion, when the scale
had to be completed rather more quickly, no one volunteered comments.

The children's rankings on the first occasion

TABLE 6.1   Occasion I

	Enjoyable	Not boring	Useful	Good at	Easy
Humanities	5	5	4.5	6	2.5
Maths	6	6	1.5	4.5	5.5
Games	1	2	6	1.5	1
Home Economics	4	3	3	3	2.5
Science	2	1	1.5	1.5	5.5
Design and Technology	3	4	4.5	4.5	4

Table 6.1 shows the overall rankings, for the total class
group, of Humanities and the five other curriculum areas.
From this table, it can be seen that Humanities, on the
first occasion, holds a relatively low position by comparison with other subjects.   On the first three scales, all
of which have a clear evaluative component, Humanities
comes lowest, or nearly lowest, among the six curriculum
areas.   It is seen as very unenjoyable, very boring, and
not very useful, as compared with other subjects.   The
children also rate themselves as less competent in this
subject than in any other.   This judgment is particularly
striking when taken together with the fact that Humanities
is seen as a relatively easy subject;   it seems to speak
of a general sense of alienation and lack of involvement.

How do other curriculum areas fare?   Among the six
subjects, Maths is the one which comes out closest to
Humanities.   Like Humanities, Maths is clearly unpopular.
It is rated, like Humanities, as boring and unenjoyable.
But unlike Humanities, Maths is seen as very useful, and
also as a difficult subject.   At the other end of the
evaluative scale, it is Games and Science which have the
most positive image.   Both are rated as highly enjoyable
and interesting;   for both, the children claim a high
level of personal competence.   However, on two other
scales, these two subjects get contrasting ratings: Games
is seen as very easy, but minimally useful, while Science
is seen as very useful, but very difficult.   The two
other subjects - Design and Technology and Home Economics
- have intermediate ratings on the various scales.

Given this overall profile of the six curriculum areas,
do the children differ in their evaluations according to
subgroup?   Table 6.2 shows subgroup differences between
13 boys and 9 girls on the combined three evaluation
scales - enjoyable, interesting and useful.

TABLE 6.2   Occasion 1

Humanities			Maths			Games		
	High	Low		High	Low		High	Low
Boys	24	15	Boys	17	22	Boys	25	24
Girls	12	15	Girls	17	10	Girls	16	9

Home Economics			Science			D and T		
	High	Low		High	Low		High	Low
Boys	9	30	Boys	21	18	Boys	28	11
Girls	21	6	Girls	17	10	Girls	13	14

It can be seen that there are some differences in the
way the subjects are evaluated.   Humanities is rated more
favourably by boys than girls, as also is Design and Technology.   Girls rate Maths and Home Economics more favourably, especially Home Economics.   (It is worth noting
that these differences are not all in accord with gender
stereotypes.)

The children's comments on the first occasion   It has
been said that 11 out of the 22 children - 6 girls and 5
boys - used the opportunity to make comments on Humanities,

at the bottom of the rating sheet.   It might have been
that such additional contributions came only from children
who felt positively towards Humanities; but this was not
the case.   Of the 11 children adding comments, 3 had made
generally favourable ratings of Humanities, 4, generally
unfavourable ratings, and 4, mixed or intermediate ratings.

What is striking about these comments is that whereas
all 5 boys refer exclusively to the curriculum, the 6
girls all focus on social aspects of the Humanities classroom.   Taking the boys' remarks first, the predominant
theme is that of the lesson as being enjoyable or boring.
Both Jonathan and Steve C. refer to Humanities in these
terms.   Don and Duncan also do so, with reference to particular types of work as interesting or boring; for Don,
ancient history can be enjoyable, and for Duncan, class
discussion is fun, but doing written work out of books is
boring.   Sandro is still more specific about the content
of the curriculum, detailing the historical periods he
enjoys working on, and comparing them with the more boring
spelling and English tests, and adding a comment about ex-
cessive homework.

The girls' concerns are quite different; their emphasis is on classroom relationships.   For Joyce, Coral and
Alex - at this stage an exuberant and predominantly disruptive clique - this means Rachel's relationship with
themselves.   All three girls express resentment towards
Rachel as favouring the boys in the class, talking too
much and picking on them.   However, both Alex and Coral
add the comment that Humanities lessons are good.   Fiona
refers to Rachel as a good teacher; she, alone among the
girls, also comments on the curriculum, comparing the enjoyment of doing independent work with the more tedious
activities of reading and writing.   Lisa and Anita take
another aspect of classroom social relationships.   Both
refer to other children, Lisa commenting on how disruptive
her peers can be, and Anita remarking on the humiliation
of classmates witnessing her own ignorance.

Brief and selective as these comments may be, they are
nevertheless suggestive as to how Rachel's collaborative
teaching approach was being received at this early stage.
The fact that comments were volunteered by a range of
children, some of whom had rated Humanities positively and
some negatively, also gives them greater weight.

As far as the curriculum is concerned - something which
boys rather than girls are concerned with - it is clear

that creative aspects - talk and interchange, independent
research - are generally valued over the more traditional,
individualized, mechanical aspects such as tests, spelling
or working from books.   This seems to promise well for a
collaborative approach.   With respect to social aspects -
to which girls are much more alive than boys - an emphasis
on the importance of relationships with the teacher is in
accord with Rachel's own values, as is the concern with
fairness and reciprocity in such relationships.   However,
the hints in some comments that other children are not
trusted to witness one's own ignorance, and seen as generally disruptive at work, are less auspicious.

<u>The children's ratings on the second occasion</u>   Inevitably,
the class group had changed by the time this scale was re-
administered two years later.   On this second occasion,
there were 14 pupils present who had done the scale two
years earlier.   Fortunately, these 14 were quite represen-
tative in their first ratings of the original group.

TABLE 6.3

	Enjoyable	Not boring	Useful	Good at	Easy
Humanities	3.5	4	2	2.5	3
Maths	5	5.5	1	5	4
Games	1	1	6	1	1.5
Home Economics	6	5.5	5	6	1.5
Science	2	2	3	2.5	5
Design and Technology	3.5	3	4	4	6

   The overall rank orders for the group of 14 are shown in
Table 6.3   Looking at rankings of Humanities, it can be
seen that a number of changes have taken place from previous ratings.   Humanities is now rated as more enjoyable, less boring and a good deal more useful, relative to
other curriculum areas.   What is still more striking is
that while Humanities is rated slightly harder than before,
the children evaluate themselves as much more competent in
it as against other subjects.   These changes are very
marked compared with those that have occurred in ratings
of other curriculum areas.   Except for Home Economics -

which has fallen quite markedly from its former positive
evaluation - the other subjects retain very similar
ratings.   It seems likely, therefore, that the rise in
evaluation for Humanities is related to the success of
Rachel's teaching approach.

Table 6.4 shows changes in ratings across the two
occasions (omitting those for which no change occurred).

TABLE 6.4

	Positive	Negative
Humanities	22	14
Other subjects	47	104

It can be seen that whereas Humanities has come to be
more positively evaluated, this positive shift is set
against a dramatic decline in the evaluation of the other
curriculum areas.

Gender differences, when compared with earlier ones,
are also interesting.   These are generally in the same
direction as before, with two exceptions.   Games is now
evaluated rather more highly by boys than by girls.   More
interestingly from our point of view, Humanities - previously evaluated more highly by boys - is now more positively rated by girls.   This is the only subject for
which the original gender preferences have been reversed.
The ratings are as shown in Table 6.5

TABLE 6.5

Humanities

	High	Low
Boys	12	15
Girls	10	5

On this evidence it seems that there has been a reorien-
tation towards Humanities on the part of the girls in
Rachel's class group.

We can look more specifically at how the boys' and
girls' groups changed their ratings on all five scales.
For ease of presentation, these changes will be described,
rather than shown as figures.   For the two evaluative

scales - enjoyable and boring - it is striking that,
whereas for the boys, changes in the position of Humanities are in line with those of other curriculum areas,
this is not so for the girls. For the girls, the rise in
evaluation of Humanities is set against a marked lowering
in evaluation of other subjects. When it comes to
changes in judgments of usefulness, the differences are
less clear-cut; boys, to a greater extent than girls,
place a higher value than before on the usefulness of
Humanities, and both gender groups rate other subjects as
less useful than before.

Ratings on the last two scales, taken together, suggest
again, a differential position for girls and boys.
Whereas the boys now rate Humanities, together with other
subjects, as easier than before, they judge their own competence to be no greater in Humanities, nor in other subjects. By contrast, the girls judge Humanities as more
difficult than before - an increased difficulty not so
marked for other subjects - and yet rate their own competence in Humanities as holding up, against a declining
competence in other subjects.

Conclusion   It is clear that, as a group, Rachel's class
held a very negative evaluation of her curriculum area at
the start of the research period. Relative to other subjects, Humanities was seen as unenjoyable, boring, and not
very useful. Even though it was perceived as a relatively
easy subject, the children rated themselves as personally
incompetent at it. This picture is very different from
what emerged after two years in Rachel's class. By that
stage, Humanities was judged to be more enjoyable and
interesting and much more useful. Perhaps more strikingly still, the children rated their own competence in it
much more highly, despite judging it to be relatively difficult at this stage. That these changes are not just
part of an overall shift towards positive evaluation of
the school curriculum is clear from the comparison of
these changes in ratings with those of the other five subjects, where changes are dramatically downward rather than
upward.

Within this overall change towards a positive evaluation of Humanities, are certain differences between the
boys and the girls in Rachel's class. At the beginning
of the period it was the boys who evaluated Humanities
more favourably; by the end of the period the position is
reversed, with girls expressing a more positive view.

This reversal does not happen for any other subject.   Nor
does the change in girls' ratings of Humanities accord
with similar changes in their perception of other subjects
- it runs counter to it.   What might account for this
marked change, for the girls in Rachel's class group, in
their evaluation of Humanities?   Perhaps a hint exists in
the differential focus of the comments made on the first
occasion by the small groups of girls and boys.   It was
the girls who expressed a concern with social aspects of
Humanities, in contrast with the boys' emphasis on curriculum content.   It may be that Rachel's increasing focus,
in her lessons, upon social relationships and social
interaction, as time went on, tuned in with the girls' own
interests, while to some extent by-passing the interests
and expectations of the boys.   Whatever the underlying
reasons, it is clear that Rachel's collaborative teaching
met with a more strongly positive response among the girls
in her classroom group, and that this was against the
background of their apparently increasing alienation from
other school subjects.

(ii)   Perceptions of schooling

At the end of the summer term of the first year of the
project and the beginning of the autumn term of the second
year of the project, we conducted two sets of interviews
with boys and girls from Rachel's class.   The four groups
were made up as follows:

    Group 1, which consisted of Paulette, Jackie S., Suzanne
and Jackie T., was interviewed at the end of year 1.
This group had worked together and got on well as a group.

    The children in Group 2 were Rodney, Andrew, Warren,
Don and Steve C.   They were interviewed early in year 1.
This group formed a viable friendship group and was felt
to represent the 'average' boys in the class.

    Group 3, interviewed at the start of year 2, consisted
of Jackie T., Jackie S., Alex, Coral and Anita.   This
group was chosen by Rachel to represent a range of opinion
among the girls in the class.   Two girls, Jackie T. and
Jackie S., had been part of group 1 in the summer.

    Group 4, interviewed at the start of year 2, consisted
of Rodney, Don, Warren and Frank.   This group was chosen
by Rachel and represented 'average' opinions in the class.
Rodney, Warren and Don had been in Group 2 and were interviewed in the summer.

Of the 13 children who took part in the interviews, 5
were black: 3 girls - Jackie S., Paulette and Coral - and
2 boys, Don and Frank.   All were of working-class origin.
Andrew was exceptional in the sample in presenting special
behavioural difficulties; by the second set of interviews,
he had been sent to a unit for children who found integration into school difficult (not, however, a Disruptive
Unit).   None of the children was really a high achiever,
and some of them found quite a lot of difficulty with academic work in some subjects.

The first two interviews focused more specifically on
the immediate content of the curriculum in Rachel's
lessons, on pupils' understanding and response to collaborative work, and attitudes to different teaching methods.
The second two interviews were designed not only to follow
up these themes, but also to investigate areas which had
not been probed before.   Since the pupils were by then in
their third year and experiencing a slightly different
curriculum and organization, it seemed opportune to ask
them about their perceptions of change.   We were also
interested in their attitudes to the introduction of
social issues into the curriculum generally, as a backdrop
to Rachel's concern with personal relationships as the
subject matter for new (newly begun) English syllabus.   A
third theme of the interviews conducted in the autumn was
boys' and girls' views on the traditional gender-related
subjects.   This tied in with Rachel's concern with
stereotyping and poor relationships in schools between the
sexes.

The interview with Group 3 involved a lengthy discussion initiated by the girls themselves, about their experience at the school's country house, Belvedere.

One of Rachel's central concerns had to do with the
quality of teacher-pupil relationships.   She felt that
discipline, though firm, should be non-authoritarian, and
tempered with personal honesty as well as with a real concern for pupils' welfare.   The remarks of these children
suggest a view with somewhat different emphases.   Like
Rachel herself, they all stress the very great importance
of the relationship between teacher and pupils; and it is
clear that personality differences among teachers are
highly salient.   There is a consensus that teachers could
get children interested in subjects they had felt indifferent about, and, conversely, that an antipathetic
teacher can put them off previously enjoyed subjects.   As
Jackie S., in Group 3, puts it, with general accord:

'Because if you kind of put your trust in them and they
trust you as well, then you get on together as a teacher
and a pupil.'   Suzanne, in Group 1, also expresses the
group's consensus in her description of Rachel herself:
'She's strict, quite strict; but she's really nice when
she wants to.   If you get on the right side of her, then
she's a good friend, the teacher I mean, trusting her.'

Where the girls stress trust between teachers and
pupils, the two groups of boys emphasize sharing fun and
having a laugh.   Steve, in Group 2, compares Rachel with
another teacher: 'Like as where she would make a joke,
and then get down to work, not him, he always wanted to be
strict all the time.'   Later, talking of this same, disliked teacher, Don remarks: 'He weren't like, you'd never
think he'd been a kid like you.'   Conversely, in Group 3,
Rodney expresses appreciation of a well-liked PE teacher:
'Mr F. doesn't go straight into the lesson, he messes
about with you and everything.   He goes, right, we've had
a joke, now settle down, and we just get on with the
lesson.'

It is clear from what all four groups say, however,
that friendly teacher-pupil relationships are viewed as
viable only within a context of clear teacher control.
The children put considerable emphasis on this.   Group 2
talk about why a particular teacher is good:

Steve: 'Mr McC.'s a good teacher.'
Don: 'He makes sure he gets through to you.'
Steve: 'You know he's strict.'
Rodney: 'But that's the best way to be a teacher.'

The girls in Group 3, approving of their form teacher,
agree that 'He can control us, he can control us, but
other teachers can't.'   These girls, discussing lesson
discipline, endorse Alex's judgment that 'Some of the
teachers are a bit soft.   The children kind of take advantage.'   In Group 1, whose members tend to be rather
shy and conformist, there is a slightly different reason
for disapproving of teachers who are unable to control the
class.   As Jackie S. comments: 'Miss B., she shouts at
you, because most of them muck about, and you get fed up
with it, you find your work all boring and everything.'
From what they say, all the children seem to feel that
strictness and discipline are an essential part of a
teacher's role, because pupils would otherwise naturally
muck about.

For the girls in Group 3, this kind of relationship with teachers is evidently context-bound.   The opportunity, at the school's country house, to share day-to-day domestic life with teachers had evidently affected things. Anita remarks: 'We played with the teachers more, we talked to them and everything.'

The girls describe, with considerable enthusiasm, how the usual teacher authority had melted away, with teachers behaving like overgrown adolescents, or playing roles which parents might have played:

Coral: 'We had this really long tube and I used to hit Mr L. on the head with it all the time, and he, he smashed me on the back with it, and we all got him on the floor....'

Alex: 'Mr L., I like Mr L. [the warden of Belvedere], we've got quite a good relationship and he's always picking me up and throwing me and things like that.'

However, this relaxation of rules and roles with teachers is totally context-bound.   Back at school it is apparently no longer possible to enjoy an easy relationship with teachers, or joke and laugh with them.   The girls see the pressures of school as inhibiting teachers themselves from offering the kind of friendship and openness that had been acceptable outside the school institution:

Alex: 'They [the teachers] forget about it.'

Jackie S.:   'Sometimes it's a lot harder when you try and talk to them.'

Coral: 'Yeh, they go, we ain't got time, we've got to go to the staff room and mark our books and everything.'

Alex: 'When I met him [Mr L.] at school on Friday he seemed to have changed a lot from when he was at Belvedere, he's still funny, but....'

Despite clear limits on the mutuality, within classrooms, of teacher-pupil relationships, all the children we talked to valued being able to learn, and see teachers as crucial mediators in this.   Don, in Group 2, sees discipline as the key.   He suggests that consistent implementation of rules makes pupil feel they are being taken seriously, and in turn encourages them to take the work more seriously:

'It's right, ain't it [that teachers are stricter as

pupils go through school], because if you keep on coming in like you were in the first or second year, then you got reason to believe that teachers ain't going to do nothing, so you'd just come in every day, so you've got to get harder, harder as you go up.'

Teachers who 'help you with your work' are clearly appreciated in Group 1, where Jackie S. speaks of direct guidance in correcting mistakes, and the use of quite traditional methods:

'Some of us get Mr F., he's really nice. We do work on the board, we work all together on the same thing. He puts the answers down, so if you haven't got the answers you can copy them down afterwards.'

The girls in Group 3 also value teachers who 'tell you your mistakes so you learn it'. For these girls, however, it is evidently very important that teachers should care; good teachers are described as 'caring for your work', and as 'taking more of an interest in you than other teachers do'. By contrast, a teacher is generally condemned for her public criticism of pupils: 'If you don't know something sometimes, she just calls you silly and stupid. You stupid girl.'

In Group 4, the boys agree that teachers are vital in school learning, which they see as not accessible to their own efforts. Phil asks:

Phil: 'Supposing you didn't have a teacher at all, and you wanted to learn French?'
Rodney: 'I couldn't.'
Frank: 'He wouldn't know what's going on in the books.'

This view of French as shut away in books and needing to be taught by teachers is quite striking, in view of the fact that these boys have participated for two years in conversational French classes, and have visited Dieppe.

In general, it seems that all these children view the personality of the teacher as crucial to making progress in school learning. For all, a context of firm control is seen as essential. Clear exposition of material, plentiful revision, and help with mistakes are emphasized by some children. For some of the more able girls, learning is the direct outcome of a good teacher-pupil relationship. As Alex puts it: 'You learn to live with the teacher, you respect the teacher, and you don't muck about as much as you would with a teacher you didn't know.'

Rachel's collaborative approach depended on pupils
seeing themselves as resources in learning.   We wanted to
explore how the children saw their own agency in the
classroom.   We asked how they felt about lessons where
the teacher does most of the talking.   In Group 1, the
girls have mixed views.   Suzanne comments: 'When Miss
reads, it gets quicker, and we enjoy it more.'   But
Jackie S. argues that people need practice to get better
in reading, and Jackie T. remarks: 'If they're reading
it themselves, they'll kind of get involved in the
stories.'

Paulette makes the point that children do not get the
chance to show lack of understanding if they are restricted to answering teachers' questions: 'We should get a
say in things. We have to be quiet.   We want to know a
question, usually the teacher's talking to someone else,
or she's telling you to be quiet.'   In Group 2, Steve
sounds a similar theme, emphasizing that pupils need to be
able to say they have not understood.

Though these children generally agree that pupils need
to have more than a minimal share of classroom talk, they
do not, on the whole, seem to see themselves as able to
inaugurate or control the content of what is said.   In
discussing talk amongst pupils themselves, there is general agreement that this could be unproductive, because of
'mucking about', but all groups agree that pupil-pupil
talk can be helpful.   Educational benefits, mentioned by
the boys in Groups 2 and 4, are sometimes seen in quite
modest terms; Rodney suggests: 'We tell each other what
we've done when they're not there.'   Steven refers to
help from more competent friends: 'In Maths, when I was
sitting next to Don, whenever I get a question, he's good
at Maths, and I'm not good at it, he always helps me out.'
However, he goes on, thoughtfully, to consider more subtle
and far-reaching benefits:

   'The thing I like is more, like, talking as a class ...
   and discussing things, so you get a better example, a
   better answer and things ... so you get each other's
   different opinions, so you know, you match them up to
   see what's the best idea, like.'

The girls in Group 1, similarly, refer to pupil talk in
explicitly collaborative terms, as 'putting little ideas
together', instancing their own joint work in producing a
poster.   Both groups of girls also emphasize the social
support functions of pupil-pupil interaction.   As Paulette

says: 'When we're going to have exams it's frightening,
but if you've got your friends they can, like, make you
less frightened, knowing they're there.'   For this group
of girls, also, the presence of friends is reassuring in
allowing feelings of incompetence to be shared.   This
theme is also sounded by the two boys' groups, who refer
to the support of peers in the tension and anxiety of unfamiliar school situations, and - for Group 2 - their
worries about the effects of option choices on their
friendship groupings.   A comment by Steve indicates the
importance and the delicacy, for some boys, of pupil-pupil
relationships:

> 'Now you can joke, like you know what not to say wrong
> to that person, how much he can take, and what another
> person can take like, you know.   But in the first year
> I think people were more petrified to talk to each
> other in case they said something wrong.'

For most children, pupil talk, if it is to be enjoyable
and productive, is apparently seen as involving those who
are already friends;   only Jackie S. suggests that for
pupils not initially friends, 'You might get quite a few
ideas from them and come to like them.'

Rachel's curriculum was a highly personal one.   We
asked the children how they felt about making personal relationships part of the curriculum.   One aspect of this
relates to tutorials.   Girls and boys are somewhat divided.   The girls in both groups express the rather generalized view that school should teach children about sex and
marriage;   but they are not able to suggest just how they
think this should be done.   Both groups of boys are unequivocally against;   as Don remarks, to general agreement:
'Sex education is a load of rubbish ... they can't tell
people more about how to lead their lives and so on, it's
wrong to tell people ... it's nothing to concern the
school.'   Yet if these boys are reluctant to accept direct
instruction about relationships, they express some appreciation of the use of drama to increase inter-personal
understanding.   In Group 2, Rodney, Steve and Warren discuss how being an audience for girls' plays has given them
a helpful perspective for their own performance: 'That's
how we got to get, you know, to tell them our characters,
so we made sure they would, like, in our own.'

This group of boys also comments on how greatly drama
has affected gender relationships in Rachel's class.
Steve says:

'In the first year it was all boys one side and girls
the other side, you know, not talking to each other.
Then, like, we did plays and things like that, when
you're acting out, you know, Mum and Dad, and things
like that.   In that way, you get to know the girls.'

This theme is developed still further by the girls,
particularly those in Group 3.   In discussing their experience at the school's country house, these girls describe how the taken-for-granted segregation rules of
school had gradually been supplanted by informal camera-
derie.   Alex remembers: 'Because we used to play the
boys at table tennis, tennis, all games we used to play.
It wasn't just girls and boys together, it was all mixed.
We all used to play together and have fun.'

Recalling how three boys went missing at one point in
their stay: 'No one could eat their dinner at dinner
time', and the realization that boys could also become
emotional had made a strong impact.   Individual relationships with boys had flowered outside the public glare, as
Anita and Coral describe.   However, once back at school,
relationships became attenuated;   as Alex puts it:

'We all used to play together and have fun, but when we
get back to school it's all different, because they got
different friends from different classes, and if they
come along they think they will talk about it that we
played with a boy.   The boys, their friends, probably
get the wrong ideas.'

Alex goes on to suggest: 'I'm sure some people in our
class want to sit next to someone like a boy, but they
daren't, because we'd just talk about it.'   This is endorsed by the others: 'Boys go there, we go here, that's
it, no more.'   Jackie T., however, is concerned to remind
the others that in this context, 'We do work with a boy,
Alex, sometimes, because we do a play, and we need a boy
sometimes to act as a boy.'   Considering this, the girls
agree that working with boys in a play 'about a family,
how they carried on', had, in the end, been 'really good'.
They think Rachel's fostering of boy-girl relationships
should be applied more widely: 'If a teacher do it in
their school, make you sit next to boys all the time, then
I think we'd get better, so you shouldn't be ashamed to
sit next to them.'

In general, just as it is the girls who explore more
fully the contextual constraints on teacher-pupil, and

boy-girl relationships, it is the two girls' groups who
most emphasize the significance of Rachel's curriculum for
interpersonal understanding.   The boys, in both groups,
seem to view drama largely in terms of sheer enjoyment,
and as enabling them to learn directly about the subject
at issue.   On their side, though Group 1 endorse Jackie
T.'s idea that drama 'gets your mind working', on the
whole the girls see its purpose in terms of developing
inter-personal sensitivity and understanding.

> This is clear from a conversation, in Group 3:

> Anita: 'The games help us learn the kind of people who
>   do things like that.'
> Jackie S.: 'To find out what they do in their spare
>   time and what happens to them.'
> Coral: 'To learn what kind of character they got and
>   that.'
> Anita: 'It kinds of helps you to see what kind of
>   person that is.'
> Jackie S.: 'That's how you get to know them.'

Viewing the Drama curriculum in this way, these girls seem
closer in their emphases to Rachel herself than do the
boys.

(iii)   Construing other children

The next source of information about pupils' ways of
seeing things comes from talking with them about other
children.   For this purpose, we used a set of 16 school
photographs of boys and girls unknown to the children, of
approximately their own age.   The photographs included 5
white boys, 2 black boys and 1 Asian boy, 4 white girls, 2
black girls and 2 Asian girls.   These photographs formed
the starting points from which we elicited these children's construing of their peers.

   The interviewing was carried out, one-to-one, by Dilys,
one of Phil's research students, who did not know the
children and therefore could not identify the class group
they belonged to.   This enabled us to make a comparison
of eight children chosen randomly from Rachel's class, and
eight children randomly chosen from a parallel class
taught by another teacher not committed to collaborative
learning methods.

   The composition of the two groups was as follows:

Rachel's group: 2 white boys, 1 black boy, 3 white girls,
                   1 black girl, and 1 Chinese girl.

Comparison group: 3 white boys, 1 Asian boy, 1 white girl,
                    2 black girls, and 1 Chinese girl.

However, we decided to look at the responses, not in
relation to the individual children concerned, but simply
in terms of their membership of one of the two groups.

Our idea in seeking this material was to explore the
viewpoints which members of Rachel's pupil group brought
to their relations with peers.   In what terms did they
evaluate other boys and girls?   How did they experience
diversity among children?   How did they understand relationships with and among their peers?   We were, of course,
also concerned with whether the construing of pupils from
Rachel's class differed from that of pupils in the comparison class group.   We therefore carried out this part
of our work at the end of the first year - just half-way
through our study of Rachel's class group.   Had a year
spent in Rachel's class, with its distinctive ethos,
methods and curriculum - all focused on children's inter-
relationships - brought about distinctive ways of seeing
other children, and peer group relationships?

Something of a paradox emerges in considering this
material;   the stance adopted towards other children, as
expressed in the judgments made about them, is to a considerable extent contradicted by the pattern of choices
made.

Examining the content of the responses made by this
group, it is evident that the children categorize their
peers in essentially personal rather than object terms.
Very few judgments make reference to external features or
fixed properties of people;   on the contrary, they are
typically couched in terms of personal outlook, orientation towards others and social relationships, and characteristically refer to dynamic rather than static qualities.
Friendship and antagonism are accounted for, and described,
mainly in relational terms.   Most children acknowledge
that feelings of dislike might change after further
acquaintance, thereby implying an assumption that personal
relationships are contingent rather than fixed.   Reference to interpersonal aspects also outnumber those to
static features in construing collaboration, while trouble
and success in classrooms are viewed much more often as
the outcome of relationships or personal outlook than as
due to inbuilt characteristics.

Within this overall emphasis on the dynamic and inter-
actional aspects of people, relations among peers are
viewed largely in terms of a dimension of coerciveness-
versus-mutuality.   These children, in discussing relationships both in and out of school, clearly endorse
friendliness, helpfulness and concern, as against bullying
and disregard for others.   In every context considered,
riding rough-shod over other people, dominating or exploit-
ing others carries a strong negative connotation.   The
children speak as disapproving witnesses, as victims, as
reluctant retaliators - very seldom as instigators of
aggression towards others.   Conversely, a clearly approving tone colours the many references to friendliness and
solidarity.   These are seen as the basis of positive
relationships with peers, both in general and in classroom
contexts.   In fact these qualities are more significant
in governing who is able to work with whom - particularly
if children are speaking for themselves - than academic
orientation or competence.   Lack of consideration for
others is seen as mainly responsible for getting into
trouble in class.   Similarly, getting on well with
teachers is interpreted in largely interpersonal terms;
general friendliness is seen as associated with success,
and among references to relationships with the teacher
mutuality is mentioned.

The children's judgments also contain implications
about the place, for them, of peer relationships in school
learning.   For most, there seems to be a continuity
rather than a disjunction between such relationships and
their classroom work.   For most children, school friendships are sustained out of school.   A noticeably positive
evaluation of school learning is characteristic in the
construing of classroom contexts.   Descriptions of class
collaboration imply, to a large extent, that friendship
and solidarity among pupils lead to productive rather than
unproductive class work.   Conversely, major trouble in
class is seen to arise out of disruptive and antagonistic
interactions with peers, although more positive peer relationships are implicated in minor and occasional trouble.

These themes seem to carry hopeful implications, as far
as Rachel's class is concerned, for the success of her
collaborative methods.   From this evidence, it appears
that these children are sensitive to the personal qualities of others, and set a high value on relationships
which involve mutual respect and appreciation.   It also
seems that they have positive rather than negative attitudes towards teachers and classroom learning, have a co-

operative rather than competitive ethos, and see peer relationships as sustaining rather than undermining class
work.   However, certain other aspects of this group's
response strongly suggest that the picture is more complicated.

Among the judgments made by these children about every
context involving peers are overtones of racism, and to a
lesser extent, of sexism.   At an explicit level these are
relatively rare.   Race and gender feature sometimes as an
explanation of antagonism among children, and, by a few
children, as the reason why they might reject someone for
a collaborative partnership;   race is also cited by a
minority as the reason for personal dislike.   What is
more striking is the implicit stereotyping, by race and
gender, evident in the pattern of choices made, and in the
selective use of particular interpretations.

In choosing particular children to fit the various
categories asked for, this group was clearly influenced by
both race and gender.   This is evident at many different
levels.   The choices made to represent friendly, antagonistic and collaborative relationships among peers all
show that positive relations, in and out of classrooms,
are seen as involving same-race individuals, while hostile
relations are perceived to involve individuals of different race.   Similarly, friendship and collaboration - perhaps not surprisingly - are seen as occurring within
rather than across gender lines, although antagonism is
also viewed as mainly a within-gender phenomenon.   At
another level, race and gender clearly affect who is seen
as a particular sort of person.   White children are
chosen for every category far more often than black or
Asian children;   this seems to imply a greater salience of
majority group children for the whole group of subjects,
nearly half of whom were themselves minority group children.   This means that negative stereotypes of their own
race have evidently been internalized by the ethnic
minority children in this group.   For instance, of the
three black girls in the group, none chose black children
as working partners nor as successful in school.   The
content of stereotyping differs according to ethnic category.   Black and Asian children are chosen to represent
rather different categories.   Black children feature in
both positive and negative choices.

Black girls, however, unlike white or Asian girls, are
picked to represent entirely negative aspects of classroom
adjustment, being chosen quite often as getting into

trouble and never chosen as getting on well with teachers.
Asian children appear much less visible than black children and are relatively seldom chosen.   As far as gender
is concerned, there is also a clear differentiation.
Friendship is seen as characteristic of girls' relationships and antagonism, of boys'.   Boys are also nominated
much more often as likely to evoke personal dislike.   In
classroom contexts, boys are generally more salient; they
are viewed as both more likely to be involved in trouble,
and as more likely to get on well with teachers - but this
is at least partly because of success in PE - itself
associated with negative rather than positive attributes.

    Race and gender also influence the kinds of interpreta-
tions made about peers.   Friendship among black or Asian
children is typically attributed to race or gender - an
explanation not given for friendship among whites.   A
distinctive basis is also assumed to exist for collaboration among Asian children, who are seen as sharing an introverted orientation, as against the more outgoing qualities assumed to underlie white children's collaboration.
In construing collaborative relationships, the children
also imply a significance for gender, in that girls' collaboration is viewed as more productive than boys'.
Finally, both race and gender seem to influence the kinds
of qualities attributed to people who get on well with
teachers.   Whereas white children are seen as achieving
all-round success, this is not seen as the case for Asian
or black children.   Girls viewed as successful are
assumed to be characteristically good at the traditionally
feminine subjects, while boys are seen as good at traditionally masculine subjects and PE.   Black boys are seen
as particularly successful in PE, but this carries pejorative connotations.   Finally, whereas the success of white
and Asian children is viewed as arising out of interest,
effort or personal and social qualities, the success of
black children is typically seen as the product of race or
physique.

    All this suggests a less optimistic view of this
group's ethos.   It seems clear that these children perceive mixed-race encounters as implicitly hostile and con-
flictful.   They also appear to be operating stereotyped
views about different racial groups and about boys and
girls.   In general, white children are more salient, with
Asian children in particular being relatively invisible.
The tendency to interpret black and Asian children in more
external, static, less personal terms also suggests a de-
valuation of non-white children.   To a lesser extent,

these children are stereotyping their peers by gender.
Personal and collaborative relationships are seen as
essentially occurring within, not across gender lines.
Girls are ascribed more positive attitudes and relationships, both generally and in a school context.

The question now arises why there are no clear differences in the construing of the two groups of pupils.   It
had seemed likely that, after a year in Rachel's class,
the target sample would have evolved a distinctive ethos.
We had ourselves witnessed, in the interactions of the
group during the year, a growing solidarity among the
children which cut across racial and gender boundaries,
yet this was not reflected in any apparently distinctive
way of construing themselves and their peers.   It seems
that the preparedness to transcend negative stereotypes,
which was increasingly evident in what we saw of Rachel's
class during the year, had remained limited to that class
room context, rather than being generalized to become part
of children's habitual response to others.   It remains to
be seen whether Rachel's collaborative group culture will
have achieved a wider impact after a further year.

(iv)   Construing of self and other groups

In this part of our study of Rachel's class, we wanted to
explore whether the children came to view themselves and
other pupils differently, as a result of experiencing her
teaching.   For this assessment we chose an instrument
lending itself to formal statistical analysis.   In this
way, we were able to make a strict comparison between
changes in Rachel's class and those that occurred in a
control group - another quite similar class which had,
however, experienced a different Humanities teacher.

Conventional statistical measures, within the traditional psychological research paradigm - target and control
group, test and retest - did not form a major feature of
our study.   For this reason, the results we obtained in
this part of the work are useful in providing evidence of
a different order.   The IDEX grid, derived from a personal
construct theory framework and pioneered by Peter Wein-
reich, has typically been used so far in individual case
studies.   However, it lends itself to assessment in more
general terms, and can be tailored both to group compari-
sons and the assessment of changes over time.

The task involved the children in categorizing particu-

lar kinds of individual, and particular groups, on three
dimensions.   They were: Myself as I am now, black boys,
white boys, black girls, white girls, a person who gets
into trouble, a person who finds lessons difficult.   The
three dimensions in terms of which we asked the children
to categorize these entities were: Fun to be with v. not
much fun;   Easy to understand v. hard to figure out, and
Understanding person v. person you can't talk to.   Basically, the children's categorizations provided information
as to their level of self-esteem, and their evaluation of
other children, in terms of race, gender, and orientation
to school.

The grid was administered on two occasions: in the
early and last weeks of Year 2, representing nearly one
academic year.   We were able to test 16 children in
Rachel's class across the two occasions, and 17 in the
control class.   As will be seen, the two classes in their
perceptions were not initially very different, in spite of
the fact that Rachel's class had already experienced her
teaching for a full year.   There were, however, certain
contrasts between the two groups at the later stage of
assessment, relating to some different directions of
changes in perceptions.

The results   The analysis contains an index showing how
consistently constructs were used across the entities
(subgroups and types of people to be judged) and allowed
us to check that pupils found the supplied constructs
meaningful.   It was particularly important for us to discover whether the constructs were meaningful and consistently used since we had supplied them with Rachel's goals
for her class in mind.

The means, medians and ranges of scores show adequate
consistency of use of the constructs at test and retest;
this gives confidence that the children's judgments were
made meaningfully.

Evaluation of self   Our results suggest that there were
not, at the first test, great discrepancies between the
two groups in self-esteem.   Although the grids of two of
Rachel's boys indicate very low self-esteem, means and
medians show that the groups were comparable.

From retest data, it would appear that Rachel's class
had achieved a more positive view of themselves as people
who were easy to understand, talk to and fun to be with.

In Rachel's group, both girls and boys showed positive
changes in self-esteem.   Most noticeable is the number of
girls whose self-esteem went up.   For the boys, the new
mean was slightly higher than before, although some children showed no change, or moved downwards compared to their
first test.

In the case of the control class, it is clear that the
girls in particular felt less confident about construing
themselves positively on the supplied constructs;   there
was no improvement in the boys' self-esteem.

Evaluation of black boys as a subgroup   In Rachel's class
the majority of pupils increased their regard for their
black male peers.   The control group showed the opposite
tendency: just over 50 per cent viewed this group in a
less sympathetic light.   Interestingly, the two girls in
Rachel's group to make a negative change were both black
themselves.   The two black boys in that class also failed
to improve their evaluation of their own subgroup.

In the control group two boys failed to construe the
subgroup at all, indicating that, in their opinion, black
boys did not fall within the range of convenience of the
supplied constructs.   It is striking that not a single
white boy in the control group construed black boys more
favourably at the end of the year, though four of the ten
white girls did make more positive judgments.

Evaluation of white boys as a subgroup   In Rachel's class
all but one of the girls changed to a more positive evaluation while the white boys judged their subgroup generally
more negatively.   In the control class, the figures show
that there was actually a fairly even balance between
negative and positive changes.

Evaluation of black girls as a subgroup   In Rachel's
class, the majority of the boys made negative changes;
though the girls' mean was lower on the second test, the
numbers making positive or negative changes were the same.
In the control class the figures are distorted by the numbers of pupils who did not construe the entity at all.
There was no trend for the remaining pupils to make positive or negative re-evaluations.

Evaluation of white girls as a subgroup   The majority of
Rachel's pupils changed their evaluation positively and
only two negatively.   In contrast, less than a quarter of
the control pupils made positive changes and over 50 per
cent were more negative about white girls than on the previous occasion.   The figures indicate that the change was
not confined to one sex - both girls and boys in the control class felt more negatively about this group than
before.

Evaluation of a person who gets into trouble   In Rachel's
class the girls were evenly balanced between positive,
negative and no change regarding this sort of person.
However, the majority of boys moved in a positive direction.   In this, the control girls were more similar to
the boys in Rachel's class than to control boys.   Only a
small minority of control boys made a positive change,
whereas more than half control girls did so.

Evaluation of a person who finds lessons difficult   With
only one exception, the girls in Rachel's class construed
a person with academic problems more positively than
before.   However, the boys did not alter their perceptions in this way, and only one-third felt more positive
than before about this kind of person.

     In the control class, boys were also harsher in their
judgments at retest.   Most were more negative than
before, a situation which was not quite paralleled by the
girls, among whom only a minority were more negative.

General comments   For the girls in Rachel's class, her
methods seem from their findings to have had positive
results.   Like the boys in her own class (but unlike
either sex in the control group) they showed positive
changes in self-esteem;   they also showed a positive re-
evaluation of their own subgroups and positive reconstrual
of other groups, with the exception of the black girls'
subgroup, towards whom some ambivalence was manifested.

     For part of the research period there were only two
black boys in the control class and no black girls, though
there were girls of Asian origin.   We have already described how the evaluation of black children, both boys and
girls, decreased in the control class.   No boys at all
made positive changes, and six out often girls made nega-

tive changes in construal of black boys; six children
failed to construe black girls at all.   The organization
of lessons in the school ensured that even if there were
no black children in one's own class, regular meetings and
interactions with black children from one's year group
would occur; no pupil was insulated from contact with
other racial groups.   In this context, the failure of
control pupils to construe black girls is thought-provok-
ing, suggesting minimal response to pupils outside their
immediate class.   It implies that, left to themselves,
many children will make no moves towards getting to know
and understand pupils from groups other than their own.

By contrast, black boys came to be more positively
viewed in Rachel's class, although good feelings across
racial lines did not extend across gender boundaries.

The results from the measures of change suggest that
Rachel's class had moved from their original perceptions
of themselves and their peers quite considerably.   Comparing their results with those from the control class,
where many changes were in a negative direction, the case
becomes even stronger.   Presumably, in the absence of
their experience of collaboration, Rachel's class might
also have slipped backwards in their appraisal of other
groups, and in their own self-esteem.

The most striking results are those indicating changed
evaluation among Rachel's group of black pupils by whites,
and of boys by girls.   Girls seem to have become more
open to others, more aware of areas of mutuality and more
sympathetic to difficulties.   At the same time, their own
feelings of self-worth have increased.   There is also a
tendency for boys to re-evaluate white girls (though not
black girls) in their class more highly by the end of the
period, and in general, a less sexist feeling seems to
have developed across the class.   The positive re-evaluation across racial lines, already mentioned, is particularly heartening though, as we have noted, it is not extended unequivocally to black girls.   In contrast with
the negative perceptions or non-construing of black children by the control class, this diminution of racism must
count as a positive contribution of Rachel's teaching.

(c)   THE DYNAMICS OF INTERACTION AND CHANGE

Our work with Rachel's class represents the longest contact we had with any of the classes we studied.   We met

them first at the beginning of their second year in secondary school, and followed them through till the end of
their third year.   During these two years, we were able
to see the children functioning as a classroom group, and
note the progress they made.   Our observational contact
with them was a good deal closer in the first year;
during the second year, our visits were more occasional.
We also assessed the children's attitudes to the work,
their teacher and each other, at three points during the
two years: at the beginning of the first year, the end of
the first year/beginning of the second year, and at the
end of the second year.   The timetable was:

Beginning of First Year	End of First Year	End of Second Year
Perceptions of Humanities	Perceptions of schooling	Perceptions of Humanities (retest)
	Construing other children (comparison group)	
	Construing of Self and other groups (comparison group)	Construing of Self and others (retest, comparison with group)

Drawing on this quite extensive material, we can look
at what happened, over the two-year period, in this group
of children exposed to Rachel's collaborative classroom
approach.   But first, it is necessary to define the significance for us of that approach.

In its bearing on issues of commonality and sociality,
Rachel's collaborative approach can be defined in terms of
the three critical features already outlined.   First, she
insisted that learning was a matter of group work, rather
than solitary, individual endeavour.   Such a message,
running entirely counter to the messages of many other
lessons, demanded that the children redefine their classroom activities.   Rather than seeing their learning as
their own private affair, to which other children could
make no contribution except by cheating, pupils in
Rachel's class needed to construe class work as essentially a joint effort, in which what they already shared with
others, and what they were able to work out together, were
the things that mattered.   This means defining learning
as an area of commonality.

Equally important in Rachel's approach was her emphasis

on pupils' personal engagement in their classroom work.
This too entails assumptions about commonality.   As long
as children separate school knowledge from what they personally know and live out in their everyday lives, the
school curriculum will continue to be alien and out-there
- something that belongs to teachers, not to children.
By demanding a genuinely personal response to herself and
the work she set up, Rachel invited pupils to cross the
barrier between school curriculum and personal life, and
thereby to claim their own expertise in 'her' area of
knowledge.   To do this means experiencing sociality with
the teacher.

The third aspect of Rachel's collaborative approach
which is critical was her concern to create integrative
social relationships within the classroom group.   For
Rachel, good relations between children were not simply
the context within which learning could occur;   they were
the actual substance of class work.   Against the usual
separation of classroom learning from peer-group relationships, she was concerned continually to focus class activities on social interactions and mutual understanding.
In doing so, she made the process of sociality the central
feature of her curriculum.

In tracing the impact on the class we studied, of
Rachel's collaborative approach, we should start by asking
what they were like, as a group, at the beginning of our
contact with them, when they first encountered Rachel.
We have two sources of evidence.   First, there are the
children's responses to the ratings of curriculum areas,
in which they evaluated Humanities on five six-point
scales, along with five other subjects.   Second, we have
our observations of the children functioning as a group
in Rachel's classroom;   it seems convenient to take the
first term's observations as a sampling of their early
adjustment.

Phase one: The beginning of the study

As far as the first feature in Rachel's approach is concerned - the development of commonality with other children in classroom work - the observational material is more
relevant than the ratings of Humanities.   However, one
additional comment, written by Anita after she had completed the formal ratings, is suggestive.   She wrote
'Teacher isn't bad but sometimes it can annoy me when the
teacher asks me a question I don't know.   Also when the

children won't shut up when I'm trying to work.'   It
seems that at this stage not only did Anita experience
other children as disrupting rather than supporting and
sharing her classroom endeavours; she also apparently
felt humiliated if she had to reveal her ignorance to
others.   From our observations, it seems that the children in general perceived their class work as an individual
activity, and were not ready to accept others' involvement
in it.   Though working quite well on writing tasks when
these could be done alone, they were typically unwilling
at this stage to take up Rachel's invitations to engage
with others in written work.   In drama, there was less
reluctance to work with others; but an individualistic
ethos persisted in so far as the children remained relatively uninvolved in dramatic improvisations in which they
played no role themselves.   They were also often bored
and impatient when they had to listen to each others'
work, or wait for their own turn.   At the beginning of
the term, comments on other children's writing were apt to
be abusive and ridiculing.   On this evidence, these
children did not begin their association with Rachel as
people who believed that classroom work entailed uncompetitive sharing and joint effort.

For the second critical feature of Rachel's approach,
the results of the children's ratings of curriculum areas
are significant.   From these, it is clear that Rachel's
curriculum was perceived highly negatively, as an area in
which personal involvement was minimal.   On the three
scales which imply the possibility of personal engagement
- Enjoyable, Boring, and Useful - the class group rated
Humanities second lowest of all six subjects; it was
seen as very unenjoyable, very boring and very much lacking in usefulness.   Equally significant is the fact that,
as a group, the children rated themselves as more incompetent in Humanities than any other subject, despite rating
it the second easiest.   This adds up to a considerable
alienation from the Humanities curriculum.   There are
some differences, however, within the class group; girls
rated Humanities more favourably than boys.   The
comments of six girls and five boys suggest that their
evaluations may have been made in somewhat different
terms.   The boys all stressed the work itself, while
the girls referred to Rachel herself, and their relationship with her.

The children's alienation from the curriculum, and from
Rachel herself, is borne out by what we saw of their
behaviour as a group, during the first term.   Particularly

at the start of the term, rude and disruptive behaviour
was typical, and Rachel's attention was more often given
to controlling disruption than to anything more positive.
There was a general lack of attentiveness to Rachel; her
suggestions were sometimes disregarded completely, and
there was seldom an enthusiastic response to what she pro-
posed in the way of work.   The children's unengagement
showed itself in their generally rushing off as soon as
the pips went.   It was also noticeable that although
there were some good relationships among the children
themselves, these typically served to undermine rather
than support Rachel's position in the class group.   One
friendship clique - Alex, Coral, Fiona and Joyce - were
exuberantly disruptive in class.   Three of these girls
had expressed a sense of alienation from Rachel in the
comments they made in their ratings of curriculum areas.
Alex, Coral and Joyce all referred to her as picking on
them, and as spending too much time with the boys.
Jonathan and Duncan, who kept a low profile in class, were
typically passive towards Rachel.   Jackie S. and Paulette,
girls who seldom took the initiative in group work, commented at this stage that Rachel ignored them when they
did.   In all these ways, it seems that the children felt
little commonality, at this stage, with Rachel and her
curriculum.   Rather, they had apparently carried over
into her class the strong anti-teacher feelings which, as
a group, they had developed during the previous year.

   The existence of good relationships between some particular children in the class has just been mentioned.
However, at the beginning, it was far from being an integrated social group.   We saw a good deal of overt hostility between the children.   Within the total group, there
were islands of sociality.   Coral, Alex, Joyce and Fiona
were typically indifferent towards other children, if not
actually provocative.   Duncan and Jonathan, quiet, hard-
working boys, and longstanding friends, kept almost total
distance from everyone else in the group.   Jackie S. and
Paulette, absorbed in their own friendship, interacted
with virtually no one outside themselves throughout the
term.   Not only did these particular friendship groupings
remain relatively isolated from the wider group; but the
absence of generally positive social feeling within the
class showed itself, at this stage, in the general unwillingness to work with anyone who was not chosen as a
partner - although there was an exception to this, when
Mick worked with Andrew, and Rodney worked with Steve Y.,
at a high level of commitment.   The group as a whole also
refused to accept two particular boys, Andrew and Alfonso,

who at this stage were often explicitly rejected.   One
girl, Jenny, was similarly very isolated.   Finally, the
lack of group feeling meant a marked cross-gender segregation - usually expressed in mutual mistrust and indifference, rather than outright hostility.   There were, however, no signs at this stage of racist hostilities or subgroups.

For this class group, often mutually hostile, characterized by a general cliquishness, and divided additionally by gender, Rachel's emphasis on social interactions and
social relationships was clearly very uncomfortable.   As
we saw, the children, often prepared to work at traditional, written tasks, were at this stage ill at ease with the
more reflexive work of group drama, particularly where its
content was highly personal.   Their discomfort was expressed, if not in actually anti-social behaviour, in
general restlessness and lack of commitment to the work.

All this adds up to quite an unpromising start.   At
the beginning of their contact with Rachel, this class
group was far from sharing the sense of commonality and
sociality, towards their class work, their teacher, and
each other, which we have defined as the critical features
of Rachel's collaborative approach.   How did things turn
out during the first year, which represents the first
phase of our study of these children?

The first year: What happened in class?   In any classroom, the major responsibility for initiating and organizing events belongs to the teacher.   In defining the significant events in this classroom, it seems appropriate to
examine what Rachel herself actually did during this
period, as this bears on the three areas of commonality
and sociality.

Commonality in learning   The first area is that of commonality in learning, and relates to the perception of
classroom learning as involving sharing, and joint endeavour among pupils.   In many ways, this was the message of
Rachel's classroom work.   Right from the start of the
year, Rachel set up activities which required pupils to
operate on each others' ideas, feelings and experiences.
On the second occasion on which we saw the class, the
major part of the lesson had as its focus an improvised
drama brought by Coral.   This entailed not just the
active participation of some children within the group;

it was also made the basis of further work to be done at home by the whole class.   The use of particular child-dren's contributions as the basis of work by the whole class typified lessons throughout the year.   Often Rachel would take as her starting point the suggestion of one - sometimes unlikely - pupil; and the class would be asked to develop this further in writing or improvisation. Written work done in class was itself more often than not work on the mistakes in one child's homework.   By making mistakes the agenda for the group, Rachel was not merely enabling the children to work from each others' material; she was also tacitly conveying a non-competitive ethos, and a respect for imperfect productions, as providing the basis for further development.

   In many classrooms, one's own efforts, and the reac-tions which teachers make to them, are a very private affair.   Rachel's style was different.   Throughout the year, she regularly made sure that the children had access both to what others had individually produced, and to her own feelings about the work.   Lessons usually began with her reading from the written work of particular children, and making comments about it.   Such comments, often put tentatively or as questions, served not as unassailable judgments from on high, but as invitations to others to voice their own views and feelings.   These invitations were another very important aspect of Rachel's development of commonality in classroom learning.   From the start of the year, she asked the children to comment on each others' work.   This meant, at first, expressing what they felt about someone else's story, essay or poem.   Towards the end of the year, it entailed offering criticisms of the dramatic work of other individuals and small groups, in terms of how exciting, moving, or convincing the drama or particular interpretations had been, and how things might have been done better.   In inviting and treating seriously children's mutual criticism, Rachel legitimized their access to each other's work, and encouraged serious and appreciative shared involvement.

   Rachel also specifically set up classroom activities which required joint work.   Her way of using collabora-tion was one which offered children the experience of their own strengths.   Often she reacted to requests for help by suggesting that, instead, they asked each other. In setting up collaborative partnerships, she looked for pairs of children who would complement each other.   On one occasion, she made a point of asking the class why they thought she had suggested working together, and

receiving the rather weary response 'mixed ability', countered this by saying that, on the contrary, it was because
of complementary strengths, since everyone in the class
had particular areas of expertise.   The notion that children could act as consultants for each other was something
which Rachel often suggested.   In this way, she used the
work of the class to give children the experience of
mutual respect and inter-dependence in their work.   This
was extended further by the many opportunities she provided during the year for the children to organize their own
small group improvizations.

Summarizing the events, during this year, it can be
said that the classroom activities set up by Rachel supported, in a number of different ways, an experience of
learning as entailing commonality between pupils.
Rachel's lessons gave children access to each other's
work, involved them in developing each others' ideas, and
entailed joint effort in which the positive resources of
each person were made salient.

In this, she was concerned to broaden the terms beyond
merely academic ability, emphasizing, for example, the
understanding which the children possessed of their social
world.

Commonality and sociality in relations with curriculum and
teacher   This crucial area involved both the sense that
the curriculum is consonant with one's personal understanding, and, concomitantly, sociality with the teacher.
In this area, what bearing do the events in Rachel's class
have, over the first year?

On one level, the differentiation between class curriculum and personal knowledge was quite fundamentally challenged by Rachel's approach to Humanities during the year.
From the very beginning, class work took as its focus the
personal experience and feelings of pupils themselves.
By making these the material for writing, class discussion
and improvization, Rachel clearly endorsed their validity,
and their importance for 'serious' school work.   Nor was
this just one, soft, side of her curriculum, with another,
more distant, traditional side representing the rest of
the work.   Where lessons centred on other historical
periods or other cultures, or on the lives of particular
individuals, Rachel often required the children to make
their own personal interpretations of the material, and
bring it to life in their own way by their improvizations.

Potentially, therefore, the less ostensibly personal
aspects of the curriculum work were also integrated with
the children's own experience.

   Rachel's personal approach itself ran counter to the
separation of school from personal life.   At one level,
she refused the traditional polarization of teacher-
versus-pupils, by taking every opportunity to give the
children the direction of their own work.   Early on in
the year, we saw small groups in charge of their own
improvizations;   as the year progressed, the periods of
such autonomy got longer, and extended into more reflective activities, so that, towards the end of the year,
Rachel took a back seat while the class engaged in group
criticism of a drama.   She also undermined the teacher
stereotype by insisting on behaving in highly personal
ways.   On one occasion, she initiated an exercise on communication by telling a story against herself, which
emphasised her own vulnerability.   Throughout the year,
she responded in personal ways to the children, and referred freely to her own feelings and situation.

   Conversely, Rachel made many references to the children's own feelings, in ways which conveyed an understanding and sympathy with them.   At one end, this meant
articulating what children must be feeling, at moments in
class work.   For instance, she referred to the embarrassment they were all probably feeling in one particularly
personal improvization.   Towards the end of the year,
when Steve Y. and Suzanne had had a fight, she gave a good
deal of time to discussing Steve's feelings of rage and
frustration, and the general agitation which the fight had
aroused in the other children.   At the other end of the
scale, Rachel brought into her class discussion, mention
of the children's more general feelings about their situation;   for example, their frustrations and difficulties as
school children.   This recognition by Rachel of the children's feelings, both in and out of class, together with
her own emotional expressiveness, conveyed the sense that
their relationship was a personal rather than a stereotyped one.   This was endorsed by Rachel's contact with
the children outside school;   for example, at Christmas
she had the whole group to her flat for a party.

   To summarize Rachel's teaching, in relation to school-
versus-out-of-school knowledge, and commonality with the
teacher, it seems that her way of conducting her lessons
invited an integration of the curriculum with the children's own experience.   A sense of us-versus-them, so far

as Rachel was concerned, was likely to be countered by her
conduct of herself as a feeling, and potentially vulnerable person, who could share her experience with them, and
enter into theirs.

Sociality among pupils   It has already been said that
Rachel's main concern in teaching was the development of
good relationships between the children in her classroom.
For her, the involvement with others in work, the personal
engagement with the curriculum and with the teacher, which
she fostered, themselves served to make possible genuine
sharing, mutual support, and a differentiated experience
of other children.   But quite apart from these aspects of
her classroom work, Rachel made social relationships
within the group the explicit focus of many of her activities.

In most classroom groups, there are some children who
are isolated, or actually rejected, by other children.
In Rachel's class, Jenny, the Chinese girl, who was often
out of class for ESL tuition, was very much left on her
own when she was present.   The same was true of Kurdo, an
Iraqi boy who joined the class in the second term; Kurdo
was also often withdrawn for ESL tuition, and, like Jenny,
was isolated from the rest of the group.   Two boys,
Andrew (a regular member of the class) and Alfonso (often
out of class for basic skills work), were not so much ignored as actively rejected by the class group.   Both boys
tended to behave in disruptive and generally immature
ways.   With these particular pupils, Rachel actively
sought to change their status within the group.   Rather
than allowing the children's natural preferences to govern
working partnerships, she specifically asked particular
children to work with Jenny and Kurdo.   She also made
these two children salient within the group, from time to
time during the year, by asking the class to note the progress they were making.   She gave similar public acknowledgment to Steve Y., a member of the basic skills group,
who, when he was present in class, tended to be somewhat
apart from the main group.

Rachel also took active steps to alter the position of
Andrew and Alfonso.   She frequently ignored the anti-
social and attention-seeking behaviour of these two boys,
while generally calling attention to any positive contribution they made.   On occasion, she gave them prominent
roles within class activities, as, for instance, when in
the first term she asked Andrew to take the limelight as

William the Conqueror, whom the other children were to
interview.   Rachel also mediated directly in the interpretation of their class behaviour.   She said of Andrew,
'Andrew often starts by being horrid, but he generally
ends up being nice.'   This comment offered both Andrew
and the rest of the class a way of construing his class
role positively.   Towards other pupils who tended to disrupt class work, Rachel took a similar approach.   Early
on in the year, she gave central roles in dramatic work to
Coral and Joyce, both of whom were at that stage disruptive and hostile.   At the same period, she selected the
written work of Alex and Rodney - also generally disruptive in class at that time - for comment and general
praise.   Rachel also gave similar prominence to a different category of pupil - those who were particularly unob-
trusive and reticent.   In her conduct of class discussion, she often called on very quiet children, such as
Paulette, to make a contribution (although, in the noisy
early part of the year, she did not always notice such
children when they volunteered something).

Rachel's concern to establish good social relationships
went beyond her dealings with particular individuals.
Mention has been made of the three groupings within the
class: the three 'Latin' children, the three basic skills
children, and the two children who had ESL tuition.   Not
only did these special categories mean the regular absence
of those concerned from the class group, with their potential lack of social integration.   Their existence also
made explicit, differences in ability levels between the
children in Rachel's group, carrying the possibility of
ability categorisation among the children.   In the way
she set up class work, Rachel tried to forestall these
possibilities.   She regularly partnered the children from
the basic skills and ESL groupings, with members of the
wider class group.   Her public acknowledgment of the progress of less able, and second language pupils, has
already been mentioned.   So has the use she made of the
children's errors in their written work;   in selecting
particular pieces of work, she regularly chose those done
by the majority group, never exposing the mistakes of the
less able children.   More widely, the very use of mistakes for class work did perhaps carry the implication of
the irrelevance of hierarchies of attainment.

Rachel also used classroom work to establish relationships between children who were initially indifferent or
even hostile to each other.   In setting up collaborative
partnerships, she often suggested groupings which broke up

or widened friendship cliques.   In the first term, for
instance, she asked Fiona, who wanted to work with her
friend Coral, to pair up instead with Jenny.   At several
points in the year, she set up working groups which required Paulette and Jackie S. to include other girls in
their very exclusive relationship.   On a wider level,
Rachel sought to overcome the barrier between boys and
girls in her class group.   She did not try to do this by
suggesting mixed collaborative groups, although occasionally such groups did arise in dramatic work.   Her method
was sometimes to take as the content of class work, areas
of experience in which boys and girls had different perspectives, and to encourage each to consider the others'
context and feelings.   However, during this year, Rachel
did not set up any activities which necessitated a more
active and personal involvement in the experience of the
opposite gender.

   Throughout the year, Rachel's concern with relationships among the children in her class showed itself in her
continual monitoring and comments on their interactions.
When the children worked together, she insisted that they
were mutually attentive, and used each others' ideas.
'You should be working together, not against each other,'
she said at one point, and added, 'You're not always very
good at listening to each other.'   The recognition of
other children as resources, the appreciation of each
others' progress, which have already been mentioned, were
further dimensions in Rachel's efforts to foster positive
relationships throughout the group.   Towards the end of
the year, she began to set up exercises which necessitated
the development of psychological understanding of others
in the group, and were likely to overcome the stereotyping
of other children.   In the 'guess-who' exercise, for
instance, the children had to listen carefully to an
account of someone's personal experience, and draw on
their knowledge of the other children's background, history, and outlook to identify the person concerned.   In
trying to do this, they were obliged to move beyond any
stereotyped categorizations, and recognize the particular
personhood of others in the class.

   In summary, Rachel's fostering of sociality among the
children in her classroom group took the form of attention
to particular individuals, to friendship groupings and
cliques within the class, and to group dynamics generally.
Her concern with particular individuals was to integrate
marginal children, and to create a positive role for children who might otherwise remain withdrawn, disruptive or

antisocial.   In her approach to existing social groupings, Rachel tried to prevent cliquishness, and forestall
the divisive character of any friendship or organizational
groups.   Finally, she continually monitored and guided
the moment-to-moment interactions of children in the
group, so as to create positive feeling.   Towards the end
of the year, this meant setting up class work which called
for the development of mutual understanding.

Phase two: Halfway through

There are four sources of evidence which need to be considered at this stage, as bearing on the impact which
Rachel's collaborative approach had on the group after
they had been a year in her classroom.   First, we have
our observations of them; for convenience, the final term
in the year can be taken to represent how they functioned
at this point.   Next, there are three assessments of how
the children saw things at this stage.   First, we have
the constructs they used about other children generally,
for a sample of the class, and for a sample of children
from another class, to serve as a comparison.   Second, we
have the perceptions of the whole group, of themselves and
of particular categories of other children.   Again, we
can consider these kinds of evidence as they bear on the
three key areas of developing commonality and sociality.
Finally, we have small group interviews ranging across
work and relationships in school.

Commonality in learning   After their year in Rachel's
class, oriented to the development of a sense of commonality with others in classroom work, how far had the group
come to see their learning as the outcome of joint effort,
and other children as partners rather than as rivals in
school?

   From our observations, it seems that the children had
indeed become both more committed to sharing their classroom work, and better able to use collaborative opportunities productively.   In the three main kinds of activity
which Rachel set up, we saw a much greater involvement in
working with others.   One of these activities was feedback from Rachel, to the whole group, on the written work
of particular people.   Here, where previously we had seen
the children bored and restless, at the beginning, unless
their own work was in the limelight, by this stage there
was typically interested attentiveness throughout this

stage of the lesson.   Not only were the children visibly
interested in what others had written, and in how Rachel
reacted to it.   They also were ready to respond seriously
to the writings of others, not just their own friends, but
including class members who were relatively marginal in
the group.   The second category of work was that of
writing done in pairs.   Here, too, we saw the children
generally involved together in what they were doing;
their level of engagement was very different from their
earlier reluctance to do written work jointly.   For the
last sort of activity - improvized drama - we had earlier
seen rather greater ease in working with others.   However, we had also noted that the children tended to lose
interest if they were not directly involved.   In this
area too, improvement was evident.   By this stage, the
group often divided up, with some children doing an improvization while the others watched.   As audiences, the
children typically watched the performances closely, and
showed every evidence of enjoyment.

The quality of joint work also seemed to have improved.
In written work done in pairs, the children showed a capacity for organizing things themselves which we had not
seen at the beginning of the year.   Perhaps the most
impressive piece of work which we saw during the whole
year was the criticism made in the last term of the girls'
improvization by the rest of the group, who rose to the
occasion with a sustained seriousness.   In general, the
children were visibly easier with the relatively unstructured parts of the lesson, in which they were thrown back
on their resources, as pairs or small groups, than they
had been at the beginning of the year, when they seemed
very dependent on Rachel's constant oversight.

From these observations, the children did seem to have
developed a co-operative rather than an individualistic
attitude towards their work in Rachel's class, together
with a familiarity with working jointly.   How far were
these features incorporated in the views and feelings they
expressed in our other assessments?   Our assessment of
constructs is relevant in one aspect: the children's construing of working partnerships in school lessons.   For
the small group sample whose constructs we elicited, the
evidence suggests a generally positive attitude to sharing
work, but in this, the sample was not different from the
control group sample.   Both groups of children expressed
ideas of shared work both as generally productive, and as
involving friendly and helpful interactions between working partners.   To this extent, the children had by this

stage come to see joint work in school as feasible, and
friendships as supporting rather than undermining learning.   However, since the two groups were no different, we
cannot conclude that these attitudes had come about as a
consequence of experience of Rachel's approach.   Perhaps
this age group's general experience in school had fostered
a generally positive view of shared classroom learning.

The third kind of evidence which is relevant is interview material.   Here, for all four small groups of children we talked to, there was general consensus that working
with others was both enjoyable and worth while.   Most
children talked about Rachel's class; this seemed to represent their major experience of working with others.
The terms in which they talked about the learning which
could occur were sometimes quite close to Rachel's own;
they mentioned the value of getting to know other people,
particularly those who were previously strangers, and of
coming to understand others better, particularly through
seeing them perform.   To this extent, these children
seemed to have assimilated Rachel's idea of social relationships as a focus of classroom learning.   In terms of
more academic aspects of learning, there was rather more
ambivalence.   Some children mentioned sharing ideas, and
coming to know what others thought and felt.   But there
was a general reservation about shared work from the
standpoint of academic standards, with the fun and enjoyment of group activity being set in contrast with the possibly boring but necessary acquisition of knowledge.   To
this extent, it seems that these children still envisaged
'serious' learning as incompatible with the freedom and
pleasure of Rachel's class; and it may be that for them,
her curriculum, and the shared work it entailed, were implicitly separated from the more individualistic kinds of
learning seen as the real business of school.

Commonality and sociality in relations with curriculum and
teacher   In the bearing which they have on questions of
commonality and sociality with curriculum and teacher, our
observations are mostly highly positive.   It has been
said already that the children were, in the final term of
the year, typically involved in their classroom activities.
It was noticeable that they rapidly stopped whatever they
were doing when Rachel came into the classroom, and waited
eagerly for her to start the lesson.   At the end of the
period, there was often a reluctance to stop work, particularly if this was drama, which by that stage had become
obviously the most popular kind of activity.   There was

one exception to this generally high level of involvement.
In one lesson we observed, the children were markedly
passive and apparently unengaged.   However, this was a
lesson in which Rachel deliberately allowed little opportunity for participation, and operated a high level of
teacher control.   Apparently, the children felt alienated
in a class which offered none of the usual social interchange.   Much more typical for this stage of the year was
their general engrossment in what they were doing, and the
personal enjoyment, evidenced by much laughter and enthusiasm, which they apparently felt in the work of the class.

If their generally high level of involvement denotes a
lack of alienation from the curriculum, so does the children's acceptance of references to personal feelings and
out-of-school experience.   By this stage, Rachel was
using a number of exercises which demanded that pupils
drew on personal areas of experience, and expressed their
own feelings.   On the whole, the group coped well with
these demands, offering personal incidents and personal
feelings, and listening with interest to those of others,
although we noted some lack of interest in the experience
of the other gender.   This general readiness to bring
personal areas into the classroom suggests that the children were not operating a dichotomy between school and out-
of-school knowledge.   However, it must be remembered
that, in interview, they contrasted 'fun' classroom activities from the more boring but necessary acquisition of
knowledge.   It is possible that the integration of personal understanding and the school curriculum, achieved
within Rachel's classroom context, may not have been
generalized beyond this.

A genuinely personal engagement with the curriculum
implies a positive relationship with the teacher, and a
sense of the teacher as a genuine person rather than a
stereotyped authority figure.   Certainly this is borne
out by what we saw of these children in their interactions
with Rachel.   In marked contrast to the inattentiveness,
even actual hostility and disruption, characteristic of
the first term, the group was, as a group, very positive
towards her.   Not only did the children attend closely to
her, and respond, usually, with some eagerness to her suggestions;   they also seemed aware of her particular personality and outlook.   One way in which this showed
itself was the fact that some children - particularly some
of the boys - regularly teased her and joked with her
about herself.   Not all the children were equally free or
forthcoming with Rachel, of course.   Those who were most

positive towards her were, in general, children who were
well liked by their peers, such as Coral, Jackie S.,
Jackie T., and Anita, among the girls, and Steve C., Frank
and Don among the boys.   It should be said that Coral
herself had changed markedly during the year, from someone
who was initially unco-operative and hostile towards
Rachel, to one of the most enthusiastic members of the
class.   From our observations, it seems that by this
stage the class group were positively oriented towards
Rachel, and had in general achieved a differentiated
rather than a stereotyped relationship with her.   Their
general ease with participant rather than teacher-dominated lessons also suggests an equality of relationship, in
which genuine sociality could occur.

    As far as evidence from elicited constructs is concer-
ned, this again seems positive, but, again, is not confined to children from Rachel's group.   Both groups expressed largely favourable attitudes towards school work
and teachers.   This emerged from constructs about people
who make trouble at school, and those who do well with
teachers.   For the first category, both groups described
trouble-makers in disparaging terms, and, while sometimes
acknowledging that they got into trouble themselves, took
care to differentiate themselves from real trouble-makers.
It seems that neither group of children identified with
those who set themselves against teachers, and who were
generally seen as alienated from peers - implying that
good relations with teachers and peers were viewed as consonant rather than contrasted.   When it comes to construing people who get on well with teachers, attributions
from both groups were characteristically positive; success at school was favourably rather than unfavourably
viewed.   From this evidence, these children were generally sympathetic to school work, and were not operating an
us-versus-them orientation towards teachers.   But this,
again, seems to have been part of their general school
culture, not simply the outcome of their experience in
Rachel's class.

    Interview material also throws some light on this area.
Not surprisingly, teachers were highly differentiated by
the children we talked to; but comments on Rachel were
mainly highly positive.   There was for all the groups
some sense of Rachel as a person with whome genuine
sociality was possible, in so far as the fun and laughter
available in her class were common themes.   However,
these children also emphasized the importance of control,
implying definite limits to the equality of pupil-teacher

relationships within classrooms.   One group of girls
articulated the differences between such relationships in
and out of the school context, and in doing so, showed an
appreciation of teachers as themselves people who are subject to the constraints of social contexts.   On this evidence, these children certainly saw teachers as differentiated individuals rather than stereotyped figures, and,
so far as Rachel herself was concerned, viewed their relationship with her very positively.

   Did this sense of commonality, and possibilities of
sociality, in relation to Rachel, extend towards her curriculum?   The general expression of enjoyment and involvement in her classroom work which these children mentioned,
has already been described.   To this extent, they clearly
saw personal engagement as possible in her kinds of school
work.   But not all those we talked to accepted the integration of personal areas of experience with their classroom activity.   Whereas the girls expressed a sense that
quite intimate aspects of feelings and relations with
others could be talked about in an encouraging and supporting class atmosphere, the boys had more reservations,
seeing school work as generally instrumental, and personal
relationships as none of its business.   For these boys at
least, therefore, the work in which we saw them engaged in
Rachel's class had not broken down a general sense of distinction between school work and private life.

Sociality between pupils   In drawing on our observational
material for what it tells us about any development of
sociality between the children themselves, we should start
by noting the changes that took place in the composition
of the class.   During the year, some children left, and
others joined the class, so that the group was not quite
the same at this stage.   During the first term, Joyce and
Fiona were withdrawn from the group, in order to break up
the boisterous anti-teacher clique they had established
with Alex and Coral.   Sandro, one of the Latin children,
also left during the year.   Four children had joined the
class by the final term: Kurdo, Suzanne, Frank and Jeff.
By this stage, four boys were frequently absent from the
group, for different reasons: Andrew, Alfonso, Dave and
Steve Y.

   Given this altered group composition, what were relations like between the children at this stage?   Mention
has already been made of the marked change in Coral's
attitude to Rachel and the class work, which must have

been at least partly due to the enforced absence of Fiona
and Joyce.   Coral maintained and developed her friendship
with Alex, but within the context of a generally good
relationship with the rest of the group;   more than the
other girls, she often engaged in friendly banter with the
boys in the class.   Paulette and Jackie S. were less
cliquish as the year went on.   A private island in the
group during the first term, these two quiet black girls
now regularly admitted Suzanne, a white girl, and, to a
lesser extent, Jenny, who was Chinese.   Warren, whose
regular friend in class had been Sandro, appeared at this
stage to be quite happily integrated in the loose friendship group comprising most of the boys.   Don, from the
start a good mixer, had evidently widened still further
his sphere of friendly relations by this stage;   during
this term he was generally popular, and often actively involved in good-natured talk, with girls as well as boys.

   Generally good group feeling is also conveyed by the
greater integration which we saw of marginal children.
Though Andrew and Alfonso were frequently absent, when
they were there we saw little evidence of overt rejection
by the other children, and both boys appeared to respond
to their changed position by behaving in generally more
mature ways.   The progress of the children who had joined
the class is also revealing.   By this stage, Suzanne and
Frank seemed to have been easily integrated within the
group, and certainly did not stand out as 'new' members,
although Jeff was not so well integrated.   It seems that
the class group, though generally cohesive, had not evolved an exclusive feeling which shut out newcomers.   However, Kurdo remained largely apart.   From what we saw of
his relations with the group at this stage, though there
were some friendly overtures to him from some of the other
boys, attempts at working partnerships involving him uni-
versally failed, and he remained socially quite isolated.
Like Jenny, whose social integration seemed only partial,
his own reserved personality, combined with his language
difficulties, may have been mainly responsible for this
isolation.   With these exceptions, the social relationships we saw during this term were markedly less cliquey,
and more generally expressive of positive feeling, than
during the first term.   However, the complete or partial
absence from the class of some of its initially most difficult and disruptive members must not be forgotten.

   Our observations also suggest that at this stage,
though the earlier mutual indifference had disappeared,
there were gender-governed limits to mutual trust and

appreciation between children.   We saw clear evidence
that girls were able to respect and enjoy the dramatic
improvizations of boys, and boys, of girls.   However,
when it came to more personal spheres, some barriers were
apparent.   We noted that, in the exercise involving the
children in guessing the person whose experience was described, much less interest was taken by boys in girls'
stories, and by girls in boys' than in those of their own
gender.   On the only occasion during the term in which we
saw a serious fight, a boy and a girl were involved.

    The constructs we elicited from our class sample and a
control group sample also throw some light on the degree
to which sociality with other children had become possible.   Once again, the constructs the children offered
us were not different as between the two groups, so we
have to infer that they were the product of a wider culture among the children, and not merely the effect of experience in Rachel's classroom.   In general, what was
most striking about both groups' perceptions of peers is
that their overall theme of consideration and helpfulness
towards other children was to some extent contradicted by
their use of demeaning racial and gender stereotypes.
These stereotypes were apparent in the perception of black
boys as troublesome and naughty, but good at sport, of
black girls as failures in school, of Asian boys and girls
as quiet and introverted, and of boys generally as antagonistic where girls were friendly and helpful.   The general perception of conflict as having a largely racial
basis, and of the two genders as, at best, mutually indifferent, was also significant.   These findings suggest
that the characteristically harmonious interaction in
which we saw these children engaged, in Rachel's mixed and
multi-ethnic classroom, had not fundamentally altered
their sense of racial and gender barriers in their relations with other children - barriers which clearly limited
their capacity for genuine sociality towards some of their
peers.

    Race did not emerge as a topic in our interviews, but
gender did.   Both boys and girls expressed an awareness
of problems in cross-gender relationships in school.
There was general consensus that hostilities and indifference, in their own class, had been partly overcome by the
experience of working together, particularly in drama.
However, some of the girls implied that peer-group norms
strictly limited the possibility of genuinely personal
involvement between boys and girls in school;   these
girls' account of the liberating effect of an out-of-

school context, on boy/girl mutual enjoyment and appreciation, suggested that the potentiality for true sociality
might sometimes exist, even if it was unrealisable in a
classroom context.

The last source of evidence we have for this stage of
the children's progress is their perception of themselves
and other children, as obtained at the end of the year
from a grid format.   As with the constructs we elicited
at the same period from a sample of the group, this
assessment included a comparison with a control group -
another class, generally comparable except that their
teacher was not Rachel.   Just as with the constructs,
perception of self and other children did not seem to be
noticeably different for the children in Rachel's class.
In their self-esteem, both groups held a similar range of
estimates.   In perception of particular groups of other
children, and of particular categories of individuals, the
two groups were also highly similar.   Both groups expressed generally negative views of the category of black boys
in their class.   Towards white boys in their class,
though boys in both groups held generally positive evaluations, girls in both groups expressed negative ones.
There was a slight difference in the estimates of the two
groups of black girls in their class, with Rachel's group
expressing more favourable perceptions.   Towards white
girls in their class, however, the situation was reversed,
with children in the control group expressing more positive
views, while for those in Rachel's class, boys and black
girls expressed negative evaluations.   For the two other
kinds of category, Rachel's class and the control group
expressed very similar perceptions; both a person who
gets into trouble, and a person who finds lessons difficult, were negatively evaluated.

On this evidence, the children in Rachel's class had not
by this stage evolved a distinctive way of perceiving themselves and other children.   There was no sign either of
enhanced self-esteem, or of a greater sympathy with other
racial groups, or the opposite gender; as a group, they
were no more positive than the class chosen for comparison.
Both race and gender seemed at this stage to act as barriers to positive feeling.   In Rachel's group, black boys
were particularly poorly evaluated; and perception of
white children by black and black children by white, was
generally low.   The same thing was true of cross-gender
perception.   Boys took a poor view of girls, and girls,
of boys.   These findings generally confirm those we saw
in the construct elicitation and suggest that, despite the

absence of any overt racial tensions and the partial
breaking down of gender barriers in what we saw of
Rachel's class, the impact of this experience, for the
children themselves, had been limited. When drawing on
their more general perception of other children, out of
Rachel's special classroom context, it was to another peer
group culture to which they turned - one much less tolerant of race and gender differences.

The position of the group at the end of the first year
Drawing together all the evidence we have, we can try to
see what it indicates about where the class group stood,
in our three critical areas, after their year of Rachel's
teaching. In the first sphere - that of developing a
sense of commonality in classroom learning - Rachel's
methods had entailed providing children with the fullest
possible access to each others' ideas, enabling them to
develop each others' work, and setting up activities that
were designed to highlight the positive strengths of working partners. How far had this resulted, after a year,
in the children actually feeling their learning to be
something which they could share with each other, and
arrive at through common endeavour?

    In this sphere, our evidence seems to be largely posi-
tive. From our observations, the children certainly used
opportunities for collaborative work very differently from
the early part of the year. Characteristically, they engaged themselves in joint learning to a degree which
allowed them to be relatively independent of Rachel; and,
so far as we could see, often made their joint work productive. They also expressed positive feelings about
work with others, in construing collaborative situations,
although it is noteworthy that in this they were no different from children who had not experienced Rachel's
teaching. The response of those we interviewed was similarly positive towards working jointly, and some of the
children documented the social and personal gains that
could arise, in terms which suggested sympathy with
Rachel's particular approach. But some reservations were
expressed about the fun and freedom of shared work, as not
contributing to the acquisition of knowledge. For the
boys who expressed these feelings, the commonality in
learning to be gained in Rachel's class may have been seen
as irrelevant to the serious, individualized, work of
school, and perhaps to be increasingly suspect as secondary schooling progressed.

The second critical area, from our point of view, is
the development of commonality and sociality towards the
curriculum and the teacher.   What seems particularly
important in Rachel's approach was her continual effort to
integrate personal with school knowledge, by drawing on
pupils' own feelings and out-of-school experience.   She
also worked to eliminate an us-and-them polarization
between herself and pupils, by behaving in personal ways
towards the children, and inviting a similarly personal
response from them.   What effects had this approach had,
after the year?

Again, we witnessed a remarkable change in the children's approach to class work, from what we had seen of
them at the start of the year.   Their personal engagement
in lessons was obvious.   They also seemed ready both to
draw on quite intimate aspects of their experience, and to
attend to that of others.   In their relations with
Rachel, the earlier hostility and disregard had been replaced by an eager responsiveness, and several of the
children had developed an easy, affectionate relationship
with her.   To some extent, this lack of alienation, and
generally pro-school work and pro-teachers stance, seems
to have been an aspect of peer group culture rather than
specifically resulting from contact with Rachel's methods;
this is implied by the results of construct elicitation.
Interview material suggests some caution about the meaning
of what we saw in our observations.   The fact that some
children emphasized the importance of teacher control
implies that for them, at least, there were definite
limits on the mutuality of teacher-pupil relationships
within the classroom, while the critical comments by some
of the boys about the involvement of personal experience
in the curriculum suggests that they may have had some
inner doubts about some of the work which Rachel's class
entailed.

Finally, there is the area of sociality between the
children themselves.   Here, Rachel's approach meant working to integrate marginal children, and to enable difficult and rejected children to achieve more positive roles.
She was also concerned to overcome cliques and divisive
barriers within the group, and to promote a high level of
mutual tolerance and understanding.   How far had these
efforts succeeded in establishing genuine sociality in the
children's attitudes to each other?

What we saw in our observations was encouraging.
There was evidently a more positive, and more widespread,

group spirit.   Marginal children appeared better integrated, and children who had previously been markedly anti-
social and disruptive were now behaving in much less provocative ways.   Friendship cliques had generally opened
up, and there were no evident group barriers to interaction, although there was still some mutual mistrust and
lack of positive involvement between boys and girls.
This enhanced sociality within the group may have resulted, not just from the children's year with Rachel, but
also from the fact that some of the most disturbing members of the class had either left or were frequently
absent.   The existence of difficulties in relating to
those of the opposite gender was recognized by the children we interviewed, and some of the girls referred to the
strength of peer group norms operating against boy/girl
interaction in school.   What emerges from our two remaining sources of evidence is how far these children had
themselves internalised such norms, and, in addition, the
extent to which they held racist stereotypes.   In construing other children, our sample, just like our comparison sample, expressed generally negative and demeaning
images of black and Asian children, and portrayed boys as
provocative and belligerent.   They also saw race, and, to
a lesser extent, gender, as underlying conflict and strife
between children.   Similarly poor images of minority
races, and the other gender, were evident in their perceptions of other children on the grid;   and here again, the
children in Rachel's class did not differ from children in
another class.   There was a marked lack of sympathy
across race and gender, with black boys in particular
having a poor image, black children expressing generally
negative views of white ones, white children of black
ones, boys of girls, and girls of boys.   All this is very
different from the inter-racial harmony which we witnessed
in Rachel's class itself, and the partial transcendence of
gender barriers.   What it suggests is that the positive
changes of attitude which were evident in the children's
behaviour towards each other in Rachel's classroom were
themselves highly context-bound.   In their general feelings towards each other, and other children, outside that
special setting, these children clearly drew on a very
different philosophy, which they shared with their peer
group, and on which, as yet, their experience of Rachel's
classroom had made no impact.

The second year: What happened in class   There were also
some changes during the year in the composition of the
class group.   Two boys, Andrew and Mick, left the class

in the first term.   Two girls, Maria and Claire, joined
during the year;   Juliet came in the last month of the
final term.

Not much need be said about classroom events during the
second and final year in which we observed Rachel's class.
For one thing, we set out to maintain only occasional contact with the group during this period, rather than monitoring closely the events of each term as we had done in
the first year.   We felt that over the first year we had
achieved a close understanding both of Rachel's distinctive teaching approach, and of the particular children who
composed the class group.   It therefore seemed most
appropriate, for this second year, to keep in touch with
the class sufficiently to note any major changes, rather
than attempting any more detailed observation.

From our occasional visits, and from our general contact with Rachel, it seemed that her teaching continued to
incorporate the focuses already described, aimed at developing a sense of learning as shared with others, a feeling
of integrating school knowledge with personal understanding, and the capacity for differentiated personal relationships with herself and other children in the class.
What distinguished this year from the previous year, as
far as we could see, was Rachel's increasing demands that
in their classroom work the children drew on highly personal and intimate areas of their experience, and ventured
to enter personally into the role of other people, both in
and out of the class.   It is particularly significant,
for us, that these undertakings were apparently often concerned with interactions between boys and girls, and with
the perspective of members of the other gender.   For
instance, at the end of the year we saw one pair of children - Anita and Don - in a cross-gender role-playing exercise concerned with the behaviour and feelings of boy/girl
pairs in a public place.   By this stage, the children
were becoming used, through the work Rachel set up, not
just to sharing their experience with class members of the
opposite gender, but to themselves attempting to express
and interpret what members of the opposite gender thought
and felt.

Phase three: The end of the second year

We can now draw on what evidence we have about the cumulative impact of Rachel's collaborative teaching approach,
over two years, on this group of children.   This evidence

consists of our somewhat scanty observations in the last
term of the second year, and two assessments of changes in
the children's attitudes: towards their curriculum, on
the ratings of Humanities, and towards themselves and
their peers, on the grid format.   Again, this can be considered in relation to each of the key areas in turn.

Commonality in learning   In so far as the few observations we have bear on this area, it appeared that by the
end of the year the children were generally happy to
accept the involvement of others in their classroom work.
Indeed, by this stage, they had apparently come to expect
that class activity would consist of drama, which characteristically meant taking as the content of learning, the
ideas and feelings of members of the group.   When class
work involved each others' writings, we also saw a high
level of shared involvement.   The children listened with
general respect to the written work samples which Rachel
read out.   On one occasion, when the content of writing
was very personal, we noticed several children expressing
support for those whose work was being exposed.   From
this rather impressionistic evidence - derived from only
three visits - it seems that by this stage the children
were operating from a standpoint in which sharing class
work, and entering into the work of others, were seen as
natural and easy.

   Neither of the two assessments of attitude have any
clear bearing on commonality in learning.

Commonality and sociality towards curriculum and the
teacher   By this stage, the work set up by Rachel was
highly personal, and characteristically required the children to bring into the classroom their experience of contexts and relationships outside school.   Our few observations suggest that the group had come fully to accept
such a curriculum.   We saw the children working with
apparent familiarity and expertise on role-taking exercises
which called for imaginative exploration of out-of-school
encounters and roles.   There seemed to be no avoidance of
the emotional aspects of such work.   Improvizations, once
embarked on, seemed to arouse a very personal involvement,
with real immersion in the role among some children.
From what we saw, not only were the children generally
willing to express quite intimate feelings on their own
part, but they also listened without hostility or embarrassment to the feelings of other, rather different children in the class.

Another aspect of the sense of commonality between
school and out-of-school knowledge is the feeling that
school work is one's own endeavour, not merely something
imposed.   It is significant that during this last term,
from what we saw of them, the children were working with
real enthusiasm.   Delight and enjoyment were unmistakable
concomitants of the role-taking we witnessed, and many
children tried to prolong the work after the end of the
lesson.   The group as a whole also seemed by this stage
to have assumed a good deal of personal responsibility for
the work they did in Rachel's class.   Although we saw a
few children who were not able to sustain improvizations
unless Rachel was there to guide and support them, this
was not typical.   Most children developed their role-
playing a long way without Rachel's mediation.   This
freedom to use a very unstructured kind of task also
speaks of considerable development of autonomy in learning.

This general seriousness and personal involvement in
class work could probably not have happened without a high
degree of sociality between the children and their
teacher.   From our three observations, it seemed that the
children had, as a group, developed both in their interest
and awareness of Rachel, and in their ease in relating to
her.   We saw a generally attentive, often eager, responsiveness to Rachel's comments and suggestions, and, on one
occasion, the children listened to her with apparent fasci-
nation throughout her very long initial talk;   during the
whole ten minutes, no one moved.   The fact that by this
stage the children were so free in sharing intimate personal feelings with the class does itself imply a high
degree of trust in Rachel herself.   This seemed to be
borne out by the generally confident and easy way in which
we saw them relating to her.

The ratings of curriculum areas are also relevant to
how the children were, at this stage, experiencing Rachel's
curriculum.   There were some clear changes from their
perceptions two years previously.   It is evident that
this was not just part of a general re-evaluation of all
curriculum subjects, because all the other subjects except
Home Economics retained much the same relative position as
before.   Home Economics, previously quite popular, was
now the least popular subject.   With Humanities, the
group's ratings showed that they felt much more personally
involved in the curriculum;   it was seen as more enjoyable,
less boring, and much more useful than before.   Perhaps
still more significantly, the children rated themselves as
very much more competent at the subject, while rating it
as slightly more difficult than before.

There are some subgroup differences in these ratings,
and changes in ratings across the two year period.   Girls,
who had previously rated Humanities more favourably than
boys, by this stage had developed still more favourable
attitudes relative to boys.   Looking at the changes in
ratings across the two years, for boys and girls, it is
clear that girls came to see Humanities as less boring and
more enjoyable, and to see themselves as much more competent at it.   This last change seems particularly significant since it goes against the strong trend, for all other
subjects, for girls to see themselves as less competent
than before.   For boys, on the contrary, although Humanities was rated as rather more useful than previously, it
was seen as more boring and less enjoyable.   As far as
competence is concerned, boys rated themselves as less
competent than previously, in line with a general lowering
of self-rated competence across other subjects.   These
differences seem to add up to a rather different perception of Rachel's curriculum, at this final stage, by boys
and girls, with girls holding a much more favourable view,
and a much more confident sense of themselves in relation
to it.

Again, our observational evidence is scanty; but some
changes, in the direction of greater sociality, were
apparent in the way the children dealt with each other at
this stage.   On the level of individual members of the
group, it seemed that further progress had been made in
integrating isolated children, and those who previously
had threatened to divide the group.   We noticed that
Kurdo, though still somewhat marginal, was actively supported and encouraged by some children, while the two new
girls seemed to have become well integrated group members.
We also saw that Coral, who at the end of the first year
was still a rather egoistic member of the group, by this
stage was prepared to put the group work first, and resist
the temptation of being in the limelight.

It has been said that the class work during the second
year was to a large extent focused on the mutual perceptions of boys and girls, and on boy/girl relationships.
These topics were, of course, naturally interesting to
children of this age.   What we saw of their class work,
however, suggested that their interactions with each other
in the course of Rachel's lessons went a long way beyond
generalized excitement about the opposite sex, or interest
in individual pairings.   In exchanging experience with
each other, many of the boys and girls, from what we saw,
showed trust and freedom on the one side, and support and

appreciation on the other.   When it came to the exploration of the other gender's perspectives, we witnessed a
general willingness to enter the world of the other, and,
in some cases, a real empathy in understanding the other's
situation and feelings.   It was also noticeable, on the
few occasions that we saw them, that the children's interactions were generally more friendly and easy.   Nevertheless, it looked as though some residual gender barriers
remained, though we saw no signs of any barriers of race
or ability.

We have another source of evidence about the children's
mutual sociality at this stage, in their perception of
themselves and other children, as assessed via a grid.
As before, we also assessed, for comparison purposes, the
same control group class.   Here, there were several
changes on the part of Rachel's class group which suggested a general development of mutual sociality - changes
which did not occur in the comparison class group.
First, Rachel's group, whose self-esteem had initially
been no higher, expressed an enhanced self-esteem, where
that of the comparison group remained the same.   Rachel's
group also expressed generally more favourable cross-race,
and cross-gender perceptions, where, again, the perceptions
of the comparison group remained the same, or deteriorated.
Black boys in the class, who a year previously had been
poorly perceived by both groups, were now more positively
viewed by Rachel's group.   This improved image was not
extended to black girls, however;   previously positively
viewed in Rachel's class, they were now somewhat less
highly regarded.   A striking difference was evident in
the two groups' perceptions of cross-gender white subgroups.   In Rachel's class, girls generally viewed white
boys positively, while girls in the comparison class
viewed them negatively.   The same situation occurred with
white girls;   in Rachel's class, boys viewed them positively, while boys in the comparison class held negative
views of them.

There were also some differences in how the two groups
changed in their evaluation of particular categories of
people.   A year before, both class groups had held negative views of people who get into trouble, and people who
find lessons difficult.   By this last stage, people who
get into trouble, still negatively viewed by the comparison class, had come to be more positively seen by the
boys, though not the girls, in Rachel's class.   Conversely, people who find lessons difficult, less favourably
viewed than before by the comparison class, were more

favourably seen by the girls in Rachel's class.   From
this rather slight evidence, it seems that the boys had
perhaps begun to align themselves with those who felt disaffected in school, where the girls had extended their
sympathy to those who were less able in school work - with
whom, judging from their general ratings of themselves as
incompetent in most lessons - they may have felt some
identification.

The position of the group at the end of the second year
In the three areas we are concerned with in this study -
commonality in learning, commonality and sociality towards
curriculum and teacher, and sociality among children - we
have more evidence in this final phase about the last two
than the first.   All we can say about the children's
sense of commonality in learning at this stage, is that,
from our observations, they seemed to have developed an
ease and familiarity with sharing and joint work, and a
capacity to use this in often very productive ways.   What
we do not know is how far this experience of learning as a
shared endeavour was generalized beyond the confines of
Rachel's classroom.   We saw, at the end of the first
year, that some children were differentiating between the
freedom and enjoyment of Rachel's class, and the more academic learning of other classes.   It is possible that by
this stage, when the children were at the end of their
final year, and about to choose their options, school
learning as traditionally defined was increasingly salient
for them, and that Rachel's classroom work, personally
engrossing as it may have been, was seen as at a tangent
to the real work of school.

    Our evidence about commonality and sociality towards
the curriculum and teacher is rather more substantial,
because, here, our scanty observations are backed up by
attitude assessment.   The conclusion, from our visits to
the class, that the children had by now become very personally engaged in their class work, and in their relationships with Rachel, is generally borne out by their ratings
of curriculum areas.   The results from these ratings show
a greatly enhanced evaluation of Humanities, as against
its earlier very poor image for these children.   However,
these results also show something else which was not
apparent to us when we visited the class: the very different attitudes to Rachel's lessons on the part of boys
and girls.   In general, girls had a much more favourable
view of Humanities.   More specifically, despite feeling
themselves to be less competent than before in other

lessons, they judged their competence as better in this subject, where boys saw their competence as lower all round.

On the last area, sociality in relationships between the children themselves, our observational and attitude assessment results are consonant.   In our few visits, we saw generally high group integration, and a lot of good feeling between the children.   Mutual trust and openness seemed characteristic of their dealings with each other, and some children showed a high level of empathy with others.   That mutual appreciation and respect had developed during the year, was borne out by our grid findings. Most striking among these was the improved image of black boys in the class, and the more favourable view of the opposite gender.   The fact that these changes did not happen in the comparison class implies that they were a function of experience in Rachel's classroom, in which the development of understanding and sympathy with others across race and gender boundaries was a constant underlying theme.   It seems that the impact of this experience was gradual and cumulative.   A year earlier, when we assessed these children's attitudes towards their peers, after one year with Rachel, racial and gender hostilities and mistrust, not apparent in their visible interactions in class, were clearly evident in the way they construed their peers, and in their evaluations of subgroups within the class.   In these perceptions, these children did not differ from the control groups we used.   It was not, apparently, until two years had passed, that the influence of Rachel's methods was personally assimilated, and came to govern the way in which these children perceived their peers.

It looks from our findings as though Rachel's approach achieved a greater impact among the girls than among the boys in her classroom group.   At least, this seems to be true as far as perceptions of the curriculum are concerned. Half-way through the period in which we studied them, we had some hints that the girls in the group might be rather more receptive to messages of commonality and sociality in their classroom work.   In interviews, it was the girls who dwelt on the value, as well as the complexity, of classroom relationships, while some of the boys had reservations about the involvement of school lessons in personal relations.   In writing their own comments, at that stage, about Humanities in the ratings of curriculum areas, all the girls who volunteered such comments spontaneously brought up issues of social relationships;   none of the

five boys who wrote comments referred to these.   As a
group, the girls in the class thought more highly of
Humanities than did the group of boys.

From this point of view, perhaps it is not surprising
that by the end of our contact with them, it was the girls
who seemed to have assimilated a relatively stronger sense
of commonality and sociality.   Certainly their increased
appreciation of Humanities, together with their confidence
in their own ability in the subject - contrasting with
their general feelings of incompetence in other curriculum
areas - suggests that they had come firmly to identify
with the standpoint from which Rachel taught.

Chapter 7

Reflections on the study

This study has been concerned with the degree of commonality and sociality between teachers and pupils, and
between pupils themselves, within the framework of meanings which each brought to their classroom situation.
Collaborative learning has been the central focus of
study. On the one hand, it was through this mode that
the teachers interacted with their pupils, and the pupils
with each other. To the extent that these classroom
participants shared similar perceptions of learning, and
of collaboration, and had some understanding of each
other's perceptions - to that extent, such modes were
likely to be used in ways that were personally and socially fruitful. On the other hand, collaboration in learning also represented a channel of communication between
those involved. It offered possibilities, therefore, for
the development of common ground and mutual understanding.

In considering those questions in relation to the four
classrooms we studied, it is possible to separate the
material we gathered into two broad spheres - to do with
the meaning of learning and the curriculum, and to do with
the meaning of social relationships. For each sphere in
turn, we can look at the way the teacher saw things, and
then examine how far these perceptions were like those of
the pupils in her or his classroom. To understand the
meanings we are concerned with, it is important to consider not just what teachers and pupils said about aspects
bearing on classroom collaboration, but also what they did
in learning situations. This means paying attention to
the ways in which the teachers set up collaborative classroom work, and the ways in which their pupils responded.
For this final evaluation of the study, it seems appropriate to cast the discussion in non-theoretical language.

THE MEANING OF LEARNING AND THE CURRICULUM

Mac's second year Design and Technology class

For Mac, the possibilities which collaboration in learning
offered were closely geared to the way he defined his subject.   As he saw it, the practical, technical aspects of
Design and Technology were secondary to its essentially
intellectual and creative character.   Its scope was very
broad, reaching well beyond the immediate workshop situation, and ultimately encompassing the functional, aesthetic and economic meaning of human artifacts within the physical and social environment.   As curriculum, Mac defined
D and T in terms of process rather than product, and saw
it as covering a complete cycle from the preliminary
stages of planning to a critical evaluation of the finished article.   It was within this emphasis on process that
Mac saw the potential of collaborative modes.   Although
the making stages of D and T might necessarily be individualized, the more crucial, thinking stages lent themselves
to a common endeavour, in which children could pool ideas,
refer to shared out-of-school experience, and generally
spark each other off.   Mac thought his subject was a
natural for this kind of spontaneous activity;   he
believed it was generally enjoyed by boys and girls alike,
so long as no artificial barriers were set up by masculine-
type artifacts.

   Mac's perception of his curriculum, and the learning it
entailed, was not altogether shared by his pupils.
Unlike Mac, these children focused very much on technical
skills as the crucial feature of this part of the school
curriculum;   they generally saw D and T as a strictly
practical subject.   Because of this, their sense of collaboration in D and T was very different.   Rather than
seeing themselves and their peers as resources for joint
exploration of ideas, they defined help between pupils
quite narrowly in terms of superior levels of technical
skill.   In line with this emphasis on practical aspects
of learning, these children clearly saw the physical product as the prupose of D and T work, and felt that, beyond
the technical expertise that had gone into its construction, its practical utility represented a further measure
of its value.   Another aspect of this view was the perception of D and T work as learning a particular, correct
way of doing things.   Most of these children did not
apparently see design as open to their own creativity, but
were preoccupied with the possibility of making mistakes.
In terms of the personal involvement which Mac saw as

underpinning collaborative work, the situation was very
different for boys and for girls.   Over and over again,
it was the boys who spoke with enthusiasm about the subject, and defined it as personally relevant.   For these
boys, Mac's assumption that D and T had a natural attraction certainly seemed borne out.   On the whole, however,
this was not the case for the girls in his class who, as a
group, expressed much less liking for the subject, and, in
several cases, rejected it as personally inappropriate.

Given this partial consensus between Mac and his
pupils, as to what learning in D and T actually meant,
what function did collaborative learning have within his
workshop?   It seemed that, in general, the opportunities
which Mac set up were used in rather more limited ways
than he hoped for.   Where the children involved each
other in their work, this was typically on the basis of
substituting for the teacher - relaying instructions about
the task, giving practical help, cross-checking progress,
showing their own work, or giving the answer to calculations.   Individual children were sought out for consultation because they were seen as having superior information
or technical skills.   This made collaboration generally
asymmetrical, though pupils who sought help on one occasion might themselves be giving it in others.   The opportunities provided by Mac to 'help each other' were interpreted, and used, by these pupils to obtain extra help
from their friends in tasks which were essentially individualized.   In line with the perception that learning
meant producing an artifact that could be respected, the
children, where they worked together, used each other to
aid practical construction or improve finish.   In the
case of George W., access to this kind of help was crucial
in enabling him to meet at least some of the practical
demands of the task.   For most of the boys, at least, if
not for all the girls, the collaborative nature of Mac's
lessons seemed to further their own positive educational
purposes - different though these were, in their scope, to
Mac's objectives.

Mac's class represents a context in which the teacher's
goals for classroom collaboration were only partly
achieved.   Probably there were a number of reasons for
this.   Most obviously, the generally authoritarian ethos
of the school itself - informing the children's previous
educational experience, and the large part of their current school lives - mitigated against their understanding
of Mac's innovative classroom methods.   More subtly, the
particular ways in which Mac defined the function of

collaboration in his curriculum may not have been viable,
given the school context in which he worked.   His goals
for collaborative learning were very ambitious intellectually, and were probably particularly difficult for children unused, in their schooling, to exercising autonomy
and responsibility for their learning.   Had Mac used collaborative modes to foster and develop these qualities
themselves, it seems possible that the children might have
made more creative use of their learning opportunities.
As it was, he did not see the function of collaboration
primarily in these terms, and, in his classroom practice,
did not fundamentally challenge traditional expectations
of teacher authority.   Finally, Mac's curriculum area
may itself have imposed constraints on collaboration.
Certainly, given the children's essentially practical
definition of the subject, it is difficult to see how they
could have used collaborative working in other than rather
limited ways.

Islay's fifth year Social Studies class

Islay believed her curriculum area involved knowledge as
lived experience to be understood, rather than knowledge
as extraneous facts to be regurgitated.   This was why she
saw collaboration as important and necessary in learning
within Social Studies.   In her view, pupils were themselves the central resource in their own learning, as
people whose own personal and social situations and experience were directly at issue, or at least formed the base
from which social questions needed to be considered.
Talk with peers who shared broadly similar situations, but
might bring somewhat different perspectives to bear on
them, was intrinsically valuable in helping pupils articulate their own ideas and reflect on social issues and
practices.

    Within this definition of Social Studies, Islay never-
theless saw its meaning, for the pupil group we studied,
as involving some special considerations.   Most centrally,
she viewed her goal, for those nearing school-leaving age,
as being the certification of their learning.   This was,
of course, a practical necessity, given the contemporary
situation within the labour market.   But quite apart from
this, Islay thought it vitally important that the boys she
taught should experience the stamp of public recognition
on the value of genuinely personal learning.   To this
extent, the domination of the curriculum, in the fifth
year, by public examinations did not mean only a con-

straint.   Since the Mode 3 exam requirements allowed some
room for the kind of learning Islay hoped to foster, this
exam could potentially serve to validate it for the
pupils.   Within its terms, not merely did talk form part
of the syllabus to be examined;   but the project it included was allowed to be done jointly.   To this extent,
the exams at which the class was aiming could be worked
for collaboratively.

Like Islay, the boys in her fifth year class set a very
high premium on passing their Social Studies examination.
Its value, for them, however, lay entirely in its instrumental capacity of certification for work.   Hardly surprisingly, they were as a group highly conscious of entering
a world of scarce employment.   But apart from this, these
boys perceived school learning in terms that were very
different from Islay's sense of her curriculum.   For them,
knowledge was very much 'out there' - the property of
books and teachers.   Concomitantly, it embodied correct
answers, and was in no sense a process of personal construction.   They did not see the curriculum as intimately involving their own lives and concerns, and they generally
had a very low opinion of themselves as learners.   In
line with these perceptions, talk among friends was not
seen by these boys as representing learning at all;
instead, learning was seen as exclusively embodied in
individualized written work.   As such, it was certainly
respected.

From what we saw of the way these boys responded to
Islay's encouragement to talk together about personally
relevant and involving questions, the meaning of her collaborative opportunities was strictly limited by their
definition of learning and the curriculum.   It was clear
that they made a definite demarcation between the enjoyable but un-serious period of classroom talk, and the
period of individualized writing, seen as more boring but
much more important.   Because the boys did not view their
classroom discussions as being real work, they did not use
them to more than a very slight extent for questioning or
extending their own understanding, reserving class talk
instead for pleasant banter and essentially social interchanges.   Nor did they, in a single case, take up the
option of doing a project jointly.   Again, these boys
clearly viewed writing - real work - as essentially an
individual effort.

It seems that Islay's attempt at a different kind of
learning experience was, ultimately sabotaged by these

boys' prolonged socialization within a competitive, individualized schooling system.   The fact that this system
had, further, clearly categorized them as generally unable, and unlikely to achieve responsibility for their own
learning, must have further undermined their chances of
responding to Islay's positive expectations.   Islay's
learning invitations were, besides, probably very much at
variance with other messages which these boys received in
other lessons they were doing.   Against the weight of all
these factors, not even Islay's two-year contact with the
group, nor her quite lengthy lesson periods, could act
effectively to reverse these boys' traditional views of
school learning, or their general sense of their own in-
adequacies as learners.

Terry's second year Humanities class

Terry's definition of his Humanities curriculum was one
which strongly emphasized the importance of writing.   He
saw it as absolutely essential that children should learn
to read and write in school, and to some extent viewed his
own role, in teaching Humanities, as enabling pupils to
produce good written work.   This perception governed his
judgment of the value of collaborative classroom modes, in
that he expected pupils to use their talk together to prepare, ultimately, better pieces of written work - without
this outcome, such talk was merely time-wasting.   However, because of the way Terry defined 'good' writing, his
emphasis on collaboration carried connotations of potential enjoyment in class work which were unlikely to be
available in more traditional learning styles.   As he saw
it, the quality of good written work was a function of the
depth of personal involvement, personal thinking and feeling, about what was at issue.   He thought that pupils,
freed from continuous teacher direction, could, at least
sometimes, enter into the material in genuinely personal
ways, and thereby participate more deeply in their own
learning.   Through relatively unconstrained talk with
their friends, children could potentially express and
develop their ideas about particular areas of the curriculum.

    Another crucial aspect of Terry's definition of his
curriculum was his rejection of its simple, literal 'relevance' to his pupils' lives.   The personal involvement in
learning, on which he laid so much stress, was, in his
perception, a function of implications drawn out from
personally quite remote events, for present-day events and

situations.   Personal involvement did not lie, for Terry,
in focusing on pupils' intimately personal experience -
something he saw both as an unwarranted intrusion on the
part of school, and as a failure to extend children's
understanding into wider spheres.   Terry viewed this
aspect of his curriculum as particularly significant in
teaching black pupils, whose engagement in learning he
thought would proceed not from Black Studies as such, but
from the ability to see ramifications, into the contemporary world, of perhaps quite distant events.

If Terry particularly related his definition of the
relevance of his curriculum to the black pupils he taught,
it was out of concern for another group - working-class
boys - that he particularly emphasized the importance of
unambiguous parameters in classroom work.   Aware of the
traditional expectations which this group of pupils typically held, Terry thought it essential that teachers were
explicit about the demands they were making, and the
nature of the task they were setting.   In his own teaching, as we saw, he frequently alternated between 'straight'
teaching and collaborative work.   In introducing either
kind of work, he was clearly at pains to reduce ambiguity
by explicitly spelling out the rules of the game - the
time-scale, the kind of activity expected, and the end-
product.   In his monitoring of collaborative working, he
frequently reminded pupils of these parameters, and re-
sumed control if they were being disregarded.

Terry's classroom group was unusually diverse in its
social and educational composition.   Nevertheless, there
seemed on the whole to be a high level of consensus
between himself and his pupils as to what it meant to
learn his curriculum.   Particular pupil subgroups echoed
particular themes more than others.   It was the middle-
class children who most strongly endorsed Terry's definition of Humanities as personally meaningful, and his view
of collaborative talk as developing the expression of
ideas, and enlarging personal understanding.   Conversely,
it was the working-class boys and girls who echoed Terry's
insistence on the instrumental value of his curriculum -
its demands for written work.   Working-class children
also separated school learning from intimate personal experience, whereas the middle-class children conveyed the
sense of much greater integration between the two.
Again, it was the working-class children who most clearly
implied appreciation of clear teacher direction - 'strictness' - and unambiguous learning parameters.   These
children also saw learning as more individualized, and

concomitantly, as more dependent on teachers.   Beyond
these differences in perception, however, the whole classroom group perceived Terry's curriculum positively and
valued his lessons, not only for the enjoyment they carried, but also because Terry enabled them to learn - different though their definitions of learning may have been.

In the way in which they responded to Terry's collaborative working modes, these pupil subgroups seemed to live
out their somewhat different perceptions.   On their side,
middle-class girls, and still more, middle-class boys,
were able to use the intimate context of friendship to
enter personally into the material, to draw on out-of-
school experience, to negotiate differences of viewpoint
and, often, to produce written work which embodied a real
development of shared understanding.   For the working-
class children in Terry's group, the opportunities of
small group talk were used more variably, and, usually, in
more limited ways.   For the black girls, class work remained largely individualized, talk maintaining an essentially social function.   For the white girls, and at
least some of the white boys, talk was used in partially
work-related ways, to remind about the task demands, cross-
check progress, give help or make particular suggestions -
and, in general, for mutually sustaining the effort of
written work.

Rachel's second year Humanities class

For Rachel, her English/Drama lessons involved, most fundamentally, building upon children's personal experience.
So far from seeing her curriculum as entailing essentially
extraneous material to be assimilated, Rachel viewed her
teaching role as focusing explicitly upon what pupils knew,
what they thought, what they felt.   This meant that the
life experience and situations of the individual children
in her class were not excluded as irrelevant to classroom
business, but, instead, formed the basic raw material on
which work was to be done.   This definition of the curriculum as essentially personal carried the implication
that quite intimate aspects of children's lives - their
personal feelings, their closest, or their most tentative
relationships - could, potentially, be matters to which
the whole class had access.   Dramatic work did, of course,
often provide a relatively indirect, tangential exploration
of such aspects.   Because Rachel saw her curriculum as
shared understandings, her approach also meant that aspects
of school work normally kept private between individual

pupils and their teachers formed another legitimate part
of lesson work.   So in her classes, children's writings,
and her own response to them, could serve as the starting-
point for group work.   Finally, the moment-by-moment
lived experience of children in their classroom was itself
relevant raw material.   Social interchanges, with all
their undercurrents, between pupils, and between pupils
and Rachel herself, could, if they were discussed with
honesty and sensitivity, help children extend their
understanding of their own and others' feelings and
reactions.

Given this definition of the curriculum, collaborative
learning modes stood, for Rachel, as clearly the most
meaningful.   Only in the context of genuinely personal
relations, between teacher and children and between children themselves, could pupils share feeling and experience,
and listen to what others were saying.   Social exchanges
and dramatic work with other people also carried, potentially, the enjoyment and spontaneity which alone made
learning vivid and personal - a character totally lacking
from learning within formal and repressive authoritarian
teaching.   Finally, material which was newly created
rather than predetermined could itself be negotiated only
within the freedom of children's personal interactions.

As far as the children were concerned, Rachel's class
only partly shared her definition of learning and the curriculum within her Humanities lessons.   In the way they
saw her lesson material and her methods, there was a
marked difference between boys and girls - a difference
which intensified over the two years.   On their side, the
boys in Rachel's class, as a group, quite clearly perceived her lessons as enjoyable and interesting, but, for
that very reason, felt them to be at a tangent to the real
work of school, which they defined in relatively traditional terms, as personally uninvolving, individualized
writing on set topics.   Early on, these boys apparently
saw 'real' school work as important instrumentally, boring
though it might be.   By the end of the two years, however, it seemed that most of them were beginning to be
disaffected with school learning as a whole.   Another
factor which may have influenced these boys' attitudes
towards Rachel's curriculum had to do with its intimately
personal character.   Despite their general enjoyment of
her lessons, many of the boys had definite reservations
about the involvement of school in their personal lives.
There was some resentment that teachers should presume to
intrude into out-of-school experience;   as Don remarked,

'People can lead their own lives, it's nothing to concern
the school.'   For all the vigour and inventiveness with
which many of these boys entered into Rachel's role-playing, such invasions into the personal went against their
general philosophy about the legitimate business of
school.

This orientation was apparently quite different to
that of the girls in Rachel's group.   As far as we could
see, most of the girls not only had some insight into the
purpose of Rachel's methods - an understanding of the
kinds of learning which she promoted - but also endorsed
the very personal focus she adopted.   Quite unlike the
boys, these girls, as a group, seemed to see personal
relationships as matters of over-riding concern, and, as
such, welcomed the kinds of exploration which Rachel's
lessons allowed.   It seemed that over the two year
period, as her curriculum became more fully personal, its
value, for most of the girls, came to be still greater.
Part of this enhanced appreciation was a sense of greater
confidence in their own ability to participate in Rachel's
classroom structures.

It is interesting that despite clear differences in the
perceptions which boys and girls had of Rachel's curriculum and learning modes, their response to the collaborative tasks she set up in class was not visibly different.
From what we saw, boys, as well as girls, entered with increasing depth and personal commitment into lesson work
which, more and more, demanded trust and confidence, on
the one hand, and tact and understanding on the other.
Though the direction of Rachel's curriculum and methods
ran counter to the expectations of many of the boys in her
class, they were apparently able to suspend their reservations temporarily within her particular classroom context.
This may have been because of Rachel's own very active and
constant engagement with the children in her group.
Rather than setting up tasks and then withdrawing, leaving
pupils to manage things as best they might, Rachel continually monitored how pairs and small groups were working.
Where children were stuck, at odds with each other, or
just playing about, she suggested other approaches, or
drew directly on their own resources to enable them to
engage more effectively with the task.   In this way,
Rachel constantly acted to forestall potential alienation,
and to secure the moment-to-moment engagement of pupils
who might have remained apart from the work of her class.

THE MEANING OF SOCIAL RELATIONS

Mac's class

While emphasizing the intellectual character of his subject, and the contribution which collaboration could make
to this, Mac was also concerned with personal and social
factors in D and T workshop practice. One of these concerns was that children should adopt a non-competitive
approach to their D and T work, and he saw collaboration
as a mode which fostered co-operation, rather than rivalry
in achievement. The general ethos which Mac tried to
cultivate through his workshop approach was one in which
mutual respect, compassion and concern for others would
inform children's behaviour towards each other. In particular, he wanted to ensure that less able pupils did not
experience failure and humiliation; and he saw collaborative work as potentially enhancing the self-esteem of such
pupils.

On their side, the pupils in his class group viewed
social relationships in somewhat different terms. It
seemed that an expectation of friction and tension between
people formed part of the everyday consciousness of most
of the boys. For the group as a whole, there were potential divisions on the basis of gender and race. Ability
differentials also seemed quite salient, and several children had feelings of contempt towards the less able.

Some of these perceptions seemed to govern how the
children behaved in Mac's collaborative context. Pupils
did not always show concern for each other's needs; we
saw several instances of children ignoring or rebuffing
the appeals of others. To this extent, the less able
pupils (who were mostly girls) were left to fend for themselves as best they might, making it likely that they
would experience failure, and low self-esteem. Yet, to a
much greater extent, Mac's values seemed to prevail in
these children's interactions. They did not divide up on
lines of race or academic ability; despite some gender
segregation, feeling across groups was definitely positive
rather than negative. Vulnerable pupils were not victi-
mized or rejected. Attitudes towards differences of
ability in D and T were broadly uncompetitive, able children being generally modest, and less able ones generous in
acknowledgment. It seems that by affirming and encouraging his pupils to base their work on the existing friendships among them, Mac largely succeeded in establishing a
classroom ethos of good feeling towards others.

If Mac's social goals were not always achieved in the
way the children in his classroom behaved towards each
other, this is not altogether surprising.   D and T
classes claimed a mere two hours in the whole school week.
In the remainder of their school experience, these children worked within a learning ethic which was essentially
individualized and competitive.   The occasional instances
we saw in Mac's class of mutually uncaring behaviour
should probably be seen, therefore, as signs of how difficult it is to operate different values within one section
of the everyday social world.

Classroom interactions also involve those between
pupils and teacher.   Mac valued a human, rather than a
purely authoritarian relationship with the children he
taught;   and he saw collaborative learning as facilitating
this.   From our evidence, it seems that his approach
within the D and T workshop generally contributed more to
his relationship with the boys in his group, than with the
girls.   This must certainly have been due partly to the
different feelings and expectations which the two gender
groups initially brought to his workshop.   As a group,
the girls felt much less positively about D and T than did
the boys.   But their negative orientation may actually
have been partly confirmed by their experience of Mac's D
and T workshop.   Mac himself had a less accurate understanding of their situation and perceptions, as compared
with his high level of empathy with the boys in his class.
As we saw, although Mac was generally prompt to respond to
pupils' working needs, it was possible for a girl's appeal
for help to remain unheeded for quite a large part of the
lesson.   This occasional lack of responsiveness on Mac's
part was the outcome of his own concern to help pupils
develop their own resources.   He tried to tread a difficult path between not neglecting children's learning
needs, and not himself being too easily available when
minor difficulties arose.   However, this seemed to work
generally better for the boys in his class, who on the
whole had achieved greater confidence.   Given that, for
most of the girls, the D and T workshop involved at least
some experience of difficulty and frustration, and for
some, of personal irrelevance, it is perhaps not surprising that towards Mac himself, they did not generally
achieve the highly positive relationship which held
between him and most of the boys in his group.

Islay's class

For Islay, the use of collaboration in classroom work
meant more than just an educationally productive method.
She was also concerned with the social functions of collaborative talk between pupils. Islay thought that encouraging young people to talk about their own experience,
their own views, their own feelings, carried, potentially,
a message of personal respect. Not only was the teacher,
in doing this, acknowledging the validity of pupils' experiences; but pupils, through hearing about each other's
lives and situations, could come to appreciate and respect
both the common ground and the diversity among themselves.
Islay also saw collaborative talk as altering the political character of classrooms, by removing central authority
from the teacher and giving pupils responsible roles which
acknowledged their maturity and power.

    Again, there were some marked differences between
Islay's view and those of the boys in her classroom group,
as expressed both in what they said and in the use to
which they put her collaborative classroom opportunities.
Most basically, their view of learning as an extraneous
body of boring material, to be individually assimilated,
carried the connotation, for school situations, of friends
as distracting and of teachers as necessarily coercive.
So far from accepting a responsible role for themselves in
classroom work, these boys generally saw their school role
as inevitably irresponsible: 'Remember, if you've got
plenty of liberties, so you mess about.' To some extent,
this was the role they lived out in Islay's class discussions. This group of boys also had their own interpretations of social relations among pupils - interpretations
which emphasized potential conflict and violence, and in
which racial group divisiveness and inter-racial group
mistrust were highly salient. Their classroom seating
patterns and interchanges with each other came increasingly to reflect ethnic group divisions; the fact, however,
that these divisions did not apparently carry mutual hostility seems to be related to the values which Islay herself conveyed.

    As far as Islay's own relationship with these pupils
was concerned, we were very much struck by the liking and
general ease which most boys evinced in their interactions
with her. Islay herself was concerned to create, through
her classroom approach, a much more equal relationship
than the usual teacher-pupil one. She clearly conveyed a
personal liking and respect for the boys in this class.

On their side, not merely did the boys in her group see
teachers as necessarily coercive, but, for some of them,
teachers were highly punitive and profoundly uncaring.
In the light of these perceptions, it seems remarkable
that at least some of the boys were able to establish a
relationship with her that was both genuinely friendly and
respecting.   However, one aspect of this may have been
that, in some sense, Islay was experienced as less of a
teacher than other teachers in school.   Her curriculum
was apparently valued not for its own sake, but for its
instrumental value as involving writing.   And the main
arena of the boys' encounters with her - class discussion
- was generally seen as not work.   To this extent, these
boys may have been able to relate to Islay as a person
precisely because they did not view her as essentially a
teacher.

Terry's class

Terry set a high premium on social relationships in the
classroom, and valued collaboration partly because it endorsed and encouraged them.   He thought lessons devoid of
human warmth and interaction were entirely lifeless and
dessicated, and felt that he could not personally endure
teaching in that kind of context.   Again, within Terry's
differentiated perceptions of particular pupil groups, it
was for working-class children - particularly working-
class boys - that classroom social relationships were
especially crucial.   As he saw it, the social lives of
many working-class children were based in a strong sense
of community, in which personal encounters were often
emotionally expressive, even passionate.   This particularly needed taking into account where boys were concerned, given that by the second or third year of secondary
schooling so many of them were involved in an anti-school
culture.   At least potentially, teachers who made room in
their lessons for the normal, enjoyable interactions among
children, rather than trying to suppress them, might act
to mitigate potential alienation.   Terry's perception of
the importance for children of their collective identity
and their individual relationships carried the implication
that existing patterns of friendship needed to be respected as they stood;   he did not think teachers should try
to modify or extend social relationships among pupils.
Nevertheless, Terry saw it as his goal to establish a
general good feeling, in which, for example, differences
of ability would be de-emphasized.

The implication that children's social feelings might
be confined within particular pupil categories certainly
fitted with the perceptions of most of Terry's pupils.
There were many indications that, among the working-class
children, there was a strong sense of personal distance
from middle-class school pupils - a distance often denied
both socially ('posh') and academically ('brain boxes').
For the black pupils in the group, racial barriers were,
additionally, highly salient, not merely through their
particular experiences of discrimination, but even by
virtue of the small proportion of black pupils in Terry's
class.

In the interactions through which this group of children set up and used their classroom talk together, this
sense of subdivisions was very clear.   Though there was a
generally positive group ethos, and occasional friendly
interchanges across subgroups, voluntary collaboration
was, throughout the year, confined to pupils of similar
class, race and gender.   The 'natural' character of these
groupings must have been a major reason for the evident
enjoyment the children felt.   This public acknowledgment
of existing divisions between pupils - something which
Terry did not see it as his role to counter - must have
acted to confirm a sense of separate group identity among
many of these children.   For working-class, and particularly black children, this may have carried a sense of
personal alienation from school values, in so far as it
was the middle-class children whom they perceived as educationally favoured and successful.

Part of Terry's concern with classroom social interactions had to do with his own relationship with the
pupils he taught.   He valued relations that were, as far
as possible, human, open and honest.   However, this was
within the context of an essentially asymmetrical relationship, since the teacher was in no sense 'one of the boys'.
Though teachers could respond personally to children, and,
in particular, share in their fun, this went alongside
being clearly seen to be in charge, and drawing the line
where pupils took advantage by just mucking around.

On their side, Terry's class group seemed very much to
endorse these attitudes to pupil-teacher relationships
although, again, middle- and working-class children expressed rather different emphases.   Throughout the
group, relations with teachers were seen as important,
and, throughout the group, Terry himself was valued.   On
the whole, the middle-class children saw teachers in terms

of much greater equality, and mutuality.   For working-
class pupils, strictness and control on the part of
teachers were viewed with approval, and this was one of
the reasons why Terry himself was so much appreciated.

These perceptions accorded closely with how the children related to Terry, as we observed this.   Over and
above his friendly relationship with the pupils generally,
Terry seemed to have particularly high rapport with the
white working-class children;   and their generally enthusiastic personal response to him was apparently furthered
still more by the easy, happy relationship he had established with certain 'pivotal' members of these groups.
Terry's special, insider's, understanding of the experience of working-class children in school was thus clearly
evident in the pupil-teacher relations which we witnessed.

Rachel's class

In contrast to the conventional separation of children's
interpersonal relationships from the educational curriculum, Rachel's approach, in some senses, actually equated
the two spheres.   Her teaching goals, ultimately, were
social ones.   What she aimed for was the development, in
the children she taught, of an appreciation of others as
people - not to be seen merely as objects, or roles.   As
Rachel saw it, children could afford to acknowledge others
only if they felt secure in themselves, and were not constantly threatened by their own low self-esteem.   It was
in these areas that, for her, collaborative ways of working were crucial.   Through their interactions with others
on a basis of equality, rather than one of submission to
superior authority, children could realize their own
strengths, and gain confidence in their own initiatives.
Conversely, working co-operatively rather than competi-
tively enabled children to discover each other as unique
individuals.   In this way, good feeling and mutual respect could develop across the divides which so often preclude them;   ethnic or gender exclusiveness could be
broken down, tight friendship cliques could be opened out,
and marginal children could be socially integrated.

Within the context of such explicitly social goals,
Rachel saw it as legitimate, and necessary, actively to
intervene in their relationships.   She did this in several ways.   She often deliberately set up working partnerships which cut across friendship patterns, so that children were called upon to work together who did not know

each other very well, and, sometimes, did not like each
other.   On such occasions, she monitored the interactions
quite closely, encouraging and supporting the children in
any efforts they were making, prompting them to try
another approach if they became stuck, or suggesting other
ideas they might use.   In this way, Rachel worked to
forestall the early breakdown of a relationship which had
not been freely chosen, and which might, without her
interventions, serve merely to confirm mistrust and dislike.   Instead, she tried to enable the children to experience each other positively, and thereby overcome
mutual ignorance and antipathy.   Another way in which
Rachel tried actively to foster good feeling throughout
the whole class group was by incorporating into her curriculum areas of mutual incomprehension or misinterpreta-
tion.   She did this particularly with the differentiated
perspectives of boys and girls, demanding that boys, for
example, not merely heard, but perhaps even enacted the
experience of some of the girls in the group.

Rachel's social goals also encompassed her own relationship with the children in her class.   Again, she saw
collaborative modes as critical.   Only through classroom
work which gave responsibility and initiative to children,
could pupils come to see the teacher as a person.   By
talking and interacting with a teacher on terms of relative equality, children learned to see her as a particular
human being, rather than as representing an undifferentia-
ted, remote group of authority figures.   But this did not
of itself bring about reciprocity and mutual respect,
unless the teacher, on her side, responded in genuinely
personal ways, rather than just acting out the teacherly
role.   This meant not only being genuinely honest and
open with pupils;   even beyond this, it meant acknowledging personal vulnerability.   As with pupil-pupil relations, Rachel saw pupil-teacher relations as a legitimate
part of the curriculum.   So, for example, she asked the
children to think about, and try to predict, the aspects
of school which teachers might find frustrating, and used
this material as a basis for discussing her own experience
as a teacher.   Rachel also extended her relationship with
this group outside the classroom context - inviting them
all back to her flat, for instance, for a Christmas party.

As far as pupils' perceptions are concerned, it is
clear that some changes took place over the two years -
changes which, in general, accord with Rachel's own goals,
and which seem likely to be related to the children's experience in her classroom.   Half way through the two-year

period, the children's ethos about their own relationships
was, so far as we could tell, quite a divisive one.
Although consideration for others was clearly valued,
mutual respect and good feeling were seen as constrained
by barriers of race and gender, viewed as a source of conflict in relations between children, and highly stereotyped views prevailed of minority ethnic group children.
By the end of the two years, this mutual mistrust and
antipathy across race and gender lines was greatly dimin-
ished.   However, the change was much more marked for
girls than for boys.   It was also girls who, in regret-
fully acknowledging barriers which operated between the
genders, considered the part played by constraints intrinsic within the school institution, as against the informality of the residential unit, for instance, where boy-
girl relations were far freer and more personal.   For the
girls, mutual ignorance and dislike seem to have been experienced, not as inevitable attitudes between boys and
girls, but as built in, at least to some extent, to the
social set-up of large mixed classrooms.   By the same
token, these girls may have held more pessimistic expectations than Rachel herself of how far such barriers could
be broken down in classroom interactions.

As a whole, the group also came to perceive themselves
more positively.   At the end of the first year, we had
evidence of low self-esteem among the girls generally, and
minority group children; but - although this was not the
case for the control class group - perceptions of self
were generally enhanced among such pupils by the end of
the second year.   This also seemed borne out by the use
which the children made of Rachel's collaborative working
modes.   From what we saw, these modes promoted increasingly free and confident initiatives on the part of the
children - initiatives which at the end of the period involved some interactions across gender lines, and some
involvement of previously isolated children or exclusive
cliques.   To this extent, their classroom work served to
enhance both self-respect and mutual appreciation among
the children there.

What of the children's attitudes to Rachel herself?
From all the evidence we have, it seems that both boys and
girls were increasingly appreciative of her personally,
and lived this out within the classroom in the attentiveness, liking and obvious enjoyment with which they responded to her.   For the group as a whole, this appreciation
seemed to relate to the children's sense of Rachel as a
very caring person.   There was a general consensus, when

the children were talking about teachers, that good
teachers were concerned, while to bad ones, pupils did not
ultimately matter very much.   It seemed that these children took as important evidence of caring, the quality and
extent of teachers' response to written work.   From this
point of view, Rachel's extended, careful and very personal response to her pupils' written work may have been
critical in confirming her, in their eyes, as committed to
their interests.

Though they clearly valued Rachel's personal qualities,
many of the children in her class - particularly the boys
- also stressed the importance of teacher control, and saw
definite limits to reciprocity in teacher-pupil relations.
These attitudes did not apparently diminish over the two
years.   For some children, Rachel was probably particularly appreciated for the confidence and ease she habitually showed in controlling her class.   One index of the
authority with which the children vested her was the fact
that they allowed her to intervene in their own social
relationships.   No one disputed Rachel's right to set up
classroom partnerships - partnerships in which two children who mistrusted or disliked each other were asked to
talk quite personally together, or share problems in working.   In this, very personal intervention, which Rachel,
alone among the teachers we studied, regularly set up, the
children, whatever their initial reluctance, were prepared
to work along with her; supported and guided by her as
they were, these artificial collaborative partnerships
seldom actually broke down.   This was all the more striking because this particular class was, at the start of our
contact with them, a very divisive and fragmented group.

SOME CONCLUDING COMMENTS

If there is a single message from this study, it must be
that the cognitive and the social in school learning are
inextricably intertwined.   In setting up the project, we
ourselves failed fully to appreciate this.   Though recognizing that learning occurs within a social context - even
arises through the medium of social relationships - we
still kept a clear distinction between context and content,
and between social and cognitive aspects of classroom collaboration.   Our focus upon collaborative modes of learning both highlighted the large significance of social factors in secondary school classrooms and pointed up the
extent to which these factors influence the impact, and
the meaning, of educational material.

From the evidence we gathered in our four classrooms,
it is quite clear that, for pupils themselves, school
lessons are essentially social situations.   The invitation to work collaboratively is, at the very least, an
acknowledgment of this fact.   In all four classrooms we
studied, teachers' endorsement and encouragement of their
pupils' relationships with each other had very positive
social effects.   The freedom of interaction, the absence
of the traditional suppression of social interest, led to
a generally friendly and benign classroom atmosphere.
One aspect of this was a characteristically positive
pupil-teacher relationship.   The role of all four
teachers we saw contrasted strongly with that of the coercive authority figure, and this clearly enabled each
teacher to communicate more fully and to respond more personally to pupils.

As far as children's own relationships were concerned,
the effects were, in every classroom, apparently just as
beneficial.   In place of competitive attitudes to school
work, reactions were typically tolerant, sometimes even
generous.   This itself is very striking.   Mac's class
operated within a fairly traditional school context, and
many of the pupils were keenly aware of ability differentials.   Islay's class group had received still stronger
messages, and for a longer time, about the salience of
academic ability, and their own inferior position.   Given
that within their group there were obvious, publicly
accessible differences in literacy skills, the general
mutual acceptance and tolerance among these boys and the
absence of reference to contrasting levels of competence,
seems very significant.   Terry's and Rachel's pupils,
too, might well have evinced competitive and individualistic attitudes towards each other.   In Terry's class, the
spread of academic ability was quite unusually wide, including as it did a girl categorized as ESN, together with
a large subgroup of children given the special, elite,
school status of musicians.   The non-integration, in the
classroom, of the pupil subgroups, which tended to embody
academic differences, might have contributed still further
to a consciousness of differentials.   Yet this did not
happen.   Rachel's class was equally striking in this respect.   Here, the general social currency between pupils
at the start of her contact with them - a currency involving much rivalry, mutual depreciation and ridicule - increasingly gave way to relations of mutual tolerance and
respect, in which, quite often, one saw more able children
offering tactful support and encouragement to their less
competent peers.

Just as impressive is the effect which, from what we saw, the collaborative conduct of learning had on racial aspects of children's relations. In the three years of this study, we witnessed a great deal of unmistakable evidence of the existence of racial hostility and mistrust within the school contexts we were looking at. It seemed likely that to most of the pupils we were studying, incidents of inter-racial conflict and tension would be quite familiar in their daily school lives. This was confirmed by many comments and judgments from pupils in all four classrooms. Not surprisingly, it was those from minority ethnic groups to whom such experience was most obviously salient. The boys in Islay's group spoke fully, often with considerable bitterness, about their social status as young black people. For them, this entailed not merely the prospect of discrimination in the job market, but a familiarity with low personal standing, if not actually persecution, in the world of school, in which teachers as well as other pupils were implicated. Similar references to the experience of racial victimization in school were made by black and Asian children in the other classes we studied; and the black girls in Terry's class expressed the sense of discrimination implicit in the very fact of being a racial minority within that group itself. While white children referred explicitly less often to the theme of racial hostility, we had indications that, for many of them, it was implicit. This was most evident in the judgments made by the pupils in Rachel's class, when they considered other children who were white or black. Those who, after a year in contact with Rachel, made judgments about black, white and Asian children, whose photographs they saw, strongly endorsed a sense of conflict and divisiveness on the basis of race, and expressed stereotypical and demeaning perceptions about their minority group peers. At much the same time, the class group as a whole expressed low esteem for black children.

Despite this strong evidence as to the existence of racial barriers and tensions among the pupil groups we studied, instances of inter-racial hostility were markedly absent in the interactions of pupils within all four classrooms. In Islay's and Terry's classes, the somewhat separate grouping of pupils on racial lines was not accompanied by any apparent sense of mutual suspicion and dislike; on the contrary, we saw evidence of general mutual tolerance and interest across the four ethnic subgroups in Islay's class, while incidents of friendly interaction occurred, in Terry's, between some of the black and white girls. In Mac's class, Lenworth, one of two black pupils,

was the object of obviously high esteem from the other
children - a status which contrasted with his notably poor
standing in school generally.   But of all pupil groups,
those in Rachel's class most clearly showed the positive
effects of classroom collaboration on inter-racial relationships.   In that classroom, racial differences, along
with others, had initially formed part of the repertoire
of mutual hostility, and were also the basis for the marginality of some pupils, in the case both of individuals,
and of an isolated pair of friends, Jackie T. and Paulette.
As time went on, this became less and less the case, previously isolated individuals being increasingly integrated
within the class group, and children being increasingly
appreciated by others as persons regardless of their
ethnic origins.   That this situation reflected a change
in general feeling, towards ethnic minority boys at least,
is confirmed by the judgments these pupils made at the end
of the two years.

It is, of course, generally acknowledged that children
are less likely to act in overtly racist ways within their
school classrooms than elsewhere in school or on the
streets.   Nevertheless, this evidence of a general shift
of attitude on the part of Rachel's pupils towards at
least some of their ethnic minority peers suggests that
the absence of racist behaviour as time went on in
Rachel's class was not just context-specific.   In hers,
as in the three other classrooms, this lack of racial hostility was also characteristic of the children's interactions when the teacher left them alone for long periods;
and for this reason, it cannot just be attributed to close
teacher supervision.

Collaborative learning modes, as we saw them in action,
also had a visible impact on gender relations between
children.   In all three mixed classrooms the potential
existed for mutual mistrust between boys and girls.   In
Mac's class, the fact that the curriculum, for most of the
girls, was seen as gender-inappropriate could have carried
a sense of boy-girl alienation.   Yet even among the four
girls who invariably segregated themselves from the rest
of the class, we saw no sign of hostility towards the
boys.   On their side, the boys in the group regularly
avoided making reference to these girls' relative lack of
competence in D and T.   Friendly interaction quite often
happened between boys and girls in this group, and there
was, of course, a regular mixed working trio.   Terry's
class, to a greater extent than Mac's, involved a voluntary segregation between boys and girls.   However, this

did not connote a sense of mutual hostility; on the contrary, we regularly saw instances of friendly mutual
interest between members of boys' and girls' groupings.
But again, it was in Rachel's class that the impact of
collaborative modes had their clearest effect on boy-girl
relations.   Gender hostilities, endemic in the early
interactions we saw, gradually gave way, as Rachel actively intervened in them, to relations of increasing mutual
understanding and appreciation.   After a year in her
classroom, it was clear that some children still retained
a sense of gender as inevitably divisive, and that most
pupils in this group held the other gender in low regard.
By the end of two years, this had changed quite markedly;
boys valued girls much more highly and girls, boys.

Taking all three contexts, it seems that making learning a collaborative affair in mixed classrooms may carry a
positive spin-off for gender relations.   Even where
teachers, like Mac and Terry, pay no specific attention to
boy-girl relationships, the general ease and enjoyment of
this way of working can defuse potential hostility between
the sexes.   Where a teacher, such as Rachel, concerns
herself explicitly with overcoming mutual ignorance and
mistrust, collaborative ways of working can be used to explore jointly and sympathetically the rather different
perspectives of boys and girls.   In considering this
aspect of our study, it should of course be acknowledged
that at this stage many boys and girls are likely in any
case to be developing an interest in the opposite sex.
What seems significant, however, in our findings, is the
impact of collaborative modes on generalized tolerance and
sympathy towards the other gender group - something which
clearly goes beyond the individualized relationships that
may develop between particular boy-girl pairs.

What of the educational benefits of collaborative
learning modes?   Put negatively, it seems fair to say
that in all four classrooms, the pupils produced academic
work at least as good, if not better, than they would have
been likely to produce under more traditional methods.
This is, however, to take a very narrow view of learning.
Much more important is the question of how far these
pupils used collaborative opportunities to develop their
understanding of the curriculum, and, in so doing, to
create new, personally meaningful knowledge.   It is in
considering this question that a purely intellectual definition of school learning seems most inadequate.   From
what we saw, pupils, and pupil groups, varied a great deal
in how they used the opportunity to work together in

classrooms.   In order to understand this variability, we
need to take account of essentially social aspects of the
learning which was involved.

Two themes which emerge from the material we gathered
seem illuminative here.   The first has to do with
teachers.   Certain pupils responded fully and enthusiastically to the invitation to work with others, and characteristically put such opportunities to the greatest use
educationally.   These were usually pupils who had a particular understanding and sympathy towards the teacher and
her or his hopes, expectations, and style of doing things.
In Mac's class, it was the boys, by and large, who expressed the greatest appreciation for him and for his subject, and who applied themselves most vigorously, and most
productively, to the tasks he set.   In Rachel's class,
conversely, it was the girls who most strongly echoed her
own emphases, her own values, and who saw her very personal curriculum as most richly meaningful.

For both these classes, the gender stereotyping of the
subject followed the teacher's own gender.   The fact,
therefore, that Mac was a man and Rachel a woman must have
held additionally potent significance for the children
they taught.   Mac, embodying as he did all the interests,
all the competences which a 'proper man' possesses in the
gender stereotype, probably represented many positive
features for the boys in his group.   The subject he had
chosen was one towards which social pressures, from both
family and school, were urging at least some of them.   As
a 'practical' man, Mac may also have resembled the fathers
and other men in these boys' lives, and in this, may have
carried some sense of future direction;   certainly for
most of them, craft skills were felt to have future significance.   By the same token, the general alienation which
the majority of girls in Mac's group expressed towards his
curriculum, felt to be gender-inappropriate, must have
been further strengthened by the fact that he was a man,
and thereby perhaps experienced as neither a current, nor
a future model for them.

This situation seems to have operated in reverse within
Rachel's class.   Just as the girls readily and enthusiastically accepted her curriculum - a curriculum which dwelt
on the interpersonal relationships, the feelings and sen-
sitivities that are traditionally the province of females
- the boys in the group expressed a sense of increasing
reservation towards the subject.   Concomitantly, Rachel
herself, so salient in the perceptions of the girls she

taught, was apparently much less so for the boys, and, via her gender, may have added to their growing sense of the personal irrelevance of her subject.

Islay's gender - which, again, endorsed the gender stereotype of her curriculum - must also have been one factor in the response of her Social Studies class.   This may have been further accentuated by the fact that the group consisted only of boys (and adolescent boys at that; the occasional sexist response to Islay herself was perhaps inevitable).   The refusal of this group of pupils to accept Islay's curriculum, as she defined it, or to take seriously her collaborative methods, may have derived partly from their sense of personal separateness from her as a young woman.

Islay, like the other teachers, had a race and class identity as well as a gender one.   These must also have been very important in governing the meaning of all four classrooms for the pupils in them.   In her class, Islay was differentiated from the pupils she taught in terms of both class and race.   Given the salience of race, for the boys, and their awareness, at least implicitly, of social class barriers in their future prospects, it is perhaps remarkable that Islay was able to achieve such a genuinely friendly personal relationship with them.   Nevertheless, their readiness to engage personally with her perceptions and her meanings may well have been limited by their sense of her as 'other' in fundamental ways.

The teacher's race also seems to have represented a barrier within Terry's class, where the four black girls, with their strong sense of separate racial identity and racial solidarity, had a lesser involvement than other pupils with Terry's curriculum, and were much less prepared to use their own relationships as a medium for his work.

However, for Terry himself, his combination of gender and working-class identity held particular meanings.   It was probably these which enabled him to engage the working-class boys in his group to a quite unusual extent. While these boys may not have reached the high level of collaborative work achieved by their middle-class peers, they certainly showed an involvement and enjoyment in their lessons very different from the incipient alienation which they expressed towards school learning generally.

From our study it seems that teachers are likely to

experience special resonances with particular groups of
pupils on the basis of shared experience, in a society
which clearly differentiates its members on the basis of
gender, class and race.   Conversely, for any pupil, the
material of school learning is likely to be given a particular kind of meaning by the person of the teacher who
mediates it.   To make learning a collaborative endeavour,
rather than a matter of individualized instruction, is of
course to acknowledge this.   Collaborative learning modes
rest on the assumption that people essentially construct
their own knowledge, and cast what they learn into what
makes sense within their own experience.   From this point
of view, it is not surprising that the gender, race or
class of the teacher can come, for pupils, to imbue the
meaning of the lesson content and its style.   But potentially, at least, collaborative modes allow learning to
break free of such social categories.   In so far as they
give children autonomy and responsibility in their own
learning efforts, they remove the curriculum from its sole
possession by the teacher.   By inviting pupils to negotiate with each other, they offer the possibility of
grounding learners' understanding within their shared
everyday world.   From our study, it is clear that this
did indeed often happen, at least within the three second
year classrooms.   Even the most disaffected girls in
Mac's workshop discovered unexpectedly a moment of shared
triumph.   In Terry's classroom, boys and girls who were
occasionally visibly bored were, much more often, personally absorbed in what they were doing, and pleased with
the work they had produced.   The boys who, as time went
on, expressed increasing reservations about Rachel's
lessons, nevertheless became visibly caught up, time after
time, in the personally creative work they did in her
class.

    If these things did not happen in Islay's classroom, we
have to look to another kind of social influence.   It is
striking that, while Islay and Rachel shared many of the
same perceptions, goals and expectations, Rachel's attempt
to convey these, and to develop her pupils' personal and
social understanding, was much more successful.   These
two teachers operated within very different institutional
contexts.   Rachel, like Terry, worked in a school which
was particularly rich in many kinds of resources and where
the charismatic, energetic head gave strong support to her
department, particularly in its work in the lower school.
An indication of the value placed on this is the fact that
the normal sequence of curriculum change was interrupted
for the class we were studying, in order to maintain their

continuous contact with Rachel.   The timetable was one
which gave her long stretches with the class.   Newlands
School was also relatively sympathetic to innovative
teaching and learning methods.   Islay's institutional
context was very different.   Claremont School was poorer
in resources.   As a relatively new comprehensive, it
still carried many of the expectations and methods of the
secondary modern boys school it had been.   This meant
that Islay's collaborative modes stood out against a
general pattern of individualized instruction, and were
relatively unfamiliar to both teachers and pupils.   Nor
did Islay have the extended time for lessons enjoyed by
Rachel;   she had fewer lessons per week with the class,
and shorter ones.   Most seriously of all, the educational
history of the group which Islay taught carried clear and
explicit messages running counter to her goals.

The very different outcomes of Islay's and of Rachel's
quite similar teaching efforts demonstrate the importance
of the surrounding supports and constraints within insti-
tutions - factors which will already have affected pupils
who have spent some time in school, and which must exercise potent concurrent influences on them.   It is clear
from our study that gains achieved in one collaborative
learning classroom are unlikely to be maintained across
the other contexts of school where a different ethos pre-
vails.   As long as collaborative learning modes are confined to a few isolated, innovative classrooms within
schools, their impact is likely to be marginal and transient.   In terms of our own account, it is the potentialities, in collaborative learning methods, for the fostering of commonality and sociality between teachers and
pupils, and between pupils themselves, which are ultimately crucial in forestalling personal alienation from school
education.   Only when such modes are seen to constitute
the royal road to education of every kind will there be a
chance for all children to achieve confidence and mastery
in their learning, and a firm sense of respect for themselves and others.   It would, however, be naive to suppose that such changes are an easy matter.   As many
people have said, schools are not independent of society;
and within our own society are powerful forces against the
political implications of these educational methods.   Yet
to the extent that teachers are able to resist such
forces, and extend the use of collaborative learning
approaches, schools themselves may become points of lever-
age for wider social change.

Appendix

Questions about school and out of school life

1 What sort of person generally does well at school?
2 Pupils usually seem to learn more in some classes than in others. Why do you think this is?
3 Do you think it's a good idea for boys and girls to go to the same school?
4 Do you think that when there's trouble at school, pupils can usually sort things out for themselves?
5 Sometimes pupils like to talk to each other in class. Does this ever help with their learning?
6 Some people have told us that they are quite different people out of school. Do you think this is often true?
7 Do you think most parents really understand what it's like for young people today?
8 Suppose you like the subject, but the teacher is not much good. Do you think you'd learn much? What if it was the other way round?
9 In most schools there are groups of people who usually stick together. What kinds of things do they have in common?
10 What do you think most pupils' parents want their kids to learn at school?
11 Some schools believe in streaming, right through school, while other schools don't believe in that. What is your opinion?
12 Most schools tend to put a lot of emphasis on homework, written work and exams. What do you think about this?
*13 Have your ideas about school changed since you were a first year?
14 Is there any question you think we should have asked, but didn't?

* Islay's class only.

Bibliography

Bannister, D. and Fransella, F. (1980), 'Inquiring Man:
    The Psychology of Personal Constructs' (2nd ed.),
    Harmondsworth, Penguin.
Barnes, D. (1976), 'From Communication to Curriculum',
    Harmondsworth, Penguin.
Barnes, D. and Todd, F. (1977), 'Communication and Learn-
    ing in Small Groups', Harmondsworth, Penguin.
Deem, R. (ed.) (1980), 'Schooling for Women's Work',
    London, Routledge & Kegan Paul.
Driver, G. (1982), Classroom stress and school achievement:
    West Indian adolescents and their teachers, in James, A.
    and Jeffcoate, R (eds), 'The School in the Multi-Racial
    Society', New York, Harper & Row.
Furlong, V. (1976), Interaction sets in the classroom, in
    Stubbs, M. and Delamont, S. (eds), 'Explorations in
    Classroom Observations', Chichester, Wiley.
Hargreaves, D. (1967), 'Social Relations in a Secondary
    School', London, Routledge & Kegan Paul.
James, A. (1977), Why language matters, 'Multi-Racial
    School', Summer
Keddie, N. (ed.) (1973), 'Tinker, Tailor: The Myth of
    Cultural Deprivation', Harmondsworth, Penguin.
Richmond, J. (1982), 'The Resources of Classroom Language',
    London, Edward Arnold.
Salmon, P. (ed.) (1980), 'Coming to Know', London, Rout-
    ledge & Kegan Paul.
Schutz, A. (1932), 'The Phenomenology of the Social World',
    London, Heinemann.
Searle, C. (1978), 'The World in a Classroom', London,
    Writers and Readers Publishing Co-operative.
Spender, D. (1982), 'Invisible Women: The Schooling Scan-
    dal', London, Writers and Readers Publishing Co-opera-
    tive.
Torode, B. (1977), Interrupting intersubjectivity, in

Woods, P. and Hammersley, M. (eds), 'School Experience',
   London, Croom Helm.
Willis, P.E. (1977), 'Learning to Labour', Farnborough,
   Saxon House.
Young, M.F.D. (ed.) (1971), 'Knowledge and Control',
   London and Basingstoke, Macmillan.

Index